Colloquial Chinese

The Colloquial Series

Series adviser: Gary King

The following languages are available in the Colloquial series:

- Albanian
- Amharic
- Arabic (Levantine)
- Arabic of Egypt
- Arabic of the Gulf and Saudi Arabia
- Basque
- Bulgarian
- * Cambodian
- * Cantonese
- * Chinese
- Croatian and Serbian
- Czech
- Danish
- Dutch
- Estonian
- Finnish
- French
- German
- Greek
- Gujarati
- Hindi
- Hungarian
- Indonesian
- Italian
- Japanese
- Korean
- Latvian
- Lithuanian
- Malay
- Mongolian
- Norwegian
- Panjabi
- Persian
- Polish
- Portuguese
- Portuguese of Brazil
- Romanian
- * Russian
- Slovak
- Slovene
- Somali
- * Spanish
- Spanish of Latin America
- Swedish
- * Thai
- Turkish
- Ukrainian
- * Vietnamese
- Welsh

Accompanying cassette(s) (* and CDs) are available for the above titles. They can be ordered separately through your bookseller or send payment with order to Routledge Ltd, ITPS, Cheriton House, North Way, Andover, Hants SP10 5BE, or to Routledge Inc., 29 West 35th Street, New York, NY 10001, USA.

COLLOQUIAL CD-ROMs
Multimedia Language Courses

Available in: Chinese, French, Portuguese and Spanish
Forthcoming: German

Colloquial Chinese

The Complete Course for Beginners

Kan Qian

London and New York

First published 1995
by Routledge
11 New Fetter Lane, London EC4P 4EE

Simultaneously published in the USA and Canada
by Routledge
29 West 35th Street, New York, NY 10001

Reprinted 1997, 1998
Revised edition 1999

Routledge is an imprint of the Taylor & Francis Group

Typeset in Times Ten by The Florence Group Ltd, Stoodleigh, Devon

Illustrations and calligraphy by Matthew Crabbe

Printed and bound in Great Britain by Clays Ltd, St Ives plc

British Library Cataloguing in Publication Data
A catalogue record for this book is available from the British Library

Library of Congress Cataloging in Publication Data
A catalogue record for this book has been requested

ISBN 0–415–11386–5 (book)
ISBN 0–415–11387–3 (cassettes)
ISBN 0–415–11388–1 (book and cassettes course)
ISBN 0–415–15530–4 (CDs)
ISBN 0–415–15531–2 (book and CDs course)
ISBN 0–415–14291–1 (CD-ROM)

To my dear father and mother

给我亲爱的父母亲

Acknowledgements

My gratitude goes to Andrew Brown, who has helped me throughout the writing of this book. Not only did he spend many hours polishing my English, but also put himself in the position of a learner for this book. The criticism and comments he made were extremely helpful in enabling me to search for the most appropriate way of expressing many language points. I am also very grateful to Matthew Crabbe, who gave me some very good and useful suggestions.

My special thanks go to Charles Forsdick, Dr Rachel Rimmershaw and Lucia Woods, who willingly gave hours of their time polishing some of the chapters and provided very useful comments. I am indebted to Dr Yip Po-Ching for his many helpful suggestions. I would also like to thank Alan Edmunds, Jonathan Culpeper, Wu Zhongtao, Dong Ming, Dr Mick Short and Li Man for their help in one way or another. Finally, I wish to thank the editors and the assistant staff concerned at Routledge for their constructive comments and support.

Contents

Introduction

The Chinese language

Some people in the west think that the Chinese language is *Cantonese* whereas in fact *Cantonese* is just one of the eight major dialects of the Chinese language. Although different dialects differ immensely in pronunciation, they share the same written form. The Northern dialect (which has many sub-dialects under it) is spoken by 70 per cent of the Chinese population. Therefore, the standard language spoken nationally is based on the pronunciation of the Northern dialect. The name for this standard form is *Putonghua* (common speech) in mainland China, *Guoyu* or *Huayu* (national language) in Taiwan, Hong Kong, and other overseas Chinese communities, and 'Mandarin Chinese' in English-speaking countries. Other terms such as *Zhongwen* (Chinese) or *Hanyu* ('*Han*' language, *Han* Chinese making up 93 per cent of the Chinese population) are more formal and are often used among Chinese language learners. Native Chinese speakers often use the term '*Zhongwen*' rather than *Putonghua* when they ask non-native Chinese speakers if they speak Chinese. *Putonghua* is taught in schools and spoken by television and radio presenters in mainland China, and it is the kind of spoken language which is most understood by Chinese speakers. This book deals with *Putonghua*.

Romanization

Various systems have been devised for transcribing Chinese sounds into the Latin script. The system used in this book is called *pinyin*. *Pinyin* was adopted as the official system in the People's Republic of China in 1958, and has since become a standard form used by news agencies as well as educational institutions. *Pinyin* has now been adopted almost universally in the west for transliterating Chinese personal names and place names although in older books you may still find earlier romanization systems in use (e.g. 'Beijing' is the *pinyin* transliteration and Peking is the *Wade–Giles* transliteration). In mainland China, *pinyin* is used as a tool to teach the correct pronunciation of *Putonghua* to children starting school. In dictionaries *pinyin* is given next to the character to indicate the pronunciation. Many street signs in big cities in mainland China have *pinyin* directly underneath the Chinese characters.

The speech sounds

Chinese is a vowel-dominated language. A syllable may consist of a single vowel, a compound vowel or a vowel preceded by a consonant. A compound vowel may consist of two vowels or a vowel with a nasal sound, which is treated as one unit. This is probably why consonants are called 'initials' (*shengmu*) and vowels are called 'finals' (*yunmu*) in Chinese. Every syllable is represented by a Chinese character. For example:

e	hungry	**ai**	to love
ke	to be thirsty	**tang**	sugar

1 Initials

There are twenty-three initials (some people regard *w* and *y* as semi-vowels), in modern Chinese. Below is a table comparing the twenty-three initials with the English sounds. Some of the Chinese initials are quite similar to English sounds, others less so. Those which differ significantly from the nearest English sounds have explanations next to them. The letter in bold is the Chinese initial:

Initial	*Initial*
b like *b* in *bed*	**zh** like *j* in *jade*, but with the tongue further back
p like *p* in *poor*	**ch** like *ch* in *church*, but with the tongue further back, and the mouth in a round shape
m like *m* in *me*	**sh** like *sh* in *sheep*

f like *f* in *foot*
d like *d* in *do*
t like *t* in *tea*
n like *n* in *nose*
l like *l* in *like*
z like *ds* in *beds*
c like *ts* in *bits*
s like *s* in *sale*

r like *r* in *road*, but with the tongue loosely rolled in the middle of the mouth
g like *g* in *good*
k like *k* in *kite*
h like *h* in *hat*
w like *w* in *we*
y like *y* in *yes*
j like *g* in *George*, but with the tongue nearer the teeth and the mouth relaxed
q – raise the front of the tongue to the hard palate, place the tip of the tongue against the back of the lower teeth. It is a bit like the *ch* in *cheese* but with the tongue further forward. The mouth is held more firmly than when pronouncing **j**.
x – place the front of the tongue behind the lower front teeth near the hard palate then let the air pass through the channel between the front of the tongue and the hard palate, rather like whistling through the lower teeth.

2 Finals

A final is a single vowel, or compound vowel or a vowel plus a nasal sound, i.e. **n** (like *n* in *in*) and **ng** (like *ng* in *long*). Altogether, there are thirty-six finals in Chinese. Below is a chart comparing the thirty-six finals with the English sounds. Some of the Chinese final sounds are quite similar to English sounds, others less so. Those that bear no resemblance have explanations next to them. The letters in bold are the Chinese finals:

a like *a* in *father*
ai – between **a** and **ei**
ao like *ow* in *how*
an like *an* in *ban*
ang like *on* in *monster*

e like *ir* in *Sir*
ei like *ay* in *lay*
en like *en* in *tender*
eng like *un* in *hunger*
er – combination of *ir* in *Sir* and the retroflex *r* (**er** is never preceded by initials)

i like *ee* in *bee* (after initials such as **b**, **p**, **d**, **t**, **l**, etc.)
(when **i** follows initials **z**, **c**, **s**, **zh**, **ch**, **sh** and **r**, it is pronounced very differently from **i** preceded by **b**, **p**, **d**, **t**, **l**, etc. Try to get the initial sound right first and then keep the mouth shape of the initial and say **i**. Note that this **i** sound and the initial overlap greatly)
ia – combination of **i** and **a**
iao like *eow* in *meow*
ie like *ye* in *yesterday*
iu like *you*
ian – like the Japanese currency word *Yen*
in like *in* in *tin*
iang like *young*
ing like *ing* in *sling*
iong – combination of **i** and **ong**
(when **i** is not preceded by other initials at the beginning of a syllable, **y** replaces **i**, e.g. **yan** instead of **ian**, **yao** instead of **iao**)
o like our in *tour*
ou like *oe* in *toe*
ong like *ong* in *ding-dong*

u like *oo* in *too*
ua – combination of **u** and **a**
uo like *war*
uai – combination of **u** and **ai**
ui like *wai* in *wait*
uan like *wan* in *swan*
un like *won* in *wonder*
uang like *wan* in *wanting*
(when **u** is not preceded by other initials at the beginning of a syllable, **w** replaces **u**, e.g. **wan** instead of **uan**, **wo** instead of **uo**)

ü like *u* in *tu* (French)
üe – combination of **ü** and a short **ei**
üan – combination of **ü** and a short **an**
ün like 'une' in French
(when **ü** follows **j**, **q**, **x** and **y**, it is written as **u** without the two dots over it (but still pronounced as **ü**), e.g. **ju**, **qu**, **xu**, **yun**, **yuan**, etc. because **u** cannot occur after **j**, **q**, **x** and **y**)

Although the above two charts should give you some guidance over the pronunciation, the recording is essential if you wish to achieve a more accurate pronunciation of these sounds.

Tones

Chinese is a tone language. In *Putonghua*, there are four tones, five if you include the neutral tone. Since there are only about 400 basic monosyllables which can be combined to make words in Chinese, the use of tones is one way of substantially increasing the number of available monosyllables. Every syllable in isolation has its definite tone. So syllables with different tones may mean different things although they share the same initial and final. For example: **ma** pronounced with the first tone means 'mother' but **ma** pronounced with the third tone means 'horse'.

1 The four tones

Name	*Pitch-graph (tone mark)*
The first tone	ˉ
The second tone	ˊ
The third tone	ˇ
The fourth tone	ˋ

To illustrate these four tones better, let us first draw a short vertical line to represent the pitch variation within an average person's voice range:

5 — the high pitch
4 — the mid-high pitch
3 — the middle pitch
2 — the mid-low pitch
1 — the low pitch

First tone is a high, level tone. Pitch it at 5 and keep it at the same level for a while. It will look something like this in the pitch diagram:

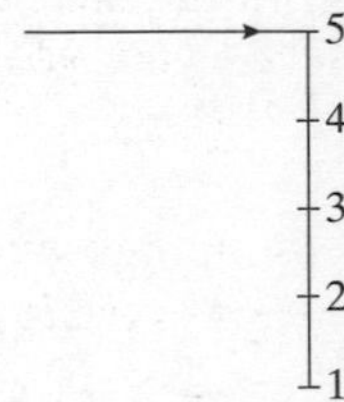

Second tone is a high, rising tone. Pitch it at about 3 and raise it quickly. It will look something like this in the pitch diagram:

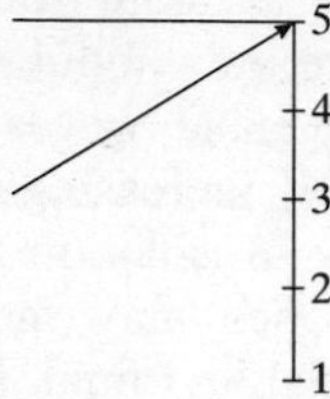

Third tone is a falling and rising tone. Start below 3 and let it drop nearly to the bottom and then rise to somewhere near 2.5. It looks something like this in the pitch diagram:

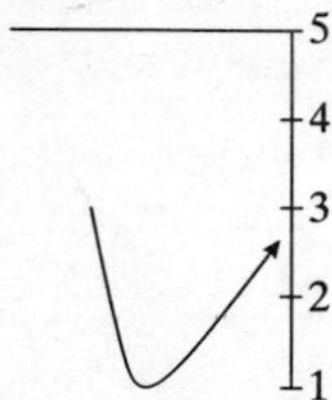

Fourth tone is a falling tone. It falls from 5 right to the bottom, 1. It looks something like this in the pitch diagram:

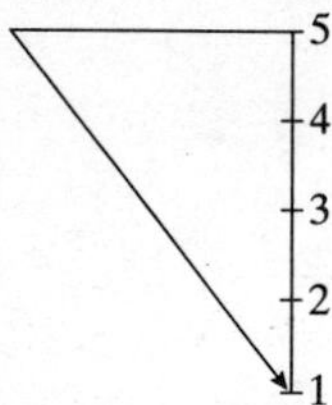

Tones are marked over the vowel (e.g. **tā)** or over the main vowel if it is a compound vowel (e.g. **táo**). The main vowel is the one that comes earliest in this list: **a**, **o**, **e**, **u**, **i**, **ü**. Whenever there is no mark over the vowel, the syllable is a neutral tone.

2 Neutral tones

Some syllables in Chinese are in the neutral tone or toneless, i.e. they are pronounced weakly, which is like unstressed syllables in English (e.g. *of* in *one of my friends*). If there is no tone mark over the vowel, it means it is a neutral tone. Neutral tones are used in the following cases:

(a) Grammar words such as **le**, **de** (see 'Word, word order and grammar' below)
(b) The second syllable in some compound words: for example, **wǒmen** (we/us)
(c) A second syllable which is a repetition of the first one: for example, **māma** (mother/mum)
(d) The measure word **ge** when it is not emphasized: for example, **sān ge yuè** (three months) (see 'Word, word order and grammar' for 'measure word' below).

3 Tone change

In connected speech, tones change depending on the adjacent tones and meaning groups. Below are some basic rules of the tone change:

(a) When a third tone is followed by another third tone and they are in one meaning group, the first one changes to the second tone. For example, **nǐ**, **hǎo**, in actual speech, should be pronounced → **Ní hǎo** (Hello).

(b) When three third tones occur one after another and they are in one meaning group, the second one changes to the second tone whilst the other two remain the third tone. For example, **wǒ**, **hěn**, **hǎo**, in actual speech, should be pronounced → **Wǒ hén hǎo** (I'm very well).

(c) In some compound words, although the second syllable, which is a third tone when used separately, has become neutral, it still carries enough weight to change the preceding third tone to the second tone. For example, **xiǎo**, **jiě**, in actual speech, should be pronounced → **Xiáojie** (Miss).

(d) The first third tone remains unchanged:

(i) If the second third tone belongs to the next meaning group. For example, **Qǐng gàosu** ***wǒ/nǐ*****de diànhuà hàomǎ** (Please tell me your telephone number).

(ii) If a third tone is followed by a neutral tone and then followed by a third tone. For example, **Tā** ***xiě le xǔ*****duō xìn** (She wrote many letters).

(e) When the negation word **bù**, which has the fourth tone, is followed by another fourth tone, **bù** changes to the second tone. For example, **bù** in **Wǒ bú shì Zhōngguórén** (I am not Chinese) should be pronounced with a second tone.

(f) When the number word **yī** (one) is used in isolation or follows other syllables, it has the first tone (e.g. **yī**, **shíyī**); but when it precedes first, second and third tones, **yī** usually changes to the fourth tone (e.g. **yìxiē**, **yìdiǎn**); and when **yī** precedes fourth tones, it changes to the second tone (e.g. **yílù**, **yíxià**).

In actual conversation, tones are rarely given their full value. The pronunciation of syllables, stress, context and facial expressions would all help in conducting a smooth conversation. So, do not be put off by the tones. If you listen carefully and mimic, you will be able to pick them up eventually.

In this book, all the dialogues and texts in *pinyin* are marked with tones. Those syllables which do not have tone marks are neutral tones.

Word, word order and grammar

1 Word

Chinese characters are called **zì**. A *zi* is a character which consists of one syllable. It is thus the building block of the Chinese language. Some *zi* have meanings on their own (e.g., **wǒ** 我 means 'I/me') and others have to be used with others to form meaningful expressions (e.g. **de** does not mean anything on its own but it can be used to form other words such as **wǒ*****de*** 我的 meaning 'my/mine'). The former are words whilst the latter are called 'particles' or 'grammar words' in this book. A Chinese word, therefore, can consist of one syllable, two syllables or more than two syllables.

For example: **xīngqīyī** consists of three syllables and is represented by three characters: 星期一

It means 'Monday'. In some books, a space is always inserted between two syllables. For example:

Jīn tiān shì xīng qī yī. Today is Monday.

In this book, for the convenience of English speakers, I have put those syllables together which can be translated into one English word. The above sentence in this book would be written as follows:

Jīntiān shì xīngqīyī. Today is Monday.

2 Word order

In English, when you ask a question, you have to put the question word first, and reverse the order of the verb and the noun (e.g. *Where are you going?*). In Chinese, you use the normal word order and say 'You are going where?'. In English, one tends to put the most important information at the end of a sentence (e.g. *It is very expensive to telephone China*). In Chinese, the important information or the topic of a sentence comes first. Thus you say 'To telephone China very expensive.' In English, time phrases such as *at 6 o'clock*, *tomorrow*, occur at the end of a sentence (e.g. *I'll finish my work at 6 o'clock*). In Chinese, time phrases always occur before the verb. Thus you say 'I 6 o'clock finish work.' These are just a few major differences between English and Chinese in terms of word order. There are many other differences between the two languages which will be dealt with later in the book.

3 Grammar

Chinese grammar is still in the process of being perfected. However, there are a few things you need to know before you start learning Chinese:

(a) Nouns in Chinese are neither singular nor plural. Thus you say 'one book' and 'three book'.
(b) Because of (a) above, verbs (i.e. doing words) have only one form. Thus you say 'I be Chinese' and 'You be British', 'I go China' and 'He go China', etc.

(c) Verbs do not indicate past, present or future. Tenses are indicated by extra grammar words (or 'particles'), time phrases or context. Thus you say 'I go + grammar word + library', 'I yesterday go + grammar word + library', 'I tomorrow go library', etc.
(d) Prepositions such as 'at', 'in', 'on' are not used before time phrases. Thus you say 'My mother Tuesday arrive.'
(e) The largest unit, be it time or place, always comes first. Thus you say 'He January the 11th arrive', 'We from China Beijing come', etc.
(f) There is something called the measure word to be used between a number and a noun. Different measure words are used for different nouns. Thus you say two + **ben** + book, but two + **ge** + people.

There is a grammar summary at the end of the book.

Chinese characters

Chinese characters are symbols used to represent the Chinese language. It is widely believed that written Chinese is amongst the world's oldest written languages. Its earliest written records can be traced back 3,500 years. Many of the earliest writings were pictures carved on oracle bones, known as 'pictographs'. Over the years, Chinese characters evolved from pictographs into characters formed of strokes, with their structures becoming systemized and simpler. Below are five different character styles showing the evolution of the characters for the sun and the moon into their present-day form:

Styles	*Meaning* Sun	Moon
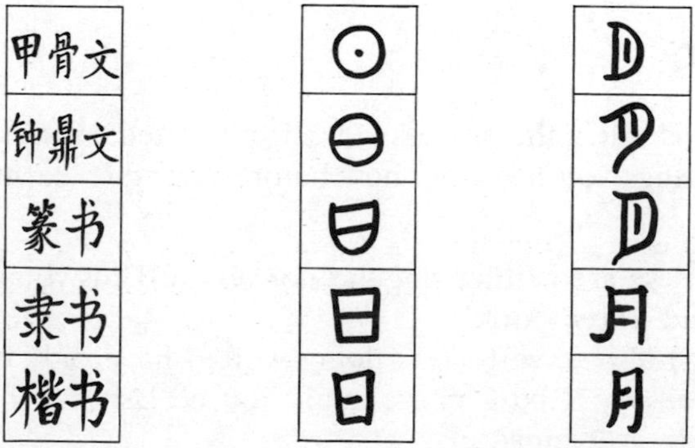 甲骨文		
钟鼎文		
篆书		
隶书	日	月
楷书	日	月

The total number of Chinese characters is estimated at more than 50,000, of which only 5,000–8,000 are in common use. And only 3,000 of them are used for everyday purposes.

1 Basic strokes

Most characters are made of two or more basic structural components (some character components can stand by themselves). These character components are limited and the basic strokes which form these components are even more limited. A stroke is a single unbroken line drawn by the writer from the time the pen touches the paper until the pen lifts off the paper. Below are the basic strokes:

Stroke	*Name* Character	Pinyin	*English*	*Explanation*
一	横	**Héng**	Horizontal	From left to right (→)
丨	竖	**Shù**	Vertical	From top to bottom (↓)
ノ 丶	点	**Diǎn**	Left-falling dot and right-falling dot	From right to bottom left (↙) From left to bottom right (↘)
丿	撇	**Piě**	Left-falling	From top right to bottom left (↙)
㇏	捺	**Nà**	Right-falling	From top left to bottom right (↘)
㇀	提	**Tí**	Rising	From bottom left to top right (↗)
亅乚㇂	钩	**Gōu**	Hook	Various hooks, all made by bringing the pen downward first then adding a hook (some are made quickly and others are made slowly) (亅乚㇂)
㇇㇕	折	**Zhé**	Turning	Various turnings, all made with a left to right stroke that turns downward at the end (some are made quickly and others are made slowly) (㇇ ㇕)

Based on the above basic strokes, there are many other combinations such as

héngpiě wāngōu
(horizontal plus left–falling plus slanting vertical hook),

héngzhégōu
(horizontal plus turning hook),

shùwāngōu
(vertical plus right-turn),

shùzhézhégōu
(vertical plus horizontal plus vertical hook),

héngzhézhépiě
(horizontal turning, and another turning plus left–falling), etc.

2 Rules of stroke order

The chart below shows the rules regarding stroke order in writing Chinese characters:

Example	*Stroke order*	*Rule*
十	一 十	First horizontal, then vertical
人	丿 人	First left–falling, then right–falling
三	一 二 三	First top, then bottom
儿	丿 儿	First left, then right
问	门 问	First outside, then inside
国	冂 国 国	Finish inside, then close
小	亅 小 小	Middle, then left, then right

3 Radicals

Most of the modern Chinese characters are formed of two components: one is called the 'radical' (known as 部首 **bùshǒu** 'common heads' in Chinese), indicating the classification of the character, and the other is called the phonetic, providing a clue to its pronunciation. The radical can be the left part, the right part, the top part or the bottom part. For example

马 **mǎ** (horse)

is a character in its own right but it is the phonetic for characters such as

妈 **mā** (mother),

骂 **mà** (to swear),

蚂蚁 **máyi** (ant).

Let us look at the radicals for these three **ma**s:

马	**mǎ**		horse
妈	**mā**	女	the woman radical
骂	**mà**	口口	two mouths on top
蚂	**má** in **máyi**	虫	the insect radical

Overleaf is a table of some most commonly used radicals:

When in isolation	*When in combination*	*Meaning*	*Example*
人	亻	people	他 **tā**, he
	氵	water	汤 **tāng**, soup
	冫	ice	冰 **bīng**, ice
	灬	fire	热 **rèn**, hot
	宀	roof	家 **jiā**, home
金	钅	metal	钱 **qián**, money
	纟	silk	线 **xiàn**, thread
心	忄	heart	懂 **dǒng**, to understand
言	讠	speech	说 **shuō**, to speak
	阝	abundant	都 **dōu**, all
	阝	cliff	陡 **dǒu**, steep
	彳	step	很 **hěn**, very
	犭	dog/animal	狗 **gǒu**, dog
	扌	hand	找 **zhǎo**, to look for
	攵	to tap/to knock	收 **shōu**, to received
爪	爫	hand/claws	爱 **ài**, to love
	艹	grass	茶 **chá**, tea
食	饣	food	饭 **fàn**, food
示	礻	sign/ceremony	礼 **lǐ**, virtue
	辶	advance	远 **yuǎn**, far
	衤	clothes	裙 **qún**, skirt
	疒	illness	疼 **téng**, painful
女	女	woman	妈 **mā**, mother
火	火	fire	灯 **dēng**, light
足	⻊	foot	跟 **gēn**, to follow
立	立	to stand	站 **zhàn**, to stand
土	土	soil	地 **dì**, floor/earth
王	王	king	球 **qiú**, ball
心	心	heart	心 **xiǎng**, to think
木	木	tree	林 **lín**, forest
目	目	eye/sight	眼 **yǎn**, eye

When in isolation	*When in combination*	*Meaning*	*Example*
日	日	sun	明 **míng**, bright
日	曰	sun	星 **xīng**, star
雨	雨	rain	雪 **xuě**, snow
口	口	mouth	吃 **chī**, to eat
月	月	flesh	脚 **jiǎo**, foot
竹	⺮	bamboo	笔 **bǐ**, pen

About 2,000 characters have been simplified in mainland China since the founding of the People's Republic so as to improve the literacy of the population. These 2,000 characters are called 'simplified characters' as opposed to 'complex characters' (also known as 'traditional form'). 'Complex characters' are still used in Hong Kong, Taiwan and other overseas Chinese communities. In this book, emphasis is laid on simplified characters.

Structure of this book

There are fifteen lessons in total. The lesson objectives are listed at the beginning of each lesson so that you know exactly what is expected of you. Each of the first fourteen lessons contains two situational dialogues. Lesson 15 has only one text, which takes the form of a personal letter. Most lessons have a character section which describes how to write some commonly used characters and sets out some character exercises. From Lesson 4 onwards character dialogues appear after the *pinyin* text and characters are also given next to *pinyin* in the vocabulary. It does not mean that you must learn characters at the same time. The choice is yours. Important language points which occur in each dialogue/text are explained with more examples in the 'Notes to dialogue/text' section. At the end of each lesson, there is a reading/listening comprehension section which reinforces what has been introduced earlier. There are also exercises in each lesson.

Lessons 1–3: These dialogues and vocabulary are in *pinyin.* After each dialogue, there is an idiomatic English translation of the dialogue and the vocabulary.

Lessons 4–5: Each dialogue is first in *pinyin*, then in character. After each dialogue, there is an idiomatic English translation of the dialogue. The vocabulary is in *pinyin* and character.

Lessons 6–15: These dialogues and vocabulary are in *pinyin* and character. However, there is no idiomatic English translation of each dialogue. You can find the English translation of those dialogues in Appendix D.

The key to all the exercises and the answers to the questions in the reading/listening comprehension in each lesson are given at the end of the book.

Finally, there are two points about the symbols used in the book: (a) the abbreviation '*lit.*' means 'literal meaning'; and (b) the apostrophe (') is used to separate two syllables whenever there may be a confusion over the syllable boundary (e.g. **qīn'ài** – **n** belongs to the first syllable not the second).

1 Chū cì jiànmiàn

Meeting someone for the first time

By the end of this lesson, you should be able to:

- say who you are
- greet people and respond to greetings
- ask, and respond to, some yes/no questions
- use some appropriate forms of address
- write your first Chinese characters

Dialogue 1

Nǐ hǎo How do you do?

David Jones has just arrived at Beijing Airport. His potential Chinese business partner, Wang Lin, is there to meet him

WÁNG LÍN: Nǐ shì Jones xiānsheng ma?
DAVID JONES: Shì de. Wǒ shì David Jones.

WÁNG LÍN: Nǐ hǎo, Jones xiānsheng. Wǒ shì Wáng Lín. Hěn gāoxìng jiàndào nǐ.
DAVID JONES: Nǐ hǎo, Wáng xiānsheng. Wǒ yě hěn gāoxìng jiàndào nǐ.
WÁNG LÍN: Qǐng jiào wǒ Lǎo Wáng.
DAVID JONES: Hǎo de, Lǎo Wáng. Jiào wǒ David ba.
WÁNG LÍN: Huānyíng nǐ lái Zhōngguó, David.

WANG LIN: *Are you Mr Jones?*
DAVID JONES: *Yes. I am David Jones.*
WANG LIN: *How do you do, Mr Jones. I'm Wang Lin. Very pleased to meet you.*
DAVID JONES: *How do you do, Mr Wang. I'm very pleased to meet you too.*
WANG LIN: *Please call me Lao Wang.*
DAVID JONES: *OK, Lao Wang. Please call me David.*
WANG LIN: *Welcome to China, David.*

Vocabulary

nǐ you
shì be (am, is, are)
xiānsheng Mr
ma [question word, see Note 5]
shì de yes
wǒ I/me
hǎo to be good/to be well/to be fine/good/fine/well
Nǐ hǎo How do you do?/hello [*lit.* 'you well']
hěn very
gāoxìng to be pleased/to be happy/to be glad/happy/glad
jiàndào to meet
yě also/too
jiào to call/to be called
lǎo old/to be old
ba [grammar word, see Note 8]
hǎo de OK
qǐng please
huānyíng to welcome
lái to come/to come to
Zhōngguó China

Notes to Dialogue 1

1 Greetings

Nǐ hǎo (How do you do?/Hello) is the most common form of greeting in Chinese, which can be used at any time of the day. In response, the person being greeted replies by repeating **Nǐ hǎo**. Further greeting expressions will appear throughout the book. Note that whenever a third tone (e.g. **nǐ**) precedes another third tone (e.g. **hǎo**), the first third tone is changed to a second tone. Thus it should be pronounced **Ní hǎo . . .** *not* **Nǐ hǎo**.

2 Names and forms of address

In Chinese, names always appear in the following order: surname, first name, title (when used). For example:

> **Wáng Lín** – **Wáng** is the surname, and **Lín** is the first name; **Dèng Xiǎopíng** – **Dèng** is the surname, and **Xiǎopíng** is the first name.

Colleagues and friends address each other either by full name (surname + first name) or by putting **lǎo** (old) or **xiǎo** (young/little) in front of the surname depending on the relative age and seniority of the speaker. For example:

> A younger person (whose surname is Li) may address a colleague (whose surname is Zhang) who is in his/her fifties as **Lǎo Zhāng** to show respect. Conversely, Lao Zhang can call this younger person **Xiǎo Lǐ.**

Sometimes, **lǎo** is used as a friendly term among men even in their thirties and forties to address each other. First names are used among families and close friends.

Titles like **xiānsheng** (Mr), **nǚshì** (Madam), **xiǎojie** (Miss) are seldom used among Chinese people in mainland China since 1949; but recently, because of the increasing number of tourists and close links with the west, these titles are increasingly used in business and tourist circles. Professional titles such as **jīnglǐ** (manager), **jiàoshòu** (professor), **lǎoshī** teacher) are used as forms of address. When titles are used, first names are usually omitted. For example:

If someone is called Li Xinzi, and he/she is a teacher, this person can be addressed and referred to as **Lǐ lǎoshī** (*lit.* 'Li teacher').

3 Personal pronouns wǒ *and* nǐ

Personal pronouns **wǒ** (I/me) and **nǐ** ('you' singular) can be used both as the subject and the object. Note the positions in the sentence. The subject comes before the verb; the object comes after the verb. For example:

Wǒ **shì Wáng Lín.** verb	I am Wang Lin.
Jiào *wǒ* Lǎo Wáng ba. verb	Call me Lao Wang, please.
Hěn gāoxìng jiàndào *nǐ*. verb	Very pleased to meet you.

This rule applies to all other personal pronouns. Below is a full list of Chinese personal pronouns:

Chinese	*English*
wǒ	I, me
nǐ	you (singular)
nín	you (polite form)
tā	he/she, him/her
wǒ*men*	we, us
nǐ*men*	you (plural)
tā*men*	they, them

As you may have noticed, 'he' and 'she' share the same pronunciation (but are represented by different characters). To make plural personal pronouns (e.g. 'we', 'you' and 'they'), simply add **men** to singular personal pronouns **wǒ**, **nǐ** and **tā**. On its own, **mén** has the second tone, but becomes toneless in **wǒmen**, **nǐmen** and **tāmen**.

4 Sentences with shì

One of the usages of **shì** (to be) sentences is to say who you are. For example:

Wǒ *shì* Zhāng Píng.	I *am* Zhang Ping.
Tāmen *shì* Zhōngguórén.	They *are* Chinese.
Tā *shì* lǎoshī.	He/she *is* a teacher.

As we can see, the verb **shì** remains the same in the above three sentences, which makes things less complicated. Thus we have:

Wǒ	shì Zhōngguórén.	I *am* Chinese.
Nǐ	shì Zhōngguórén.	You *are* Chinese.
Tā	shì Zhōngguórén.	He/she *is* Chinese.
Wǒmen	shì Zhōngguórén.	We *are* Chinese.
Nǐmen	shì Zhōngguórén.	You *are* Chinese.
Tāmen	shì Zhōngguórén.	They *are* Chinese.

5 Yes/no questions with ma

To ask a yes/no question in Chinese (i.e. a question that demands the response 'yes' or 'no'), all you need to do is to add **ma** at the end of a statement and speak with a rising tone as in English. There is no need to change the word order. For example:

Statement	*Yes/no question*
Nǐ shì Jones xiānsheng.	**Nǐ shì Jones xiānsheng *ma*?** ↗
You are Mr Jones.	Are you Mr Jones?
Tā shì Zhōngguórén.	**Tā shì Zhōngguórén *ma*?** ↗
He/she is Chinese.	Is he/she Chinese?

6 Verb–adjectives

In English, there are no verb–adjectives since adjectives can be preceded by the verb *to be*. However, in Chinese, some adjectives can incorporate the verb 'to be' and they become verb–adjectives. For example, the word **lǎo** is an adjective when it means 'old', but it is a verb–adjective when it means 'to be old'. Note that the verb **shì** (to be) is not used in this case. When these verb–adjectives are used, they are usually modified by adverbs such as **hěn** (very), **tǐng** (rather), etc. in front of them. Thus, we have:

	Tā tǐng *lǎo*.
Lit.	He/she rather be old.
	She is rather old.

	Wǒ hěn *gāoxìng*.
Lit.	I very be happy.
	I am very happy.

7 *Use of* qǐng

When the word **qǐng** (please) is used to invite someone politely to do something, as we saw in Dialogue 1, it is always placed at the beginning of a sentence/phrase. For example:

Qǐng **lái Zhōngguó.**	Please come to China.
Qǐng **jiào wǒ Lǎo Wáng.**	Please call me Lao Wang.

8 *Use of* ba

This word does not have any specific meaning on its own; however, if you place it at the end of a sentence/phrase, it makes whatever you say sound friendly and casual. It can be broadly translated as 'please' in these contexts. The difference between the word **ba** and **qǐng** is that **ba** is placed at the end of sentences/phrases, and it is less formal. For example:

Jiào wǒ Lǎo Wáng *ba*.	Call me Lao Wang, please.
Chī *ba*.	Eat, please.

9 *Adverb* yě

The adverb **yě** (also) usually occurs before the phrase it modifies whether it is an adjective phrase or a verbal phrase. For example:

	Wǒ	***yě***	**shì**	**Zhōngguórén.**		
Lit.	I	also	be	Chinese.		
	I am also Chinese.					
	Wǒ	***yě***	**hěn**	**gāoxìng**	**jiàndào**	**nǐ.**
Lit.	I	also	very	be pleased	meet	you.
	I'm also very pleased to meet you.					

Note that when three third tones are together and they belong to the same meaning group, the first and the last third tones remain unchanged whilst the second third tone changes to the second tone. Thus **wǒ yě hěn** in the above sentence should be pronounced **wǒ yé hěn**.

10 *Verb* huānyíng

If you want to say 'Welcome to China' in Chinese, you must use the structure 'Welcome you come to China'. Thus, we have **Huānyíng nǐ lái Zhōngguó**.

Exercises

Exercise 1

Solve the problems:

(a) How many ways can you think of to address the following:
  (i) a man named **Zhāng Gōngmín**, manager, whom you have just met, and who is older than you;
  (ii) a woman named **Lín Fāng**, single, whom you have known for some time on a strictly business basis, and who is younger than you;
  (iii) a very close friend whose name is **Gǒng Qíbín**, and who is younger than you.
(b) It is late in the evening, you bump into your colleague, **Wáng Lín**, and want to greet him. What do you say?
(c) If you meet a Chinese person for the first time, after the initial how-do-you-do greeting, what else can you say?

Exercise 2

Fill in the blanks:

(a) Wǒ _______ (*to be*) Tāng Píng.
(b) Wǒ hěn gāoxìng jiàndào _______ (*her*).
(c) A: Nǐ shì Wáng Lín ma?
    B: _______ (*Yes*).

Exercise 3

Turn the following statements into yes/no questions using **ma**:

(a) Nǐ shì Wáng xiānsheng.
(b) Tā (*He/she*) hěn gāoxìng jiàndào nǐ.
(c) Tāmen (*They*) lái Zhōngguó.

Exercise 4

Re-arrange the word order of the following three groups so that each group becomes a meaningful sentence:

(a) hěn, yě, wǒ, jiàndào, gāoxìng, nǐ
(b) qǐng, jiào, David, wǒ
(c) lái, Zhōngguó, nǐ, huānyíng

Dialogue 2
Nǐ lèi ma? Are you tired?

After their initial greetings, Lao Wang and David move on to talk about the trip

LǍO WÁNG: Nǐde yīlù shùnlì ma?
DAVID: Hěn shùnlì, xièxie.
LǍO WÁNG: Nǐ lèi ma?
DAVID: Yǒu yīdiǎn lèi.
LǍO WÁNG: Nǐ xiǎng hē yī bēi kāfēi ma?
DAVID: Tài xiǎng le.
(*later, inside the café*)
LǍO WÁNG: Zhè shì nǐde kāfēi, David.
DAVID: Xièxie.
LǍO WÁNG: Bù kèqi.

LAO WANG: *Did you have a nice trip?*
DAVID: *Yes, very nice, thank you.*
LAO WANG: *Are you tired?*
DAVID: *A little bit.*
LAO WANG: *Would you like to have a coffee?*
DAVID: *That would be lovely.*
(*later, inside the café*)
LAO WANG: *Here's your coffee, David.*
DAVID: *Thank you.*
LAO WANG: *You're welcome.*

Vocabulary

nǐde your/yours
yīlù trip/journey [*lit.* 'one road' or 'whole way']
shùnlì to be smooth

xièxie	thank you [*lit.* 'thank thank']
lèi	to be tired
yǒu yīdiǎn	a little bit [*lit.* 'to have a little']
xiǎng	would like/to want [when followed by another verb]
hē	to drink
yī	one
yī bēi	one cup/one glass
kāfēi	coffee
tài . . . le	extremely/very much/too
zhè	this
bù	no/not
bù kèqi	you are welcome [*lit.* 'not polite']

Notes to Dialogue 2

11 Possessive pronouns (e.g. 'my', 'his', etc.)

Simply add **de** to the personal pronouns **wǒ**, **nǐ**, **tā**, etc. to form possessive pronouns and possessive adjectives. In English, possessive adjectives are different from possessive pronouns (e.g. 'my' in front of nouns, and 'mine' at the end of the sentence). In Chinese, however, they are the same. For example:

Zhè shì *wǒde* kāfei.	This is *my* coffee.
Zhè bēi kāfēi shì *wǒde*.	This coffee is *mine*.

You must also add **de** to a person's name to indicate the relationship between the person and an object. For example:

Zhè shì Xiǎo Lǐ *de* kāfēi.	This is Xiao Li*'s* coffee.

Below is a comparison of Chinese and English possessive pronouns and possessive adjectives:

Chinese Possessive adjective and pronoun	*English* Possessive adjective (in front of nouns)	*English* Possessive pronoun (at the end of the sentence)
wǒ*de*	my	mine
nǐ*de*	your	yours
tā*de*	his/her	his/hers

wǒmén*de*	our	ours
nǐmén*de*	your	yours
tāmén*de*	their	theirs

Sometimes, **de** can be omitted. Thus we can say ***Nǐde* yīlù shùnlì ma?** or ***Nǐ* yīlù shùnlì ma?** (Was your journey smooth?/Did you have a nice jouney?). Please note that the word **de** is toneless.

12 Two verbs occurring in the same sentence

Whenever there are two or more verbs occurring in the same sentence or phrase, merely put them together. There is no link word 'to' to be used. Also remember that the verbs remain unchanged regardless of the pronoun as we saw earlier in Note 4. For example:

Wǒ *xiǎng jiào* Wáng Lín 'Lǎo Wáng'.
Lit. I want call Wang Lin 'Lao Wang'.
I *want to call* Wang Lin 'Lao Wang'.

Tā *xiǎng hē* yī bēi kāfēi.
Lit. She would like drink one cup coffee.
She*'d like to have* a cup of coffee.

Note that the verb **xiǎng** means 'to want' or 'would like to' only when it precedes another verb.

13 Negation word bù

To negate a verb, verb–adjective or the adverb 'hěn', simply put **bù** in front of them. For example:

Wǒ *bù* shì Wáng Lín.
verb
Lit. I not be Wang Lin.
I am *not* Wang Lin.

Note that the word **bù** carries the fourth tone. However, when **bù** is followed by another fourth-tone word, it should be pronounced with the second tone.

Tā *bù* xiǎng lái Zhōngguó.
verb[1] verb[2]
Lit. He not want come to China.
He does*n't* want to come to China.

Tāmen hěn *bù* gāoxìng.
verb–adjective
Lit. They very not be happy.
They are very unhappy.

Tāmen *bù* hěn gāoxìng.
adverb
Lit. They not very be happy.
They are *not* very happy.

Note that **Tāmen hěn *bù* gāoxìng** differs in meaning from **Tāmen *bù* hěn gāoxìng**. The former negates the verb–adjective whilst the latter negates the adverb **hěn**.

14 Responding to questions ending with ma

In English, yes/no questions are so called because the answers to them almost always involve a *yes* or a *no*. However, in Chinese, **shì de** (yes) and **bú shì** (no) are not often used. They are definitely used if the verb **shì** is in the question. For example:

A: **Nǐ *shì* Jones xiānsheng ma?** A: Are you Mr Jones?
B: ***Shì de.*** B: Yes.
or ***Bù shì.*** No.

When the verb **shì** is not in the question, usually the main verb/verb–adjective which occurs in the question is either repeated in the answer for 'yes' or negated for 'no'. For example:

A: **Nǐ *lèi* ma?** A: Are you tired?
Lit. You be tired [yes/no question word]?

B: **Hěn *lèi.*** *or* **Bù lèi.** B: Yes, very tired./No.
Lit. Very tired. Not tired.

A: **Nǐ *xiǎng* hē kāfēi ma?**
Lit. You want drink coffee [yes/no question word]?
Would you like to have some coffee?

B: ***Xiǎng,* xièxie.** *or* **Bù *xiǎng,* xièxie.**
Lit. Want, thank thank. Not want, thank thank.
Yes, thank you. No, thank you.

Note, if you want to say 'Yes, please' in Chinese, add **xièxie** (thank you), not **qǐng** (please), after the verb. The word **qǐng** is used for different purposes (see Note 7 above).

15 Tài . . . le

The word **tài** by itself means 'too' (as in 'too sweet', for example). It has to be used in conjunction with **le** to mean 'extremely' or 'very much'. The word **le** does not mean anything by itself. Note that you need to put the adjective or the verb (sometimes a verbal phrase) you want to modify in between **tài** and **le**. For example:

Tài* hǎo *le. adjective	*Extremely* good.
Tài* xiǎng *le. verb	I want it *very much*.
Wǒ *tài* xiǎng hē kāfēi *le.* verbal phrase	I'd *very much* like to have a coffee.

However, the word **le** is omitted when the negation word **bù** is used. For example:

Bù tài lèi.	Not too tired.
Bù tài shùnlì.	Not too smooth.

Exercises

Exercise 5

(i) Use the question word **ma** to ask Lao Wang whether:
  (a) he is tired
  (b) he is happy
  (c) he would like to have a coffee
(ii) to pretend that you are Lao Wang, and answer the questions first in the positive and then in the negative.

Exercise 6

Complete the following exchanges:

(a) A: Nǐ hǎo.
  B: ______________ (*Hello*).
(b) A: Xièxie.
  B: ______________ (*You're welcome*).
(c) A: Nǐ shì Wáng Lín ma?
  B: ______________ (*Yes*). Wǒ shì Wáng Lín.

(d) A: Zhè shì nǐde kāfēi ma?
B: ____________ (*No*). Zhè shì Lǎo Wáng de.
(e) A: Nǐ xiǎng hē kāfēi ma?
B: ____________ (*Yes, please*).

Exercise 7

Use the word **bù** to negate the following sentences:

(a) **Lǎo Wáng xiǎng hē kāfēi.** (Lao Wang does not want to have coffee.)
(b) **David hěn gāoxìng.** (David is not very happy.)
(c) **David hěn gāoxìng.** (David is very unhappy.)
(d) **Wǒde yīlù hěn shùnlì.** (My trip was not very smooth.)
(e) **Wǒde yīlù hěn shùnlì.** (My trip was very rough.)
(f) **Tā shì Jones xiānsheng.** (He is not Mr Jones.)

Exercise 8

When the question **Nǐ lèi ma?** is asked, how do you respond if you are:

(a) very tired
(b) a little bit tired
(c) not too tired

Exercise 9

Fill in the blanks:

(a) Zhè bù shì ______ (*my*) kāfēi. Zhè shì ______ (*his*) kāfēi.
(b) ______ (*her*) kāfēi bù tài hǎo.
(c) Zhè bù shì ______ (*mine*). Zhè shì ______ (*Andrew's*).

Characters

Learning to write Nǐ hǎo (hello) and Zhōngguó (China)

Now, you may wish to try writing (or drawing!) the greeting expression **Nǐ hǎo** in characters. When Chinese children start writing characters, they use square boxes, and every box has a cross in the middle. Look at the boxes below:

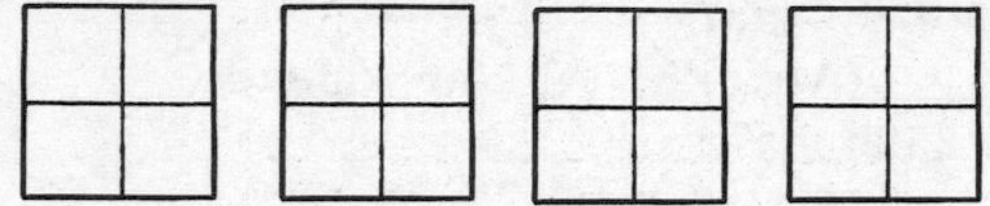

The purpose of the box is to help them get the size and the proportion of the character right, and the purpose of the cross is to help them position the character in the middle of the box. Let us see how the two characters for **Nǐ hǎo** look like inside these boxes:

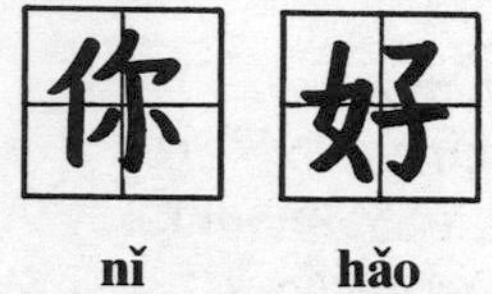

It is a good idea to use these boxes when you first start writing characters. Let us now learn how to write **Nǐ hǎo**, step by step. The first character **nǐ** has seven strokes, which are written in the following order:

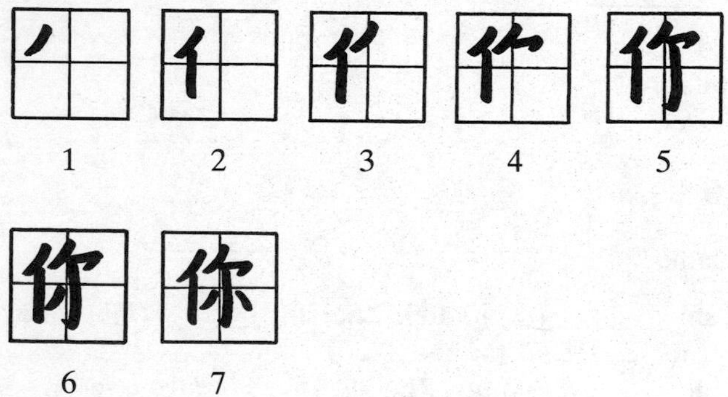

The left part of **nǐ** 亻 is called the 'person radical' because it looks rather like the character for 'person/people' (pronounced **rén**). When **rén** is written in a box, we have:

The 'person radical' is used very often to form other characters, so you may wish to make a note of it.

The second character **hǎo** has six strokes, which are written in the following order:

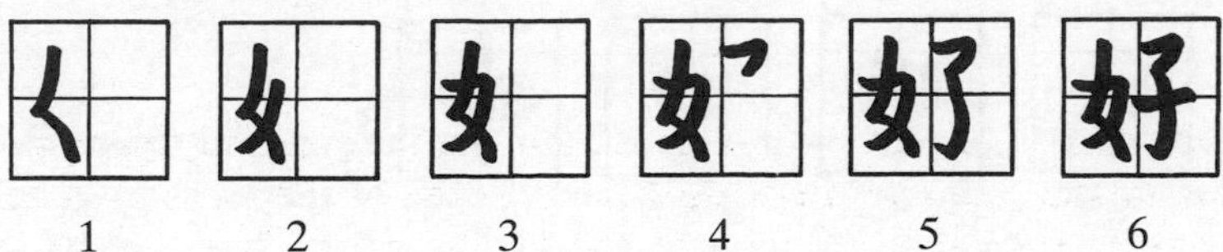

Now, let us take **hǎo** apart. The left side 女 by itself means 'woman/female' (pronounced **nǚ**), and it is called the 'woman radical', and the right side 子 is a formal word for 'son' (pronounced **zǐ**). Can this possibly reflect a culture where a woman who can give birth to a son is regarded as being capable, and hence good? When these two characters are written independently, they look like this:

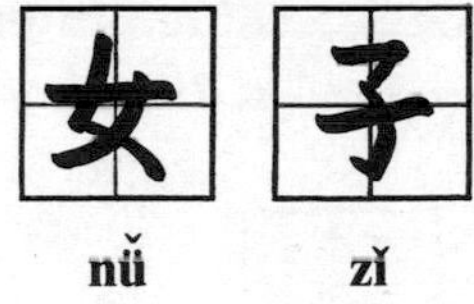

In effect, you have now learnt five characters. They are:

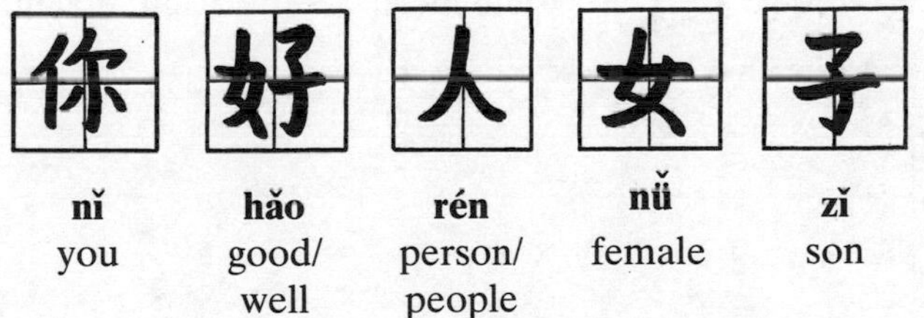

Let us now try to write **Zhōngguó** (China).

The word **zhōng** means 'central' or 'middle' by itself, and the word **guó** means 'country' by itself. So you now know what **Zhōngguó** really means! This is probably why China is often referred to in books and newspaper articles as 'the Middle Kingdom'. They look like this in boxes:

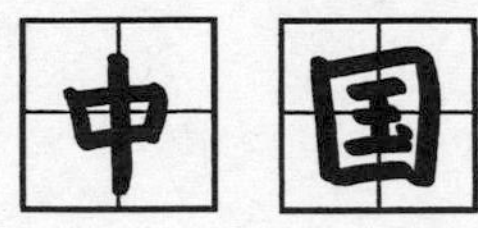

Now, let us take these two characters apart. The first one, **Zhōng**, has four strokes, which are written in the following order:

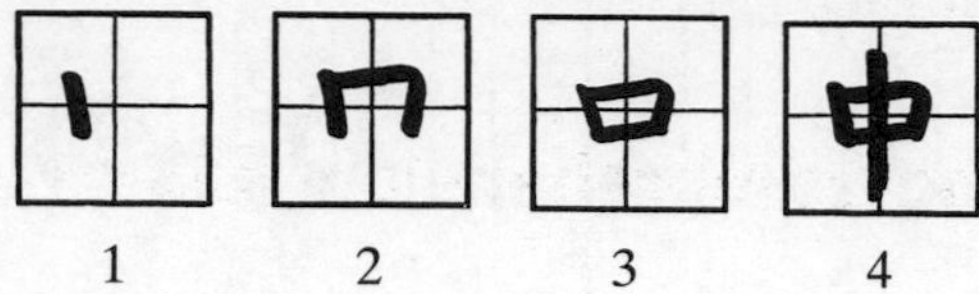

The second character, **guó**, has eight strokes, which are written in the following order:

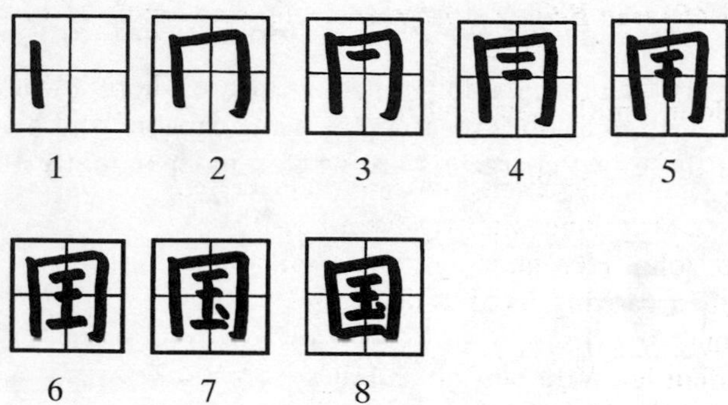

The character inside 玉 is pronounced **yù**, by itself meaning 'jade'. It looks like this in a box by itself:

A country may be interpreted as a place full of treasures such as jade surrounded by walls.

If you remember how to write **rén** (person/people) from page 30, you now know how to write **Zhōngguórén** (Chinese) in characters.

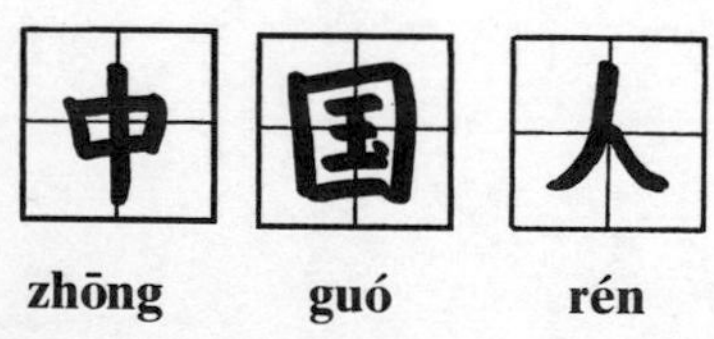

zhōng **guó** **rén**

You may now wish to write these characters on flash cards with *pinyin* and English translations on the other side of the cards so that you can practise recognizing them.

Reading/listening comprehension

Read the following dialogue, and try to answer the questions below in English. If you have the recording, listen to it first (try not to look at the script) and then answer the questions in English.

Zhang Ping (ZP) is at Beijing Airport meeting John Smith (JS) from Britain

ZP: Nǐ shì John Smith xiānsheng ma?
JS: Shì de. Nǐ shì . . .?
ZP: Nǐ hǎo, Smith xiānsheng. Wǒ shì Zhāng Píng.
JS: Nǐ hǎo, Zhāng Píng. Jiào wǒ John ba.
ZP: Hǎo de, John. Hěn gāoxìng jiàndào nǐ.
JS: Wǒ yě hěn gāoxìng jiàndào nǐ.
ZP: Nǐ lèi ma?
JS: Yǒu yīdiǎn lèi. Yīlù hěn bù shùnlì.
ZP: Nǐ xiǎng hē bēi kāfēi ma?
JS: Tài xiǎng le.

Questions

A What does John Smith prefer to be called?
B Did John Smith have a pleasant trip?
C What suggestion does Zhang Ping make?
D What is John Smith's response to Zhang Ping's suggestion?

2 Xìngmíng, guójí hé niánlíng

Name, nationality and age

By the end of this lesson, you should be able to:

- say what your name is
- say what your nationality is and whereabouts you come from
- say how old you are
- ask other people questions regarding the above three subjects
- use some of the appropriate expressions to respond to compliments
- count from 0 to 99
- say goodbye
- write more characters and recognize one sign

Dialogue 1

Nǐ jiào shénme? What's your name?

Amy, an American, is travelling in China. She sits opposite Fang Chun, a young Chinese man, on a train heading for Beijing. As Chinese people are very sociable, they soon strike up a conversation

FĀNG CHŪN: Nǐ huì shuō Zhōngwén ma?
AMY: Huì shuō yīdiǎn.
FĀNG CHŪN: Tài hǎo le. Wǒ jiào Fāng Chūn. Jiào wǒ Xiǎo Fāng ba. Nǐ jiào shénme?
AMY: Wǒ jiào Amy.
FĀNG CHŪN: Nǐ shì Yīngguórén ma?
AMY: Bù shì.

FĀNG CHŪN:	Nǐ shì nǎ guó rén?
AMY:	Nǐ cāi.
FĀNG CHŪN:	Wǒ bù zhīdao.
AMY:	Wǒ shì Měiguórén. Nǐ shì nǎli rén, Xiǎo Fāng?
FĀNG CHŪN:	Wǒ shì Běijīngrén. Nǐde Zhōngwén hěn hǎo.
AMY:	Nǎli, nǎli.

FANG CHUN:	*Can you speak Chinese?*
AMY:	*Just a little.*
FANG CHUN:	*Wonderful. My name is Fang Chun. Please call me Xiao Fang. What's your name?*
AMY:	*My name is Amy.*
FANG CHUN:	*Are you British?*
AMY:	*No.*
FANG CHUN:	*Which country do you come from?*
AMY:	*Have a guess.*
FANG CHUN:	*I don't know.*
AMY:	*I'm American. Whereabouts do you come from?*
FANG CHUN:	*I'm from Beijing. Your Chinese is very good.*
AMY:	*Not really.*

Vocabulary

huì	can/to be able to
shuō	to speak/to say
Zhōngwén	Chinese [as a language]
yīdiǎn	a little bit
tài hǎo le	wonderful
xiǎo	young/small/little/to be young/to be small/to be little
shénme	what
Yīngguó	Britain
rén	person/people
Yīngguórén	British [*lit.* 'Britain person/people']
nǎ	which
guó	country
cāi	to guess
zhīdao	to know/to be aware of
Měiguórén	American [*lit.* 'America person/people']
nǎli	where/whereabouts [see Note 6]
Běijīngrén	Beijingese [*lit.* 'Beijing person/people']
nǎli	not really/not at all [*lit.* 'whereabouts']

Notes to Dialogue 1

1 Use of huì

The word **huì**, known as an 'auxiliary verb' in grammatical terms, precedes other verbs to indicate whether a person has the ability to do something. To ask questions such as 'Can you speak Chinese?', simply add **ma** at the end of the statement. For example:

Statement	*Yes/no question*
Susan ***huì*** **shuō Zhōngwén.**	Susan **huì shuō Zhōngwén *ma*?**
Susan can speak Chinese.	Can Susan speak Chinese?

To answer a yes/no question which involves the word **huì**, you say **huì** for 'yes' and **bù huì** for 'no'. For example:

A: **Amy huì shuō Zhōngwén ma?**
Can Amy speak Chinese?
B: ***Huì.***
Yes. She can.

A: **Xiǎo Fāng huì shuō Yíngwén ma?**
Can Xiao Fang speak English?
B: ***Bù huì.***
No. *He can't.*

2 *Difference between* yīdiǎn *and* yǒu yīdiǎn

In Dialogue 2 of Lesson 1, we had the expression **yǒu yīdiǎn** (a little bit). There is no difference in meaning between **yīdiǎn** and **yǒu yīdiǎn:** however, **yīdiǎn** is usually used after the verb, and **yǒu yīdiǎn** (**yī** can be omitted here) is used before the verb–adjective. For example:

Tā huì shuō *yīdiǎn* Yīngwén.
verb
He/she can speak *a little bit* of English.

Wǒ *yǒu yīdiǎn* (or ***yǒu diǎn***) **lèi.**
verb–adjective
Lit. I a little bit be tired.
I'm *a bit* tired.

3 *Question word* shénme

When **shénme** (what) is used in a question, it occurs in the same place as where the information required should appear in the reply. For example:

A: **Nǐ jiào *shénme?***
Lit. You be called what?
A: *What*'s your name?

B: **Wǒ jiào *Lín Hóng.***
Lit. I be called Lin Hong.
B: My name is *Lin Hong.*

This rule applies to the positioning of all the question words.

4 Nǐ jiào shénme?

When you ask a Chinese person **Nǐ jiào shénme?** (What is your name?), you are usually given the full name (i.e. surname + first name). If you simply want to find out someone's surname, you ask **Nǐ *xìng* shénme?** (*lit.* 'You are *surnamed* what?'). If you want to be really formal, you ask **Nín guì xìng?** (*lit.* 'You honourable surname?'). The personal pronoun **nín** is a polite form of **nǐ** (you).

5 Question word nǎ

Whenever the question word **nǎ** (also pronounced **něi** by some people) precedes nouns, such as **guó** (country) in Dialogue 1, it means 'which'. For example:

	Nǐ	**shì** ***nǎ***	**guó**	**rén?**
			noun	
Lit.	You	be	which country	person?
	Which country do you come from?			

6 Question word nǎli

The question word **nǎli** (where/whereabouts) is used if you already know someone's nationality, but want to find out whereabouts this person originally comes from. For example:

	A:	**Nǐ**	**shì Zhōngguó**	***náli***	**rén?**
Lit.		You	be China	whereabouts	person?
		Whereabouts in China do you come from?			
	B:	**Shànghǎirén.**			
Lit.		Shanghai person.			
		Shanghai.			

Note that both **nǎ** and **lǐ** carry the third tone in isolation. Although **lǐ** becomes toneless when used with **nǎ**, it still changes **nǎ** into the second tone in actual pronounciation.

7 Names of countries

Names of countries are translated into Chinese arbitrarily. Some of them are based on the pronunciation, but others are not. Some of them have the word **guó** (country) in them, but others do not. By adding **rén** (person/people) to country/place names, we refer to the people who live in that country/place. For example:

Country/city		*Its people*	
Fǎguó	France	**Fǎguó*rén***	French
Déguó	Germany	**Déguó*rén***	German
Àodàlìyà	Australia	**Àodàlìyà*rén***	Australian
Xīnxīlán	New Zealand	**Xīnxīlán*rén***	New Zealander
Rìběn	Japan	**Rìběn*rén***	Japanese
Xīnjiāpō	Singapore	**Xīnjiāpō*rén***	Singaporean
Táiwān	Taiwan	**Táiwān*rén***	Taiwanese
Xiāng Gǎng	Hong Kong	**Xiāng Gǎng*rén***	Hong Kongese
Yìdàlì	Italy	**Yìdàlì*rén***	Italian
Lúndūn	London	**Lúndūn*rén***	Londoner

8 Ways of referring to different languages

To refer to the language spoken in a particular country, in most cases, you can add either **wén** or **yǔ** (language) to the first syllable of a country's name or add **huà** (speech/talk) to the whole name of a country. For example:

Country		*Its language*	
Yīngguó	Britain	**Yīng*wén*/Yīng*yǔ*/Yīngguó*huà***	English
Fǎguó	France	**Fǎ*wén*/Fá*yǔ*/Fǎguó*huà***	French
Déguó	Germany	**Dé*wén*/Dé*yǔ*/Déguó*huà***	German
Rìběn	Japan	**Rì*wén*/Rì*yǔ*/Rìběn*huà***	Japanese

However, this rule does not apply to some countries. For countries such as Italy and Spain, you must add **wén**, **yǔ** or **huà** to the whole name of the country. For example:

Country		*Its language*	
Yìdàlì	Italy	**Yìdàlì*wén*/Yìdàlì*yǔ*/Yìdàlì*huà***	Italian
Xībānyá	Spain	**Xībānyá*wén*/Xībānyá*yǔ*/Xībānyá*huà***	Spanish

There are many ways of referring to the (Mandarin) Chinese language. These include: **Hànyǔ** (literally '**hàn** language' since the **hàn** Chinese race comprises the vast majority of the population); **Zhōngwén** (a more formal term); **Zhōngguóhuà** (a less formal term); **Pǔtōnghuà** (*lit.* 'common speech', which is the Modern Standard Chinese); **Guóyǔ** (used in Taiwan, *lit.* 'national language' as opposed to regional dialects); and **Huáyǔ** (used among Chinese communities abroad, **huá** is another adjective for 'Chinese'). However, Chinese people realize that the terms most commonly used by Chinese-language learners are **Zhōngwén** and **Pǔtōnghuà.**

9 *Use of* zhīdao

The verb **zhīdao** (to know/to be aware of) is mostly used to talk about things you know or people you know of but not personally. It can be followed by a noun phrase or a sentence. For example:

	Nǐ	***zhīdao***	**tā**	**jiào**	**shénme**	**ma?**	
Lit.	You	know	he/she	be called	what	[question word]?	

Do you *know* what he/she is called?

	Wǒ	**bù**	***zhīdao***	**nǐ**	**shì**	**nǎ**	**guó**	**rén.**
Lit.	I	not	know	you	be	which	country	person.

I don't know which country you come from.

Compare the sentence order of **tā jiào shénme** and **nǐ shì nǎ guó rén** after the verb **zhīdao** to that of the questions **Tā jiào shénme?** (What is he/she called?) and **Nǐ shì nǎ guó rén?** (Which country are you from?) in Notes 3 and 5 above. You will notice that the sentence order is exactly the same.

10 *Polite talk* nǎli, nǎli

It is part of Chinese culture to be over-modest. When a person is complimented, he/she is supposed to deny the compliment. One of the expressions used on such occasions is **nǎli**, meaning 'not at all' or 'not really' and it is usually repeated. Another way of responding to a compliment is simply to deny what has been said. For example:

A: **Nǐde Zhōngwén hěn hǎo.**
A: Your Chinese is very good.

B: ***Bù hǎo, bù hǎo.***
B: *Not good, not good.*

Exercises

Exercise 1

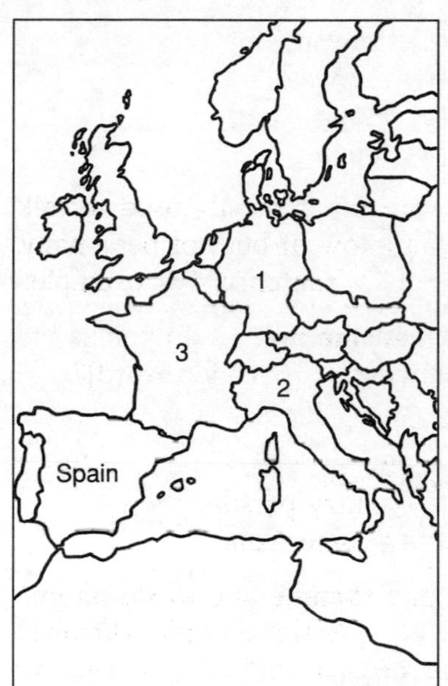

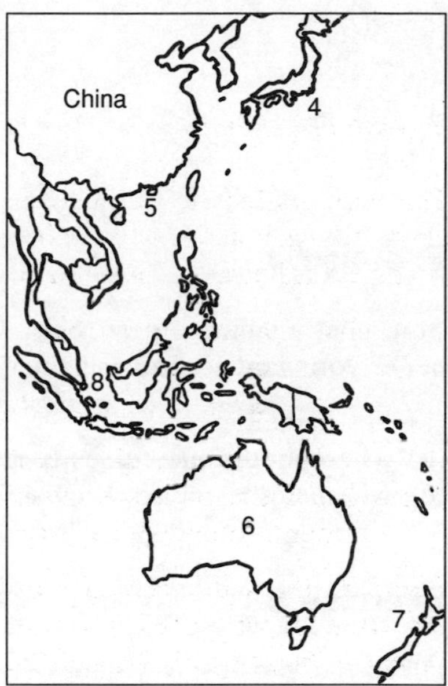

Look at the maps and match the number of each country/region with the corresponding Chinese name listed below. Then translate each name into English:

(a) Rìběn
(b) Fǎguó
(c) Déguó
(d) Àodàlìyà
(e) Xiāng Gǎng
(f) Xīnxīlán
(g) Xīnjiāpō
(h) Yìdàlì

Exercise 2

Give the Chinese terms for the people who live in the following countries/places:

(a) Britain
(b) America
(c) China
(d) Italy
(e) Taiwan
(f) Hong Kong
(g) Australia
(h) Japan

Exercise 3

Give the Chinese terms for the language(s) spoken in the following countries/places:

(a) Britain
(b) America
(c) China
(d) Italy
(e) Taiwan
(f) France
(g) Hong Kong
(h) Japan

Exercise 4

You meet a Chinese person for the first time. What do you say to her if you want to find out the following?

(a) her name
(b) whereabouts she comes from
(c) whether she speaks English

Exercise 5

Fill in the gaps using **yīdiǎn** or **yǒu yīdiǎn**:

(a) Amy shuō ____________ Zhōngwén.
(b) John ____________ lèi.
(c) Wáng Lín ____________ bù gāoxìng.
(d) Xiǎo Lǐ xiǎng hē ____________ kāfēi.

Exercise 6

Complete the other half of the exchange:

(a) A: ____________?
B: Wǒ shì Měiguórén.
(b) A: ____________?
B: Tā shì Běijīngrén.
(c) A: Nǐde Zhōngwén hěn hǎo.
B: ____________ (*Not really.*)
(d) A: Nǐ huì shuō Rìwén ma?
B: ____________ (*No, I can't.*)

Exercise 7

Translate into Chinese:

(a) Do you know which country Amy comes from?
(b) I cannot speak English.
(c) She is not Japanese.
(d) I don't know what he is called.

Dialogue 2
Nǐ duō dà le? How old are you?

Amy and Xiao Fang get on very well with each other. The conversation becomes more personal

AMY: Xiǎo Fāng, nǐ jīn nián duō dà le?
XIǍO FĀNG: Wǒ sānshí'èr suì le.
AMY: Zhēn de? Nǐ kànshangqu zhǐyǒu èrshíwǔ suì zuǒyòu.
XIǍO FĀNG: Guòjiǎng. Nǐ duō dà le?
AMY: Wǒ èrshíyī.
XIǍO FĀNG: Nǐ zhēn niánqīng. Zhème shuō, wǒ yīnggāi shì Lǎo Fāng.
AMY: Bù dùi, bù duì. Nǐ shì 'Xiǎo Fāng'.
(*five minutes before the train arrives at Beijing, they say goodbye*)
XIǍO FĀNG: Rènshi nǐ, wǒ hěn gāoxìng, Amy.
AMY: Wǒ yě shì, Xiǎo Fāng.
XIǍO FĀNG: Zàijiàn, Amy.
AMY: Zàijiàn, Xiǎo Fāng.

AMY: *Xiao Fang, how old are you this year?*
XIAO FANG: *I'm thirty-two.*
AMY: *Really? You look only about twenty-five.*
XIAO FANG: *I'm flattered. How old are you?*
AMY: *I'm twenty-one years old.*
XIAO FANG: *You are really young. In that case, I should be 'old Fang'.*
AMY: *No, no. You are 'young Fang'.*
(five minutes before the train arrives at Beijing, they say goodbye)
XIAO FANG: *I'm so pleased that I met you, Amy.*
AMY: *Me too, Xiao Fang.*
XIAO FANG: *Goodbye, Amy.*
AMY: *Bye, Xiao Fang.*

Vocabulary

jīn nián	this year
duō	how
dà	to be old/to be large/to be big/large/big
le	[grammar word, see Note 13]
sānshí'èr	thirty-two
suì	years old
zhēn de?	really?
kànshangqu	to appear/to seem/to look
zhǐyǒu	only
zuǒyòu	about/approximate [*lit.* 'left right']
guòjiǎng	to be flattered [*lit.* 'over-praising']
èrshíyī	twenty-one
zhēn	really
niánqīng	to be young/young
zhème shuō	in that case [*lit.* 'so speak']
yīnggāi	should/ought
duì	to be correct/correct
bù duì	to be incorrect/incorrect
rènshi	to know [somebody]/to get to know [somebody]
wǒ yě shì	me too/same here [*lit.* 'I also am']
zàijiàn	goodbye [*lit.* 'again meet']

Notes to Dialogue 2

11 Nǐ duō dà le?

This question is used to ask about an adult's age. Generally, Chinese people (including women!) are not offended by the question **Nǐ duō dà le?** (How old are you?). When the verb–adjective **dà** (to be big/old) is used in this context, it refers to someone's age, not their size. The word **lǎo** (to be old) we learnt in Lesson 1 is not appropriate here because **Nǐ duō *lǎo* le?** implies that the person being asked does look very very old.

12 *Numbers*

0–9		10–19		20–29	
líng	zero	**shí**	ten	**èrshí**	twenty
yī	one	**shíyī**	eleven	**èrshíyī**	twenty-one
èr (liǎng)	two	**shí'èr**	twelve	**èrshí'èr**	twenty-two
sān	three	**shísān**	thirteen	**èrshísàn**	twenty-three
sì	four	**shísì**	fourteen	**èrshísì**	twenty-four
wǔ	five	**shíwǔ**	fifteen	**èrshíwǔ**	twenty-five
liù	six	**shíliù**	sixteen	**èrshíliù**	twenty-six
qī	seven	**shíqī**	seventeen	**èrshíqī**	twenty-seven
bā	eight	**shíbā**	eighteen	**èrshíbā**	twenty-eight
jiǔ	nine	**shíjiǔ**	nineteen	**èrshíjiǔ**	twenty-nine

Numbers 30, 40, etc. . . . 90 are formed by adding **shí** (ten) to **sān** (three), **sì** (four), etc. . . . **jiǔ** (nine). Thus we have: **sānshí** (thirty), **sìshí** (forty), **wǔshí** (fifty), etc. The numbers 31–9, 41–9, etc., use the same principle as 21–9 above. An apostrophe (') is used to mark the break between two syllables whenever there is ambiguity in pronunciation. Thus we have **shí'èr** (twelve) instead of **shíèr.**

13 *Grammar word* le

This grammar word **le** (also called 'past particle') in this context suggests a change of state. For instance, when someone says **Wǒ èrshíyī suì le** (I'm twenty-one years old), the speaker means that he/she has already become twenty-one (both **suì** and **le** can be omitted, but **suì** must be used if the age is less than ten). For example:

Mary sānshíbā. *or* **Mary sānshíbā** ***suì.***	Mary is thirty-eight.
Línlin wǔ ***suì.***	Linlin is five.

Note that (a) **le** must be used in the question **Nǐ duō dà** ***le*?** (How old are you?); and (b) in telling one's age, the verb **shì** (to be) is not used.

14 *Use of* kànshangqu

The usage of the verb **kànshangqu** is very similar to the English verbs 'to look', 'to appear' or 'to seem' when they are used in affirmative sentences. For example:

Xiǎo Fāng *kànshangqu* hěn niánqīng.
Xiao Fang *looks* very young.

Nǐ *kànshangqu* yǒu yīdiǎn lèi.
You *look* a little tired.

To negate the above two sentences, put the negation word **bù** after the verb **kànshangqu** and before the adjective. For example:

Xiǎo Fāng kànshangqu *bù* tài gāoxìng.
Lit. Xiao Fang look not too happy.
Xiao Fang does*n't* look very happy.

15 Use of zuǒyòu

When this phrase is used after numbers, it means 'about' or 'approximately'. For example:

Zhāng jīnglǐ sìshí *zuǒyòu.*
Lit. Zhang Manager forty about.
Manager Zhang is *about* forty.

16 Polite talk guòjiǎng

The expression **guòjiǎng** (to be flattered), which is often repeated (e.g. **guòjiǎng**, **guòjiǎng**), is used on similar occasions to the phrase **nǎli**, **nǎli** (not really/not at all) we saw in Dialogue 1. It is another way of responding to a compliment. For example:

A: **Nǐ kànshangqu hěn jīngshen.** You look very smart.
B: ***Guòjiǎng, guòjiǎng.*** I'm flattered.

17 Use of rènshi

Earlier in Note 9, we saw the verb **zhīdao** (to know). **Rènshi** is another verb meaning 'to know', except that in this case it is 'to know somebody personally'. Let us compare these two verbs:

Nǐ *rènshi* Wáng Lín ma? Do you *know* Wang Lin?
Wǒ bù *zhīdao* tā *rènshi* Amy. I didn't *know* that she *knows* Amy.

Note (a) between **zhīdao** and **tā rènshi Amy** (she knows Amy), there is no link word equivalent to the English word 'that'; and (b) you can say **Wǒ *zhīdao* Zhāng Yǒudé**, which means that you have heard of this person, or you know who he is, but you may not know him personally.

18 Topic structure

It is very common, but not essential, in the Chinese language to put the topic of the sentence first. For example:

> ***Rènshi nǐ,*** **wǒ hěn gāoxìng.**
> topic
> *Lit.* To know you, I very be pleased.
> I'm very pleased *to have met you.*

> ***Lái Zhōngguó,*** **wǒ hěn gāoxìng.**
> topic
> *Lit.* To come to China, I very be happy.
> I'm so happy *that I've come to China.*

Exercises

Exercise 8

Describe Amy and Fang Chun – the two characters in this lesson (e.g. their nationality, age, etc.).

Exercise 9

Complete the other half of the conversation:

(a) A: Nǐde Zhōngwén hěn hǎo.
B: ____________ (*Not really*).
(b) A: Bill duō dà le?
B: ____________ (*about 30*).
(c) A: David shì Měiguórén.
B: ____________ (*Incorrect*). Tā shì Yīngguórén.

Exercise 10

Fill in the blanks using **rènshi** (to know somebody) or **zhīdao** (to know something):

(a) Wǒ bù ____________ tā huì shuō Zhōngwén.
(b) Xiǎo Fāng ____________ Amy.
(c) Tā bù ____________ Amy shì nǎ guó rén.
(d) Wǒ hěn xiǎng ____________ Xiǎo Fāng.

Exercise 11

Turn the following sentences into questions regarding the underlined parts (the underlined part is the information you wish to obtain):

Example: Amy shì Měiguórén. → Amy shì nǎ guó rén?

(a) Tā jiào Fāng Chūn.
(b) Xiǎo Fāng shì Běijīngrén.
(c) Amy jīn nián èrshíyī suì.

Exercise 12

Translate into Chinese:

(a) She doesn't look very happy.
(b) Simon looks very young.
(c) You look a little tired.

Characters

1 Learning to write:
(a) Wǒ shuō Zhōngwén (I speak Chinese)

There are four characters in this sentence and you will be pleased to know that we already learnt one of them in Lesson 1 (**zhōng** in **Zhōngguó**). This is how they should appear in boxes:

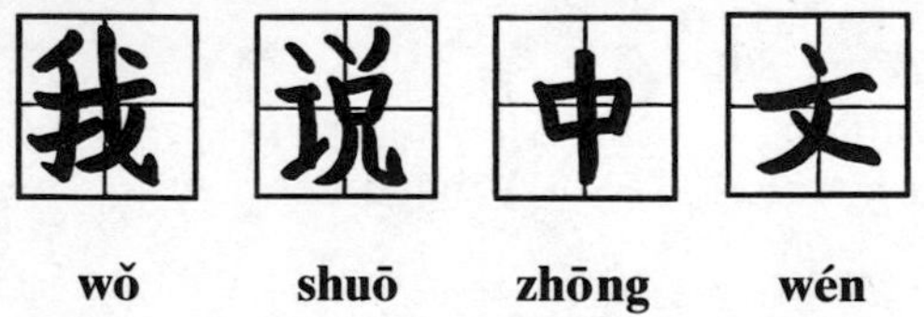

wǒ **shuō** **zhōng** **wén**

Now let us write **wǒ** (I/me) first. It has seven strokes, which are written in the following order:

1 2 3 4 5 6

7

The verb **shuō** (to speak/to say) has two parts and consists of nine strokes in total. The left part, 讠, is called the 'speech radical' which is used to form many characters concerned with speech and language. Let us see how **shuō** is written:

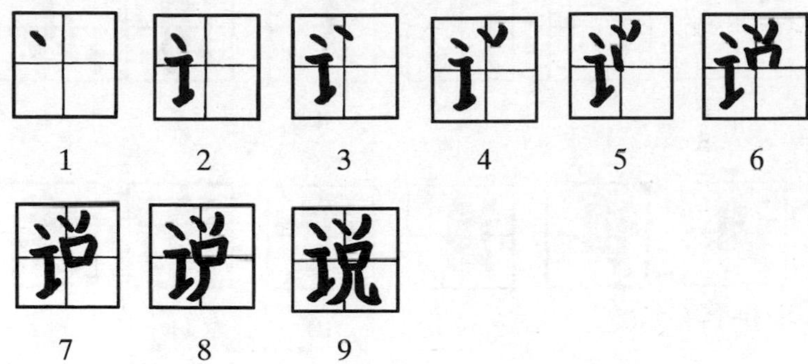

Since you already know how to write **zhōng** in **Zhōngwén** (Chinese language), let us move on to **wén**, which consists of only four strokes:

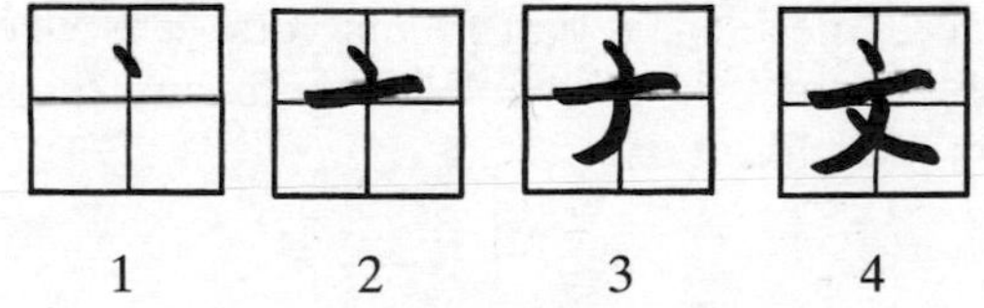

(b) Xièxie (Thank you)

The two characters representing **xièxie** are exactly the same. This is how they should appear in boxes:

The character **xiè**, although appearing to consist of three parts, is treated for descriptive purposes as having two parts. The left part 讠 is a 'speech radical', and the right part 射, pronounced **shè**, means 'to fire (e.g. an arrow)'. However, when you write this character, you must think of it as having three blocks. Each block takes up approximately the same space, which in total results in twelve strokes. These twelve strokes are written in the following order:

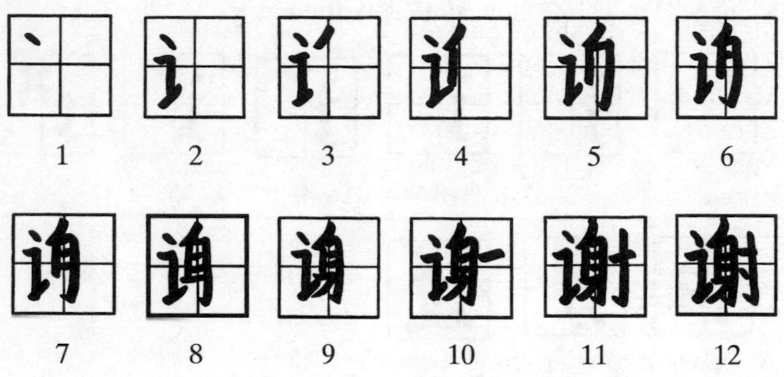

2 Recognize the following sign

The first sign we are going to try to recognize is **Běijīng** since this may be one of the first Chinese signs that greets your eyes when you arrive at Beijing Airport. Literally, **Běijīng** means 'north capital'. The characters look like this:

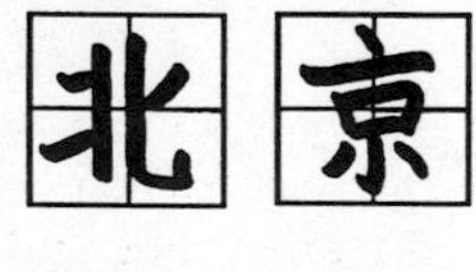

běi **jīng**

Congratulations! Now you know more than a dozen Chinese characters, and you even know how to write some of them.

Reading/listening comprehension

1 Read the following dialogue, and try to answer the questions below. If you have the recording, listen to it first (try not to look at the script) and then answer the questions in English.

Two Chinese people, Meixin and Zhongtao are talking about someone

MĚIXĪN: Nǐ rènshi Oliver ma?
ZHÒNGTĀO: Rènshi.
MĚIXĪN: Tā shì nǎ guó rén?
ZHÒNGTĀO: Yīngguórén.
MĚIXĪN: Tā huì shuō Zhōngwén ma?
ZHÒNGTĀO: Huì shuō yīdiǎn.
MĚIXĪN: Nǐ zhīdao tā duō dà le ma?
ZHÒNGTĀO: Bù zhīdao. Nǐ xiǎng rènshi tā ma?
MĚIXĪN: Tài xiǎng le.

Questions

A Does Zhongtao know Oliver?
B Which country is Oliver from?
C Does Oliver speak Chinese?
D Does Zhongtao know how old Oliver is?
E Does Meixin want to meet Oliver?

2 Read aloud the following phrases or words and add on the correct tone marks to reflect the change of tones in actual speech. If you have the recording, listen to it first, and then add on the correct tone marks. Just to remind you: (¯) first tone; (´) second tone; (ˇ) third tone; (`) fourth tone.

(a) **xiexie** (thank you) (b) **bu zhidao** (do not know)
(c) **bu dui** (incorrect) (d) **Yingguoren** (British)
(e) **shuo Zhongwen** (speak Chinese) (f) **tai hao le** (wonderful)
(g) **zaijian** (goodbye) (h) **wo ye shi** (me too)

3 Zài gōngsī de jùhuì shang

At a company party

By the end of this lesson, you should be able to:

- exchange greetings in a more sophisticated way
- use some time-related phrases
- use question words **nǎr** (where) and **shéi** (who)
- use **le** to indicate a past action or an action which has taken place
- use some measure words
- negate some verbs with **méi yǒu**
- write more characters and recognize two useful signs and some numbers

Dialogue 1

Zěnme yàng? How are you?

Rachel and Shulan are very good friends as well as knowing each other through business. Rachel also knows Shulan's husband, Yanzhong. They have not seen each other for two years. They are so pleased to see each other again at a business party in Taibei, capital of Taiwan

RACHEL: Shūlán, hǎo jiǔ bù jiàn. Nǐ zěnme yàng?

SHŪLÁN: Wǒ hěn hǎo. Nǐ hǎo ma? Nǐ kànshangqu yǒu yīdiǎn lèi.

RACHEL: Wǒ shì hěn lèi. Zuìjìn wǒde gōngzuò hěn máng. Yánzhōng zěnme yàng?

SHŪLÁN: Hái hǎo, xièxie. Tā zuótiān chūmén le.

RACHEL: Qù nǎr le?

SHŪLÁN: Měiguó. Xià ge xīngqī huílai. Nǐde nán péngyou lái le ma?

RACHEL: Lái le . . .

(*at this very moment, Stuart, Rachel's boy-friend, passes by*)

RACHEL: Stuart, ràng wǒ jièshào yīxià. Zhè shì wǒde hǎo péngyou Shūlán. Shūlán, zhè shì wǒde nán péngyou Stuart.

STUART: Nǐ hǎo, Shūlán. Rachel cháng shuōqi nǐ.

SHŪLÁN: Nǐ hǎo, Stuart. Wǒmen zhōngyú jiànmiàn le.

RACHEL: *Shulan, I haven't seen you for ages. How are you?*

SHULAN: *I'm very well. Are you well? You look a little tired.*

RACHEL: *I* **am** *tired. I've been very busy with work recently. How is Yanzhong?*

SHULAN: *Fine, thanks. He went away yesterday.*

RACHEL: *Where has he gone?*

SHULAN: *America. He's coming back next week. Has your boy-friend come with you?*

RACHEL: *Yes . . .*

(at this very moment, Stuart, Rachel's boy-friend, passes by)

RACHEL: *Stuart, let me introduce you to my good friend, Shulan. Shulan, this is my boy-friend, Stuart.*

STUART: *Hello, Shulan. Rachel is always talking about you.*

SHULAN: *Hi, Stuart. We meet at last.*

Vocabulary

hǎo	very
jiǔ	long (as of time)
bù jiàn	not see
zěnme	how
Zěnme yàng?	How are you?/How are things?
shì	[emphatic word]
zuìjìn	recently
gōngzuò	work/to work
máng	to be busy/busy
hái hǎo	to be all right/to be fine
zuótiān	yesterday
tā	he/she
chūmén	to be away/to go away
qù	to go/to go to
nǎr	where
xià ge	next
xīngqī	week
huflal	to return [*lit.* 'return come']
nán	male
péngyou	friend
ràng	to let/to allow
jièshào	to introduce
yīxià	[see Note 9]
cháng	often/always
shuōqǐ	to mention/to talk [**shuōqǐ** in connected speech]
wǒmen	we/us
zhōngyú	finally/at last
jiànmiàn	to meet

Notes to Dialogue 1

1 Hǎo jiǔ bù jiàn

This is a very common expression to be used if you have not seen someone for a long time. Literally, the phrase means 'very long no see'. The word **hǎo**, although the same **hǎo** as in **nǐ hǎo** (hello), in this instance means 'very' and is used as an adverb. There is an element of informality as well as exaggeration when **hǎo** is used to mean 'very' or 'so'. For example:

Wǒ hǎo lèi.	I'm so tired.
Tā hǎo gāoxìng jiàndào nǐ.	He is so happy to see you.

2 Zěnme yàng?

The greeting expression **Nǐ zěnme yàng?** (How are you?/How are things?) is used very often among colleagues and friends, basically people who know each other. It is one of those phrases which are difficult to analyse grammatically. Let us concentrate on its usage. If the question is aimed at the person you are speaking to, **nǐ** (you) is usually omitted. If you enquire about someone or something, you must place that person or thing at the beginning of the question. For example:

***Nǐde nán péngyou* zěnme yàng?**	How is *your boy-friend*?
***Tiānqì* zěnme yàng?**	How is *the weather*?

In response to the question **Nǐ zěnme yàng?**, you may use some of the following expressions:

Hěn hǎo.	Very well.	**Bù tài hǎo.**	Not very well.
Hái hǎo.	Fine.	**Bù hǎo.**	Not well.
Hái bù cuò.	Not bad.	**Hěn zāo.**	Terrible.
Mǎma hūhu.	Just so-so.		

3 Emphatic SHÌ

In order to emphasize certain phrases, the word **shì** (*lit.* 'to be') can be used before these phrases. Whenever **shì** is used for emphatic purposes in this book, it will be capitalized to distinguish it from ordinary **shì** (be). For example:

Měixīn ***SHÌ*** **hěn máng.** — Meixin *IS* very busy.
subject

Wǒ ***SHÌ*** **bù xiǎng hē kāfēi.** — I *DON'T* want to have coffee.
subject

When emphatic **SHÌ** is used in sentences with the verb **kànshangqu** (to look/to seem), which we saw in Lesson 2, **SHÌ** appears after the verb. For example:

Jiājia kànshangqu SHÌ hěn niánqīng.
verb
Jiajia does look very young.

Note that this rule does not apply to sentences where the word **shì** (to be) is used in the first place. Thus you *cannot say* **Wǒ SHÌ shì Yīngguórén** (another emphatic word has to be used in this case, see Note 19 below).

4 *Use of* máng

When the English sentence 'She is busy with work' is translated into Chinese, it becomes 'Her work is busy'. For example:

***Shūlán de gōngzuò* hěn máng.**
Lit. Shulan's work very be busy.

In such cases, the word **de** can be omitted. If you are asked to specify what you are busy with, you can put such information after **máng**. For example:

A: **Nǐ zuìjìn *máng* shénme?**
Lit. You recently be busy what?
A: What have you been *busy* with recently?

B: **Máng *gōngzuò*.**
Lit. Busy work.
B: Busy with *work*.

5 *Time-related phrase*

In Chinese, time-related phrases (e.g. 'next week', 'today') are placed either at the beginning of a sentence or before the verb. For example:

Jonathan *xià ge xīngqī* lái Táiwān.
Lit. Jonathan next week come to Taiwan.
Jonathan is coming to Taiwan *next week*.

***Xià ge xīngqī*, Yánzhōng qù Yīngguó.**
Lit. Next week, Yanzhong go to Britain.
Yanzhong is going to Britain *next week*.

Note that when the time-related phrase such as **xià ge xīngqī** (next week) is used, the context itself makes it very clear that it is a future event we are talking about. This sentence order applies to questions as well (see Note 6 below).

6 *Question word* nǎr

In Note 5 of Lesson 2, we saw the question word **nǎ** (which). The same word also means 'where'. When **nǎ** means 'where', it is spelt with an **r** at the end, i.e. **nǎr**, and hence pronounced with the tongue rolled up a little. As with **shénme** (what) and **nǎli** whereabouts) which we saw earlier, **nǎr** is also placed where the information required should appear in the reply. For example:

A: **Nǐ xià ge xīngqī qù *nǎr*?**
Lit. You next week go where?
A: *Where* are you going next week?

B: **Wǒ xià ge xīngqī qù *Fǎguó*.**
Lit. I next week go France.
B: I'm going to *France* next week.

7 *More on* le

In Note 13 of Lesson 2, we saw one usage of the particle **le** (in **Nǐ duō dà *le*?**). Here, in Dialogue 1, **le** is added after some verbs to indicate that an event happened in the past (especially when a time-related phrase such as 'yesterday' is used). For example:

Rachel zuótiān chūmén *le*.	Rachel *went away* yesterday.
Tā qù nǎr *le*?	Where *did* she go? [she may be back already]

Depending on the context, especially when no time-related phrases are used, **le** can either indicate a past event or an event which has happened and is still happening:

Rachel chūmén *le*.	Rachel *has been away.* [she is still away]
Tā qù nǎr *le*?	Where *has* she *gone*? [she is still away]

If there are other words/phrases (i.e. objects) after the verb, and they are not very long, **le** can be placed either after the verb or after the object. For example:

Měixīn qù Táiwān *le*. *or* **Měixīn qù *le* Táiwān.**

Depending on the context, these two sentences can either mean 'Meixin went to Taiwan' or 'Meixin has gone to Taiwan'. Note that **le** cannot be added to every verb.

8 Omission of the personal pronoun

The personal pronoun **Tā** (he) is omitted from the following two sentences in Dialogue 1: **Qù nǎr le?** and **Xià ge xīngqī huílai.** The complete sentences should be ***Tā* qù nǎr le?** and ***Tā* xià ge xīngqī huílai.** The omission of personal pronouns (e.g. 'I', 'you', 'he/she') is very common in the spoken language if they can be easily inferred from the context.

9 Use of yīxià

The word **yíxià** does not have any specific meaning in this context except that it softens the abruptness of **Ràng wǒ jièshào** . . . (Let me introduce . . .). Without the use of **yīxià**, it sounds very bossy and tactless.

10 Difference between jiànmiàn *and* jiàndào

We saw earlier in Lesson 1 the verb **jiàndào** in **Hěn gāoxìng *jiàndào* nǐ** (Very pleased to meet you). Here, we have the sentence **Wǒmen zhōngyú *jiànmiàn* le** (We meet at last). The main difference between the two verbs lies in their usage:

X + ***jiàndào*** + Y
two or more than two people + ***jiànmiàn***

For example:

Shūlán zuótiān *jiàndào* le Stuart.
Shulan *met* Stuart yesterday.

Wǒmen xià ge xīngqī *jiànmiàn*.
We are going *to meet* next week.

Exercises

Exercise 1

Solve the problems:

(a) You have not seen a Chinese friend of yours for a long time, and you have just bumped into him. What do you say?

(b) You want to introduce your good friend Amy and your Chinese friend Xiao Lin to each other. What do you say?

Exercise 2

Use emphatic **shì** to rewrite the following sentences, and then translate them into English:

(a) John bù tài máng.
(b) Shūlán de gōngzuò hěn máng.
(c) Wáng Lín kànshangqu tǐng lǎo.

Exercise 3

Translate into Chinese:

(a) A: Where did you go yesterday?
B: I went to London.
(b) A: Where are you going next week?
B: China.
(c) A: Where has Yanzhong gone?
B: He's gone to America.

Exercise 4

Place **le** in an appropriate place in the following sentences, and then translate them into English:

(a) Andrew qù Měiguó.
(b) Elena hē kāfēi.
(c) Zuótiān Xīnháng shuōqi Tiānyī.

Exercise 5

Fill in the blanks using **jiàndào** or **jiànmiàn**:

(a) Shūlán zhōngyú ___________ le Stuart.
(b) Tāmen xià ge xīngqī ___________.
(c) Rachel hé ('*and*') Shūlán zuótiān ___________ le.
(d) Wǒ bù xiǎng ___________ Zhāng Píng.

Dialogue 2
Tā jiéhūn le ma? Is he married?

Later at the party, a colleague of Shulan's, Lin Fang (female), chats with Shulan

LÍN FĀNG: Shūlán, nà liǎng ge rén shì shéi?
SHŪLÁN: Nán de jiào Stuart. Shì WP gōngsī de fù jīnglǐ.
LÍN FĀNG: Tā zhēn shuài. Nǐ zhīdao tā jiéhūn le ma?
SHŪLÁN: Méi yǒu jiéhūn. Búguò, tā yóu nǚ péngyou le.
LÍN FĀNG: Ài! Zhēn kěxī.
SHŪLÁN: Wèishénme?
LÍN FĀNG: Méi shénme. Nà ge nǚ de shì shéi?
SHŪLÁN: Tā jiù shì Stuart de nǚ péngyou. Tā jiào Rachel.

LIN FANG: *Shulan, who are those two people?*
SHULAN: *The man is called Stuart. He is the deputy manager of WP company.*
LIN FANG: *He is really smart. Do you know if he is married?*
SHULAN: *No, he isn't. But he's got a girl-friend.*
LIN FANG: *What a shame!*
SHULAN: *Why?*
LIN FANG: *Nothing. Who is that woman?*
SHULAN: *She is Stuart's girl-friend. She's called Rachel.*

Vocabulary

nà	that [see Note 12]
liǎng	two
gè	[measure word, see Note 11]
shéi	who
gōngsī	company
fù	deputy/vice
jīnglǐ	manager
shuài	to be smart
jiéhūn	to be married
méi yǒu	not
búguò	however/but
yǒu	to have
nǚ	female
ài	[exclamation word]
zhēn kěxī	what a shame/pity! [*lit.* 'really pity']

wèishénme	why
méi shénme	nothing [*lit.* 'not anything']
nà ge nǚ de	that woman
jiù	[emphatic word]

Notes to Dialogue 2

11 Measure word

Discussing quantities of things in Chinese can be a little complicated in that a measure word must be used between a number and its noun. Measure words are also used between **zhè/nà** (this/that) and its noun. In Lesson 1, we actually came across one measure word **bēi** in **yī bēi kāfēi** (one cup of coffee). Different categories of nouns require different measure words. For instance, **ge** is used for human beings whereas **tóu** is used for pigs, cattle, etc. and **tiáo** is used for fish, rivers, etc. For example:

> **Wǒ rènshi sān** ***ge*** **Yīngguórén.**
> number measure word noun
> I know three British people.

> **Tā yǒu èrshí** ***tóu*** **zhū.**
> number measure word noun
> He has twenty pigs.

At this stage, if you cannot remember which measure word goes with which category of nouns, use **gè** instead. Please also note that the measure word **gè**, which carries the fourth tone in isolation, becomes toneless when used in a phrase or sentence. More measure words will be introduced as we progress in the book.

12 Use of pronoun nà

When **nà** or **zhè** is followed by the verb **shì** (to be), they mean 'that' or 'this' respectively and function as subjects. For example:

> ***Nà/Zhè*** **shì wǒde kāfēi.** That/This is my coffee.
> verb

When **nà** or **zhè** precedes nouns, or numbers plus nouns, measure words such as **gè** must be used. Whenever the number is **yī** (one), it is almost always omitted. So **nà** ***yī*** **ge rén** becomes **nà ge rén** (that person). When **nà** (sometimes pronounced **nèi)** is followed by numbers other than one plus measure words, it means 'those'. This rule also applies to the pronoun **zhè** (which can be pronounced **zhèi** here). For example:

nà/zhè ge **Měiguórén**	*that/this* American
nà sān bēi **kāfēi**	*those three* cups of coffee
zhè sān bēi **kāfēi**	*these three* cups of coffee

Remember that **nà** (that) has the fourth tone whereas **nǎ** (which) has the third tone.

13 *Use of* liǎng

When you count, the number to use for two is **èr**. However, if you want to say 'two somethings', you should almost always use **liǎng** instead. For example:

liǎng **bēi kāfēi**	*two* cups of coffee
liǎng **ge Běijīngrén**	*two* Beijing people

14 *Changing adjectives to nouns by adding* de

Adjectives such as **nán** (male) and **nǚ** (female) can be changed into nouns by adding **de** after them. Thus we have:

Adjective		*Noun*	
nán	male	**nán** ***de***	man
nǚ	female	**nǚ** ***de***	woman
lǎo	old	**lǎo** ***de***	the old one
xiǎo	young/small	**xiǎo** ***de***	the young/small/little one

Note that we can also add the word **rén** (person/people) after **nán** and **nǚ** to form nouns **nán** ***rén*** (*lit.* 'male *person*') for 'man' and **nǚ** ***rén*** (*lit.* 'female *person*') for 'woman', which are more formal than **nán de** and **nǚ de**. On public signs, **nán** means 'men's toilet', and **nǚ** means 'women's toilet'. See the character section at the end of this lesson.

15 *Linking two nouns with* de

Another use of **de** is to link two nouns, the first being subordinate to the second. It is equivalent to the English word 'of' or apostrophe plus 's'. For example:

gōngsī *de* jīnglǐ
company'*s* manager/the manager *of* the company

Rachel *de* nán péngyou
Rachel'*s* boy-friend

16 Question word shéi

The question word **shéi** ('who') can appear at the beginning or at the end of the question depending on how you want your question to be structured. For example:

	***Shéi* shì WP gōngsī de jīnglǐ?**
Lit.	Who be WP company's manager?
	WP gōngsī de jīnglǐ shì *shéi*?
Lit.	WP company's manager be who?

17 Negation word méi yǒu

So far, we have been using **bù** to negate adverbs, verb–adjectives, and verbs for present and future events. Another important negation word is **méi yǒu (yǒu** is often omitted). It is mainly used to: (a) indicate that an action *has not* taken place; (b) indicate that an action *did not* happen; and (c) negate the verb **yǒu** (to have). You must never use **méi** to negate an adverb or a verb–adjective. It is only verbs (i.e. 'doing words') which can be negated by **méi** or **méi yǒu**. Simply add **méi** or **méi yǒu** before the verb. With the verb **yǒu** (to have), just add **méi** in front of it. For example:

Zuótiān wǒ *méi yǒu* qù Lúndūn.	I did*n't* go to London yesterday.
Stuart *méi yǒu* lái.	Stuart has*n't* arrived.
Wú Hái *méi* yǒu nán péngyou.	Wu Hai has*n't* got a boy-friend.

Remember: whenever **méi** or **méi yǒu** is used, **le** is usually not used. **Le** can only be used together with **méi yǒu** when you want to indicate that you had something before but now it is running out. For example:

Wǒ *méi yǒu* kāfēi *le*.	I've run out of coffee.
Kāfēi *méi yǒu le*.	Coffee is running out.

Another thing to notice is that there are no equivalent Chinese words to the English words 'a' and 'the'.

18 Pronoun shénme

Earlier in Lesson 2, we saw **shénme** (what) used as a question word. **Shénme** can also be used as a pronoun meaning 'anything' and it is usually used with the negation word **méi** to form negative sentences. For example:

Wǒ *méi* shuō *shénme.*
I did*n't* say *anything.*/I said *nothing.*

Tā *méi* hē *shénme.*
He did*n't* drink *anything.*/He drank *nothing.*

19 Emphatic word jiù

In Note 3 of Dialogue 1 above, we mentioned that sentences with the verb **shì** (to be) cannot be emphasized by the emphatic word SHÌ. The correct word to use in such cases is **jiù**. Simply add **jiù** in front of **shì**. For example:

Wǒ *jiù* shì Kàn Qiàn.
I *AM* Kan Qian. [often used on the telephone]

Tā *jiù shì* gōngsī de jīnglǐ.
She *IS* the manager of the company.

Exercises

Exercise 6

Referring to the two dialogues in this lesson, answer the following questions in Chinese:

(a) Shūlán rènshi Rachel ma?
(b) Rachel rènshi Lín Fāng ma?
(c) Rachel jiéhūn le ma?
(d) Shèi shì Stuart?

Exercise 7

Translate into Chinese using appropriate measure words:

(a) fifteen American people
(b) two Chinese people
(c) three men
(d) eight cups of coffee
(e) four good friends

Exercise 8

Complete the other half of the conversation:

(a) A: Nǐ yǒu kāfēi ma?
B: ___________ (*Yes, I have.*)
(b) A: Kevin yǒu nǚ péngyou ma?
B: ___________ (*No, he hasn't.*)
(c) A: Wǒ bù huì shuō Yīngwén.
B: ___________ (*What a shame!*)

Exercise 9

Turn the following sentences into questions regarding the underlined parts, which is the information you wish to obtain:

Example: Tā jiào Tāng Shūlán. → Tā jiào *shénme*?

(a) Yánzhōng qù Měiguó le.
(b) Stuart shì WP gōngsī de fù jīnglǐ.
(c) Shūlán shì Zhōngguórén.
(d) Wǒ xià ge xīngqī qù Táiwān.

Exercise 10

Use **méi (yǒu)** or **bù** to negate the following sentences, then translate them into English:

(a) Wǒ xià ge xīngqī qù Zhōngguó.
(b) Jane jiéhūn le.
(c) Xiǎo Fāng yǒu Yìdàlì kāfēi.
(d) Wáng Píng rènshi Měixīn.
(e) Zuótiān wǒmen qù le Lúndūn.
(f) Wǒ xiǎng hē kāfēi.

Exercise 11

Fill in the blanks using emphatic words **jiù** or SHÌ:

(a) Stuart ___________ shì Rachel de nán péngyou.
(b) Tā ___________ méi qù Zhōngguó.
(c) Měixīn kànshangqu ___________ hěn niánqīng.
(d) Nǐ ___________ shì Lín Fáng ma?

Characters

1 Learning to write:
(a) Pronouns tā (he) and tā (she)

First of all, there is a difference between the characters for 'he' (**tā**) and 'she' (**tā**). The difference is in the left part, whilst they share the same right part:

As you can see, the male **tā** has the 'person radical' 亻 and the female **tā** has the 'woman radical' 女

(b) Verbs qù (to go) and lái (to come/arrive)

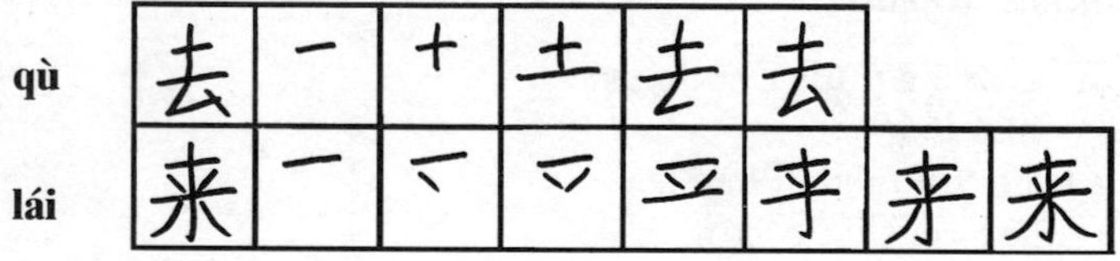

(c) Yes/No question word ma and short answers Shì de (Yes) and Bú shì (No)

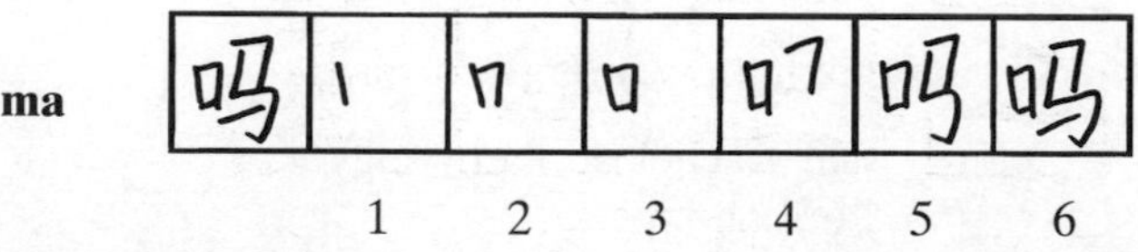

The left part of **ma** is called the 'mouth radical' 口 which is pronounced **kǒu** when used on its own. **Kǒu** is a formal term for 'mouth'.

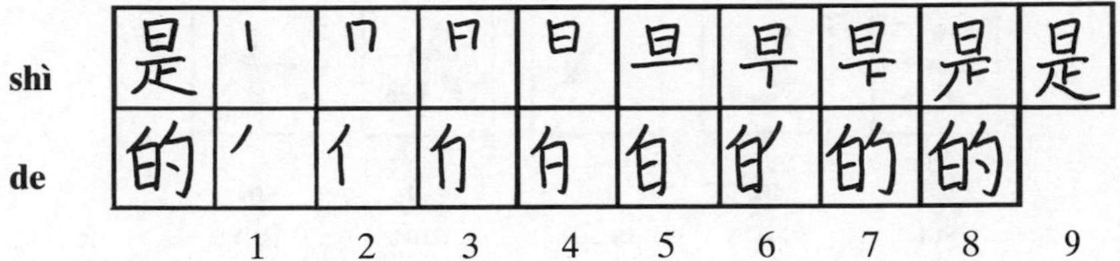

The character **shì** was introduced in Lesson 6. The left part of **de** is called the 'white radical' 白. When used on its own, 白 is pronounced **bái** meaning 'white'.

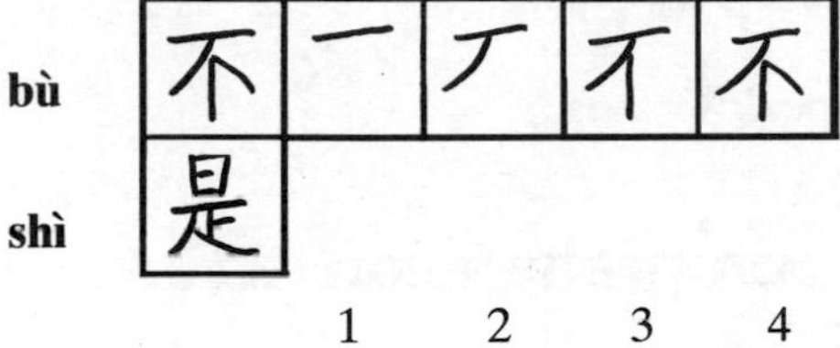

2 Recognizing two important signs

Below are two important signs to remember: one is **nán** for 'men', and the other is **nǚ** for 'women'. We actually learnt how to write **nǚ** when we were learning the character **hǎo** in Lesson 1. These two signs are useful to know if you need to use a public toilet:

3 Recognizing numbers:

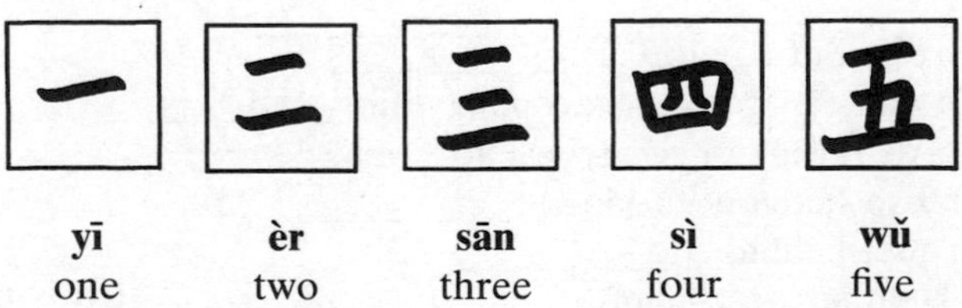

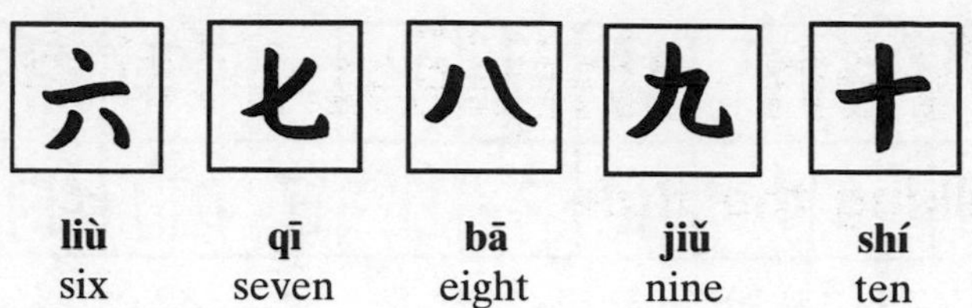

Exercise 12

Convert the following *pinyin* into characters:

(a) **nǚ rén** (woman/women)
(b) **Zhōngguórén** (Chinese person/people)
(c) **nǐ hǎo** (hello)
(d) **wǒ shuō Zhōngwén** (I speak Chinese)

Reading/listening comprehension

Read the following passage carefully, and then write 'true' or 'false' next to the sentences below. If you have the recording, listen to the passage first (try not to look at the script) and then write 'true' or 'false' next to the sentences below:

> Wǒ jiào Zhū Mǐn. Wǒ shì Zhōngguórén. Wǒ yǒu yī ge Yīngguó péngyou. Tā jiào Heather. Heather jiéhūn le. Tāde zhàngfu jiào Joe. Heather kànshangqu hěn niánqīng. Tā jīnnián sìshí suì zuǒyòu. Joe wǔshí suì zuǒyòu. Xià ge xīngqī tāmen qù Zhōngguó.

Vocabulary

zhàngfu	husband (same as the word for 'Mr')
hé	and

Questions

A Zhū Mǐn shì Zhōngguórén. ____________
B Zhū Mǐn yǒu sān ge Yīngguó péngyou. ____________
C Zhū Mǐn de Yīngguó péngyou jiào Mary. ____________
D Heather kànshangqu bù lǎo. ____________
E Heather méi jiéhūn. ____________
F Joe shì Heather de zhàngfu. ____________
G Heather hé Joe zuótiān qù le Zhōngguó. ____________

4 Wèn shíjiān 问时间

Asking the time

By the end of this lesson, you should be able to:

- tell the time
- obtain information regarding time
- use the verb **yǒu** appropriately
- ask yes/no questions in another way
- make an appointment
- apologize
- attract someone's attention
- recognize and write more characters

Dialogue 1

Jǐ diǎn le? 几点了? What's the time?

David, an Australian, and his Malaysian wife, Siti, are visiting Shanghai as tourists and staying in a hotel. They arrived very late last night, and forgot to adjust their watches to the local time. It is now morning. They ask a hotel employee the time and the time at which breakfast is served

DAVID: Zǎoshang hǎo.
HOTEL EMPLOYEE: Zǎoshang hǎo.
DAVID: Qǐng wèn, xiànzài jǐ diǎn le?
HOTEL EMPLOYEE: Bā diǎn shí fēn.
DAVID: Xièxie.
HOTEL EMPLOYEE: Bù xiè.

Siti: Cāntīng jǐ diǎn kāimén?
Hotel employee: Yǐjing kāimén le. Zǎofàn shì cóng qī diǎn yī kè dào bā diǎn bàn.

David: Hái yǒu èrshí fēnzhōng. Wǒmen kuài qù ba.
Siti: Hǎo de. Huíjiàn.
Hotel employee: Huíjiàn.

David: 早上好。
Hotel employee: 早上好。
David: 请问，现在几点了？
Hotel employee: 八点十分。
David: 谢谢。
Hotel employee: 不谢。
Siti: 餐厅几点开门？
Hotel employee: 已经开门了。早饭是从七点一刻到八点半。
David: 还有二十分钟。我们快去吧。
Siti: 好的。回见。
Hotel employee: 回见。

David: *Good morning.*
Hotel employee: *Good morning.*
David: *What's the time now please?*
Hotel employee: *It's ten past eight.*
David: *Thank you.*
Hotel employee: *You are welcome.*
Siti: *What time does the restaurant open?*
Hotel employee: *It's already open. Breakfast is from quarter past seven to half past eight.*
David: *We've got twenty minutes left. Let's hurry up.*
Siti: *OK. See you later.*
Hotel employee: *See you later.*

Vocabulary

zǎoshang	早上	morning
wèn	问	to ask
xiànzài	现在	now
jǐ	几	how many?
bā	八	eight

diǎn	点	o'clock
shí	十	ten
fēn	分	minute [see Note 5]
cāntīng	餐厅	restaurant/dining-room
kāimén	开门	to be open/to open [*lit.* 'open door']
yǐjing	已经	already
qī	七	seven
kè	刻	quarter
zǎofàn	早饭	breakfast [*lit.* 'early food/meal']
cóng . . . dào . . .	从...到...	from . . . to
bàn	半	half
hái	还	still/also
èrshí	二十	twenty
fēnzhōng	分钟	minute [see Note 5]
kuài	快	soon/quickly/to be quick/to be fast
húijiàn	回见	see you later [*lit.* 'return meet']

Notes to Dialogue 1

1 *Polite way of asking for information* Qǐng wèn . . .

Early in Lesson 1 (Note 7), we had the word **qǐng** (please) used to invite someone politely to do something. The same word is used in **qǐng wèn**, which literally means 'please ask . . .'. This is a polite phrase which is used when asking for information or help. It can be broadly translated as 'May I ask . . .?' or 'Could you tell me . . . please?' For example:

***Qǐng wèn*, nǐ jiào shénme?**
May I ask what your name is?

***Qǐng wèn*, nǐ shì Sīfāng ma?**
Could you tell me please if you are Sifang?

2 *Telling the time*

To tell the time, the key words are **diǎn** (o'clock), **fēn** (minute), **bàn** (half), **kè** (quarter) and **chà** (lacking/minus). The hour comes first, then the minute. For example:

A 7:10 **qī *diǎn* shí *fēn***
B 8:05 **bā *diǎn* wǔ *fēn*** *or* **bā diǎn líng wǔ**
C 9:15 **jiǔ *diǎn* yī *kè*** *or* **jiǔ *diǎn* shí wǔ *fēn***

D 10:30 **shí *diǎn* sānshí fēn** *or* **shí *diǎn bàn***
E 2:45 **liǎng diǎn sìshíwǔ** *fēn or* **liǎng diǎn sān kè** *or* **sān *diǎn chà* yī kè** *or* **sān diǎn *chà shí* wǔ**

Note that (a) the minute word **fēn** can be omitted once the minute is over ten; (b) if you want to omit the word **fēn** when the minute is less than ten, put the word **líng** (zero) after **diǎn** (see B above); (c) do not use the word **fēn** when **kè** or **bàn** is used; (d) use the number **liǎng** (two) not **èr** in telling the time; (e) to say '2:45', use any of the four expressions in (E) above. Because there are no terms equivalent to the English abbreviations *a.m.* and *p.m.* in Chinese, it is either the context or the adding of words such as **zǎoshang bā diǎn** (*lit.* 'morning eight o'clock), **xiàwǔ liǎng diǎn** (*lit.* 'afternoon two o'clock') or **wǎnshang bā diǎn** (*lit.* 'evening eight o'clock') which enables people to make such a distinction.

3 Jí diǎn le?

The question word **jǐ** (how many) is used to ask number-related questions and the person who asks the question expects a small number. The literal translation for **Jǐ diǎn le?** is very awkward. It is something like 'How many o'clock already?' (as **le** indicates that something has already happened). The best thing to do is simply to remember that **Jǐ diǎn le?** is the equivalent of the English 'What time is it?' or 'What's the time?' In answering the question, you can say the time with or without **le**. For example:

A: **Qǐng wèn, *jǐ diǎn le*?**	A: What time is it, please?
B: **Sān diǎn sānshí wǔ.**	B: It's three thirty-five.

Note that there is no Chinese equivalent of 'It is . . .' to be used before the time.

Similar to other question words, **jǐ** occurs in the place where the information required in the reply should appear. For example:

A: **Cāntīng *jǐ* diǎn kāimén?**
Lit. Restaurant what time open?
A: What time does the restaurant open?

B: **Cāntīng *qī* diǎn kāimén.**
Lit. Restaurant seven o'clock open.
B: The restaurant opens at seven.

Note that (a) the phrase indicating the time always occurs before the verb; and (b) no extra word like *at* in English is needed before the time.

4 *Use of* yǐjing . . . le

If you use **yǐjing** (already) before some verbs or verb–adjectives, you *must* use **le** in the same phrase/sentence. Put **le** at the very end of the phrase/sentence. However, the word **le** can be used without **yǐjing** to indicate that an event has already happened. For example:

Tā *yǐjing* wǔshí suì *le*.
He is fifty *already*.

Jane *yǐjing* qù Zhōngguó *le*.
Jane has *already* gone to China.

Jane qù Zhōngguó *le*.
Jane went to China./Jane has gone to China.

5 *Difference between* fēn *and* fēnzhōng

The word **fēn** is only used when telling the time, whereas **fēnzhōng** is used as a unit of time when referring to the length of time. For example:

Xiànzài shì liǎng diǎn shí *fēn*.
It's ten past two.

Wǒ yǒu sānshí *fēnzhōng* chī wǔfàn.
I have got thirty minutes to eat lunch.

6 *Use of* kāimén

The verb **kāimén** (*lit.* 'open door'), meaning 'to be open' or 'to open', is used to refer to the opening time of various shops and organizations. You cannot use this verb to say 'open the coffee jar', for example. That is to say, the verb **kāimén** cannot take an object. For example:

Cāntīng qī diǎn *kāimén*.
The restaurant *opens* at seven.

Xià ge xīngqī cāntīng bù *kāimén*.
Next week, the restaurant is not *open*.

7 *Position of* kuài

When **kuài** (quickly/soon) is used as an adverb, it is placed before verbs in those sentences that ask for help, or that give orders. For example:

A child begs his/her mother:

Nǐ *kuài* huílai ba.
Lit. You soon return please.
Please come back *soon*.

A mother says to a child:

***Kuài* yīdiǎn chī.**
Lit. Quickly a little eat.
Eat a bit *quickly*.

Exercises

Exercise 1

Use the clock faces to tell the time:

(a) (b) (c) (d) (e) (f)

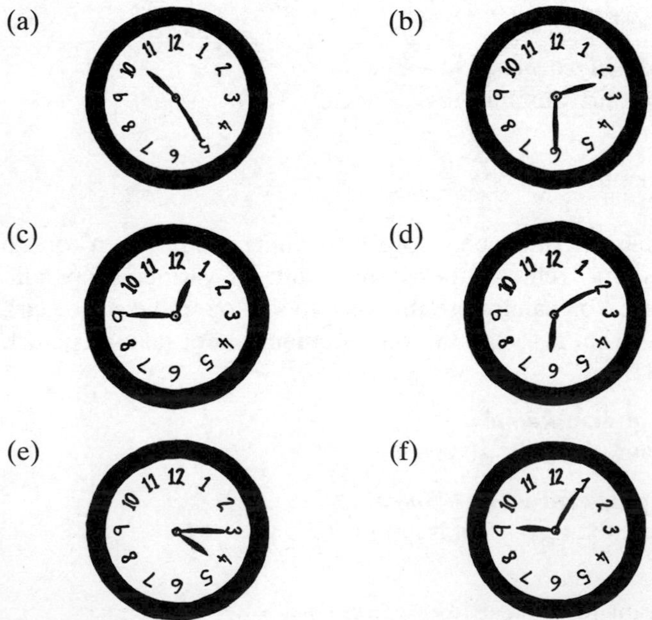

Exercise 2

Match the times to the clocks:

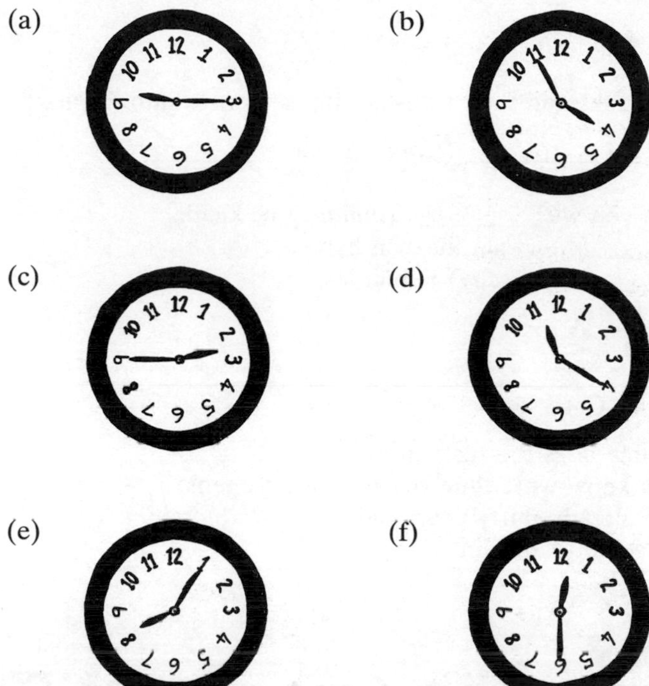

1 bā diǎn líng wǔ
2 shíyī diǎn èrshí fēn
3 shí'èr diǎn bàn
4 jiǔ diǎn yī kè
5 liǎng diǎn sìshíwǔ
6 sì diǎn chà wǔ fēn

Exercise 3

Solve the problem:

(a) You see a Chinese person early in the morning. What do you say to greet him/her?
(b) You want to find out what time it is. What do you say?

(c) You want to ask a Chinese person's name in a polite way. How do you phrase your question?
(d) How many ways can you think of to respond to **Xièxie** (Thank you)?

Exercise 4

Fill in the blanks and then translate the sentences into English:

(a) Zǎofàn shì _________ (*from*) qī diǎn _________ (*to*) bā diǎn bàn.
(b) Wǒmen yǒu wǔ _________ (*minutes*) hē kāfēi.
(c) _________ (*Now*) shì liù diǎn bàn.
(d) Tā _________ (*already*) jiéhūn le.

Exercise 5

Translate into Chinese:

(a) What time does the restaurant open?
(b) Do you know what time the restaurant opens?
(c) Alan is already thirty years old.
(d) Please come to Britain soon.

Dialogue 2
Qù yóuyǒng 去游泳 Going swimming

David and Siti want to find out if there is a swimming pool in the hotel. They first ask a Chinese woman who happens to be sitting next to them in the café

DAVID: Nǐ zhīdao zhè ge fàndiàn yǒu yóuyǒng chí ma?
CHINESE: Duìbùqǐ. Wǒ bù zhīdao.
DAVID: Méi guānxi.
(*they ask a hotel employee later on*)
SITI: Duìbùqǐ. Nǐménde fàndiàn yǒu yóuyǒng chí ma?
HOTEL EMPLOYEE: Yóu liǎng ge. Yī ge dà de. Yī ge xiǎo de.
SITI: Tài hǎo le. Nǐ kěyi gàosu wǒ kāimén shíjiān ma?
HOTEL EMPLOYEE: Dāngrán kěyi. Dà de cóng zǎoshang qī diǎn kāi dào xiàwǔ yī diǎn. Xiǎo de cóng xiàwǔ sān diǎn kāi dào wǎnshang jiǔ diǎn.

Siti:	Xièxie. David, nǐ xiǎng yóuyǒng ma?
David:	Xiǎng. Búguò, wǒ yǒu yīdiǎn è. Zánmen xiān chī wǔ fàn, hǎo bù hǎo?
Siti:	Hǎo ba. Jǐ diǎn chī?
David:	Yī diǎn, zěnme yàng?
Siti:	Hǎo de. Nàme, zǎnmen sì diǎn qù yóuyǒng, xíng ma?
David:	Xíng.

David:	你知道这个饭店有游泳池吗？
Chinese:	对不起。我不知道。
David:	没关系。

Siti:	对不起。你们的饭店有游泳池吗？
Hotel employee:	有两个。一个大的。一个小的。
Siti:	太好了。你可以告诉我开门时间吗？
Hotel employee:	当然可以。大的从早上七点开到下午一点。小的从下午三点开到晚上 九点。
Siti:	谢谢。DAVID,你想游泳吗？
David:	想。不过，我有一点饿。咱们先吃午饭，好不好？
Siti:	好吧。几点吃？
David:	一点，怎么样？
Siti:	好的。那么，咱们四点去游泳，行吗？
David:	行。

David:	*Do you know if there is a swimming pool in this hotel?*
Chinese:	*I'm sorry. I don't know.*
David:	*It doesn't matter.*

(they ask a hotel employee later on)

Siti:	*Excuse me. Are there any swimming pools in this hotel?*
Hotel employee:	*Yes, there are two. A large one and a small one.*
Siti:	*Great. Can you tell me the opening hours?*
Hotel employee:	*Of course I can. The big one is open from seven in the morning to one in the afternoon, and the small one is open from three in the afternoon to nine in the evening.*
Siti:	*Thank you. David, do you want to swim?*
David:	*Yes, I do. But I'm a little hungry. Shall we have lunch first?*
Siti:	*Fine. What time?*

DAVID:	*How about one o'clock?*
SITI:	*That's fine. In that case, shall we go swimming at four o'clock?*
DAVID:	*OK.*

Vocabulary

fàndiàn	饭店	hotel
yóuyǒng chí	游泳池	swimming pool
duìbùqǐ	对不起	I'm sorry/Excuse me
méi guānxi	没关系	It doesn't matter/It's all right /It's OK [*lit.* 'not matter']
nǐménde	你们的	your/yours [plural]
dà de	大的	the large one/the big one
xiǎo de	小的	the small one
kěyǐ	可以	may/could/can
gàosu	告诉	to tell
shíjiān	时间	time
dāngrán	当然	of course
kāi	开	to be open/to open
xiàwǔ	下午	afternoon
wǎnshang	晚上	evening
yóuyǒng	游泳	to swim
è	饿	to be hungry/hungry
zánmen	咱们	we/us [colloquial term]
xiān	先	first of all
chī	吃	to eat
wǔfàn	午饭	lunch [*lit.* 'noon meal']
nàme	那么	in that case
Hǎo bù hǎo?	好不好？	Is it all right?/Is it OK?
hǎo ba	好吧	all right/fine
xíng ma?	行吗？	Is it OK?
xíng	行	to be OK/can do/will do

Notes to Dialogue 2

8 Use of yǒu

Yǒu means 'to have'. In English, you say *There is a library at the university*; but in Chinese, this sentence becomes 'The university has a library' because there is no 'there-is/are' construction in the Chinese language. For example:

Zhè ge fàndiàn *yǒu* sān ge cāntīng.
Lit. This hotel have three restaurants.
There are three restaurants in this hotel.

Wǒménde gōngsī *yǒu* liù ge Zhōngguórén.
Lit. Our company have six Chinese people.
There are six Chinese people in our company.

9 Use of duìbùqǐ

When the phrase **duìbùqǐ** is used to apologize, it means 'I'm sorry'; and when it is used to attract someone's (usually a stranger's) attention, it means 'Excuse me'. If someone says **duìbùqǐ** as an apology, one of the appropriate things to say in response is **Méi guānxi** (It doesn't matter). For example:

A: ***Duìbùqǐ.* Wǒ méi yǒu kāfēi.**
I'm sorry. I haven't got coffee.
B: **Méi guānxi. Chá yě xíng.**
It doesn't matter. Tea will do.

A: ***Duìbùqǐ.* Qǐng wèn, jǐ diǎn le?**
Excuse me. What's the time, please?
B: **Sān diǎn shí fēn**.
Ten past three.

10 Use of kěyǐ

Another way of making your request more polite when asking for information, or permission to do something, from other people is to use **kěyi** (could/can/may) before the verb. For example:

Nǐ *kěyi* gàosu wǒ nǐ jiào shénme ma?
Could you tell me what your name is?

Wǒ *kěyi* qù Zhōngguó ma?
May I go to China?

11 Verbs used as adjectives

Some verbs (mostly verbs consisting of two syllables), without changing their forms, can be used in front of nouns as adjectives to modify nouns. For example:

Verb	*Adjective*		
kāimén	to be open	***kāimén* shíjiān**	*opening* hour/s
yóuyǒng	to swim	***yóuyǒng* chí**	*swimming* pool
jièshào	to introduce	***jièshào* xìn**	letter of *introduction*

12 Use of fàn

The word **fàn** means 'food' or 'meal'. One of the common greetings among neighbours is **Nǐ chī *fàn* le ma?** (Have you eaten?). If you have had your meal, you say **Chī le** (*lit.* 'Eat already'); and if you have not had your meal, you say **Méi chī** (*lit.* 'Not eat'). The word **fàn** is used to form the following expressions we have come across so far:

zǎo*fàn* (breakfast) *comes from* **zǎoshang** (morning) and **fàn**
wǎn*fàn* (supper/dinner) *comes from* **wǎnshang** (evening) and **fàn**
zhōng*fàn* or **wǔ*fàn*** (lunch) *comes from* **zhōngwǔ** (noon) and **fàn**

13 Yes/no question Hǎo bù hǎo?

The question **Hǎo bù hǎo?** (*lit.* 'Good not good?'), is identical in meaning to **Hǎo ma?** (Is it all right?). All questions ending with **ma** can be rephrased according to the pattern below:

(Subject) + verb or verb–adjective + **bù** + repetition of the previous verb

For example:

Nǐ shì Zhōngguórén ma? *becomes* **Nǐ *shì bù shì* Zhōngguórén?**
Are you Chinese?
(Nǐ) è ma? *becomes* ***(Nǐ) è bù è*?** Hungry?

The reply for the first question above is still **Shì de** for 'Yes' and **Bù shì** for 'No'. The reply for the second question is **È** for 'Yes' and **Bù è** for 'No'. Note that (a) the subject can sometimes be omitted; and (b) the verb or verb–adjective after **bù** must be the same as the one before **bù.** If there are two verbs in one question such as

Nǐ xiǎng hē kāfēi ma? Would you like to have a coffee?
verb¹ verb²

the pattern becomes '(Subject) + verb¹ + **bù** + verb¹ + verb² + object'. The above question thus becomes:

Nǐ *<u>xiǎng</u>* *bù* *<u>xiǎng</u>* <u>hē</u> kāfēi?
verb[1] verb[1] verb[2]

If the verb requires **méi** as its negation word, **méi** is used instead of **bù**. For example:

Nǐ yǒu kāfēi ma? *becomes* **Nǐ yǒu *méi* yǒu kāfēi?** Do you have some coffee?

14 Affirmative sentences + . . . xíng ma?, . . . hǎo ma? *or* . . . zěnme yàng?

One way of making a suggestion and then seeking agreement or asking for permission is to add one of the following phrases – **xíng ma?/xíng bù xíng?**, **hǎo ma?/hǎo bù hǎo?** (Is it OK/Is it fine?) and **Zěnme yàng?** (How about . . .?) – to affirmative sentences. Most of the time, the above phrases are interchangeable. Just remember that . . . **xíng ma/xíng bù xíng** can be used for asking for permission as well as making a suggestion whereas . . . **hǎo ma?/hǎo bù hǎo?** and . . . **zěnme yàng?** are only used for making a suggestion. For example:

Wǒ wǎnshang liù diǎn bàn lái, *xíng ma*?
I'm coming at half past six in the evening. *Is that OK*?

Wǒmen shí'èr diǎn chī wǔfàn, hǎo ma?
Let's have lunch at twelve, shall we?

Bā diǎn, zěnme yàng?
How about eight o'clock?

15 Omission of the second syllable in a two-syllable verb

Verbs such as **yóuyǒng** (to swim), **kāimén** (to be open) are two-syllable verbs. The second syllable, i.e. **yǒng** in **yóuyǒng**, **mén** in **kāimén**, is often omitted (a) in a reply to the question where the verb in its full form has already been mentioned; and (b) when the phrase **cóng . . . dào . . .** (from . . . to . . .) is used. For example:

A: **Nǐ *yóuyǒng* le ma?**
Did you *swim*?

B: ***Yóu* le. Wǒ cóng liǎng diǎn *yóu* dào sì diǎn.**
Yes, I *did*. I *swam* from two o'clock to four o'clock.

A: **Cāntīng *kāimén* ma?**
Is the dining-room *open*?

B: ***Kāi*. Cóng liù diǎn *kāi* dào jiǔ diǎn bàn.**
Yes. It *opens* from six to half past nine.

Note that the one-syllable verb always occurs before **dào** in the phrase **cóng . . . dào** (from . . . to . . .), with the exception of **shì** (to be) which is placed before **cóng**. For example:

Wǎnfàn *shì* cóng liù diǎn dào shí diǎn.
Dinner *is* from six to ten.

Yóuyǒng chī cóng liǎng diǎn *kāi* dào wǔ diǎn bàn.
The swimming pool *opens* from two to half past five.

16 Tone of nǐménde

The word **mén** carries the second tone in isolation. When it is added to **nǐ** to form **nǐmen** ('you' plural), **mén** becomes toneless. When the toneless **de** is added to **nǐmen** to form **nǐménde** ('your/yours' plural), the second tone comes back to **mén**. Thus we have **nǐménde**. This rule of tone change applies to **wǒménde** (our/ours), **tāménde** (their/theirs), etc.

Exercises

Exercise 6

Solve the problems:

(a) You want to ask the receptionist in your hotel some questions but the receptionist does not know that you are present. To attract his/her attention, what do you say?
(b) What do you say if you want to find out what time the swimming pool opens?
(c) You are late for your appointment. What do you say if you want to apologize?

Exercise 7

Use complete sentences to state the times at which you usually do the following:

(a) chī zǎofàn (b) chī wǔfàn
(c) chī wǎnfàn (d) yóuyǒng

Exercise 8

Translate the following into Chinese using **yǒu** (to have):

(a) There are twenty large hotels in Beijing.
(b) There are two restaurants in our hotel.
(c) Are there any Chinese people in this company?
(d) There isn't a swimming pool in the Beijing Hotel.

Exercise 9

Rewrite the following questions without changing their meanings, and then translate them into English:

Example: Nǐ lèi ma? → Nǐ lèi bù lèi?

(a) Tā shì Yīngguórén ma?
(b) Nǐ zuìjìn máng ma?
(c) Zhāng Bīn yǒu nǚ péngyou ma?
(d) Nǐ xiǎng qù Zhōngguó ma?

Exercise 10

The following are replies to questions or comments. Make up an appropriate question or comment which could precede the reply:

(a) Méi guānxi.
(b) Xiànzài qī diǎn èrshíwǔ.
(c) Cāntīng liù diǎn kāimén.
(d) Huíjiàn.

Exercise 11

You want to ask your Chinese friend if it is OK:

(a) to have lunch at 12:30
(b) to go swimming at 4:00pm
(c) to call her 'Xiao Li'

Characters

1 Learning to write:
(a) Xiǎng (to want)

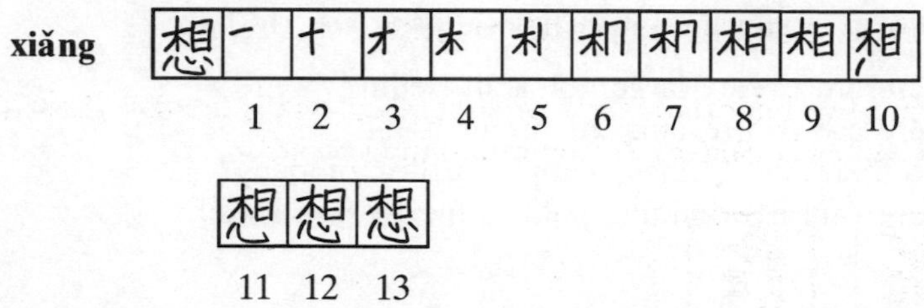

Xiǎng is a rather difficult character. The two major parts are the top and bottom parts. Let us look at the top part, which consists of the left part and the right part. The top left part 木 is called the 'wood radical' and is pronounced **mù**, meaning 'wood'. The top right part 目, which is also pronounced **mù**, is a formal term for 'eye'. The bottom part 心 is pronounced **xīn**, meaning 'heart'. Many characters in the Chinese language that involve the working of one's mind have the 'heart radical' in them. Perhaps in the old days, it was thought that the heart was used for thinking.

By learning **xiǎng**, we have in effect learnt three other characters. They are:

(b) Men [plural particle]

The suffix **men** is added to **wǒ**, **nǐ** and **tā** to form plurals **wǒmen** (we), **nǐmen** (you) and **tāmen** (they):

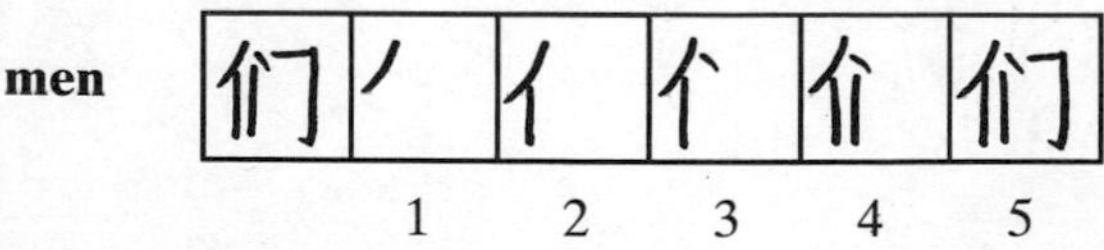

The left part of **men** 亻 is the 'person radical' and the right part 门 is pronounced **mén** as well, and it means 'door' on its own.

2 Recognizing important signs

Below are two important signs to remember: one is **fàndiàn** (hotel) and the other is **cāntīng** (restaurant/dining-room):

The character for **fàn** 饭 in **fàndiàn** means 'food' or 'meal'. The left part 饣 is called the 'food radical'. The character for **diàn** 店 means 'shop' or 'store'. Perhaps in previous times, the place you went for food also provided accommodation. However, although the term **fàndiàn** these days refers to hotels most of the time, you can sometimes find some restaurants which are called **fàndiàn**.

Since you now recognize the characters for **fàndiàn**, you may recognize the following sign. Give it a try!

It is 'the Beijing Hotel'.

Exercise 12

Put the following characters in the right order to form a meaningful sentence, and then translate the sentence into English:

说　中　想　你　文　吗

Reading/listening comprehension

1 Read the following dialogue carefully and then answer the multiple-choice questions by ticking the most appropriate phrase. If you have the recording, listen to the dialogue first (try not to look at the script) and then answer the multiple-choice questions by ticking the most appropriate phrase:

Chen Guangmeng and Xu Xunfeng share the same office at work. They are planning to do something together

Chén Guāngmèng:	Nǐ jīntiān máng ma?
Xú Xùnfēng:	Bù tài máng. Wèishénme?
Chén Guāngmèng:	Zánmen qù yóuyǒng, hǎo ma?
Xú Xùnfēng:	Hǎo zhǔyi. Búguò, wǒ xiànzài hěn è.
Chén Guāngmèng:	Nàme, zánmen xiān qù chī wǔfàn. Cāntīng jǐ diǎn kāimén?
Xú Xùnfēng:	Shí'èr diǎn bàn.
Chén Guāngmèng:	Hái yǒu shíwǔ fēnzhōng kāimén.
Xú Xùnfēng:	Shí'èr diǎn sìshí qù chī wǔfàn, xíng ma?
Chén Guāngmèng:	Xíng. Sān diǎn qù yóuyǒng, zěnme yàng?
Xú Xùnfēng:	Hǎo de.

Vocabulary

jīntiān	today
hǎo zhǔyi	good idea

Questions

A Xú Xùnfēng jīntiān máng ma?
(a) hěn máng　　(b) bù hěn máng　　(c) bù máng

B Chén Guāngmèng xiǎng gàn ('*do*') shénme?
(a) yóuyǒng　　(b) chī wǔfàn　　(c) hē kāfēi

C Xú Xùnfēng xiǎng xiān gàn (‘*do*’) shénme?
(a) hē kāfēi (b) yóuyǒng (c) chī wǔfàn

D Cāntīng jǐ diǎn kāimén?
(a) shíyī diǎn bàn (b) shí’èr diǎn sānshí (c) shí’ēr diǎn

E Xiànzài jǐ diǎn le? (*at the time when they talk*)
(a) shí’èr diǎn yī kè (b) shíyī diǎn èrshíwǔ (c) shí’èr diǎn èrshí

F Tāmen jǐ diǎn qù yóuyǒng?
(a) liáng diǎn bàn (b) sān diǎn (c) sān diǎn shí fēn

2 Read aloud the following phrases or words and add on the correct tone marks. If you have the recording, listen first, and then add on the correct tone marks:

(a) **huijian** see you later
(b) **canting** dining-room
(c) **duibuqi** I’m sorry/Excuse me
(d) **da de** the large one

5 Jiārén hé péngyou 家人和朋友

Family and friends

By the end of this lesson, you should be able to:

- describe your family and ask about someone else's family
- ask and respond to questions regarding one's occupation
- use present continuous tense
- ask after someone
- recognize and write more characters

Dialogue 1

Gàosu wǒ nǐde qíngkuàng 告诉我你的情况

Tell me about yourself

Lin Shaotang left China for America when he was only sixteen. Now, he is in his late sixties, and is currently in Sichuan province visiting his younger sister Lin Yingmei for the first time since he left China. Yingmei has told him a lot about herself and her family, and now she wants to find out about her brother

YĪNGMÉI: Gēge, lúndào nǐ gàosu wǒ nǐde qíngkuàng le.
SHÀOTÁNG: Hǎo ba. (*He goes to fetch some photos from his bag*) Zhè shì wǒ tàitai, Yīlìshābái. Tā shì Měiguórén.
YĪNGMÉI: Tā hěn piàoliang. Tā hái gōngzuò ma?
SHÀOTÁNG: Bù gōngzuò le. Wǒmen dōu tuìxiū le.
YĪNGMÉI: (*pointing at two people in one photo*) Zhè liǎng ge shì bù shì nǐménde háizi?
SHÀOTÁNG: Shì de. Tāmen yǒu Zhōngwén míngzi. Zhè shì wǒménde érzi, Zhìgāng. Zhè shì wǒménde nǚ'ér, Méilīn.

YĪNGMÉI: Zhìgāng zài shàng zhōngxué ma?
SHÀOTÁNG: Bù shì. Tā yǐjing shì dà xuésheng le.
YĪNGMÉI: Zhēn de? Tā xué shénme zhuānyè?
SHÀOTÁNG: Guǎnlǐ.
YĪNGMÉI: Hěn yǒu yìsi. Gěi wǒ jiǎngjiang Méilín.
SHÀOTÁNG: Hǎo de. Méilín yǐjing dāng māma le. Zhè shì tā zhàngfu, Línfú. . .

YINGMEI: 哥哥，轮到你告诉我你的情况了。
SHAOTANG: 好吧。(...)这是我太太，伊丽莎白。她是美国人。
YINGMEI: 她很漂亮。她还工作吗？
SHAOTANG: 不工作了。我们都退休了。
YINGMEI: (...)这两个是不是你们的孩子？
SHAOTANG: 是的。他们有中文名字。这是我们的儿子，志钢。这是我们的女儿，梅琳。
YINGMEI: 志钢在上中学吗？
SHAOTANG: 不是。他已经是大学生了。
YINGMEI: 真的？他学什么专业？
SHAOTANG: 管理。
YINGMEI: 很有意思。给我讲讲梅琳。
SHAOTANG: 好的。梅琳已经当妈妈了。这是她丈夫，林福...

YINGMEI: *It's your turn to tell me about yourself, elder brother.*
SHAOTANG: *OK.* (He goes to fetch some photos from his bag) *This is my wife, Elizabeth. She is American.*
YINGMEI: *She is very beautiful. Is she still working?*

SHAOTANG:	*No, she no longer works. Both of us have retired.*
YINGMEI:	(pointing at two people in one photo) *Are these two your children?*
SHAOTANG:	*Yes. They have Chinese names. This is our son, Zhigang, and this is our daughter, Meilin.*
YINGMEI:	*Is Zhigang at secondary school?*
SHAOTANG:	*No. He is already a university student.*
YINGMEI:	*Really? What subject does he study?*
SHAOTANG:	*Management.*
YINGMEI:	*That's very interesting. Tell me about Meilin.*
SHAOTANG:	*OK. Meilin has already become a mother. This is her husband, Linfu . . .*

Vocabulary

gēge	哥哥	elder brother
lúndào . . .	轮到	it is [somebody's] turn to . . .
qíngkuàng	情况	situation/present condition
tāitai	太太	wife/Mrs
Yīlìshābái	伊丽莎白	Elizabeth
piàoliang	漂亮	to be beautiful/beautiful
dōu	都	all
tuìxiū	退休	to retire/retired
háizi	孩子	children
míngzi	名字	name
wǒménde	我们的	our/ours
érzi	儿子	son
nǚ'ér	女儿	daughter
zài	在	[grammar word, see Note 8]
shàng	上	to go to/to attend
zhōngxué	中学	secondary/middle-school
dà xuésheng	大学生	university student [*lit.* 'big school student']
xué	学	to learn/to study
zhuānyè	专业	subject/major
guǎnlǐ	管理	management/to manage
yǒu yìsi	有意思	to be interesting [*lit.* 'have meaning']
gěi	给	for/to/to be for
jiǎngjiang	讲讲	to tell [in a sense of narrating]
zhàngfu	丈夫	husband
dāng	当	to become/to act as
māma	妈妈	mother/mum

Notes to Dialogue 1

1 Kinship terms

Kinship terms in the Chinese language are more complicated than in English. In addition to those terms in the dialogue, below are some other frequently used kinship terms:

Chinese	*English*
bàba	dad/father
jiějie	elder sister
dìdi	younger brother
mèimei	younger sister
nǎinai	grandmother (on father's side)
yéye	grandfather (on father's side)
shūshu	uncle (on father's side)
gūgu	aunt (on father's side)
wàipó/lǎolao	grandmother (on mother's side)
wàigōng/lǎoye	grandfather (on mother's side)
jiùjiu	uncle (on mother's side)
ā'yí	aunt (on mother's side)

Note that the repeated words do not carry any tones. The above terms can be used both to refer to someone and to address someone. For example:

> **Wǒde *māma* shì zhōngxué lǎoshī.**
> term of reference
> My mother is a secondary-school teacher.
>
> **Xièxie nǐ, *gēge*.**
> term of address
> Thank you, elder brother.

If you have more than one elder brother, say three, they are called and referred to as:

dà gē (*lit.* 'big brother')	the eldest brother
èr gē	the second elder brother
sān gē	the third elder brother

The third elder brother, if you have only three, can also be called and referred to as **xiǎo gē** (little elder brother). The same principle applies to other kinship terms such as **jiějie** (elder sister). However, one usually calls one's younger sister(s) or brother(s) by their first names instead of **mèimei** or **dìdi.**

2 Foreign names

Most foreign names, including personal names and place names, are translated according to their sounds. Some foreign names have standard translations. For example, 'David' is **Dàwèi**, 'Mary' is **Mǎlì**, 'London' is **Lúndūn**, etc.

3 Omission of de *from* wǒde, nǐde *and* tāde

The word **de** is most likely to be omitted from **wǒde** (my), **nǐde** (your), **tāde** (his/her), etc. if the noun that follows it is a kinship term. However, if one-syllable adjectives such as **hǎo**, **lǎo** are used before the noun, **de** *cannot* be omitted. For example:

> ***Wǒ*** **tàitai bù hùi shuō Yīngwén.**
> My wife can't speak English.
>
> ***Wǒde*** **hǎo dìdi hěn cōngming.**
> My good younger brother is very clever.

4 Titles used to refer to one's spouse

In mainland China, the term **àiren** (*lit.* 'love person') is used both in spoken and written Chinese to refer to both 'husband' and 'wife'. The formal term for 'husband' is **zhàngfu** and 'wife' is **qīzi**. The terms **tàitai** and **xiānsheng** can mean 'Mrs' and 'Mr' in one context and 'wife' and 'husband' in another context (**xiānsheng** can also be used to refer to one's teacher). In Hong Kong, Taiwan and other international Chinese communities, the terms **tàitai** and **xiānsheng** are widely used to mean 'wife' and 'husband'. Since most married Chinese women keep their maiden names, it is thus inappropriate to use **tàitai** (Mrs) to address a married woman (see Note 2 of Lesson 1 for other titles).

5 Use of lúndào

The construction **Lúndào** + pronoun + verb + **le** can be broadly translated as 'It is somebody's turn to do something'. Note that **le** is used in this construction to indicate that it is *already* somebody's turn to do something. For example:

***Lúndào* wǒ zuòfàn le.**	*It's my turn* to cook.
***Lúndào* tā yóuyǒng le.**	*It's her turn* to swim.

6 *Construction* shì bú shì

An alternative to the **. . . shì . . . ma?** question is **. . . shì bú shì . . .?** (see Note 13 of Lesson 4). For example:

Nǐ *shì* Wáng Lín *ma*? *becomes* **Nǐ *shì bù shì* Wáng Lín?** (Are you Wang Lin?)

7 *Use of* qíngkuàng

Words like **qíngkuàng** (situation/present condition), which are very vague in meaning, are often used in Chinese to express the English equivalents of 'yourself', 'about', 'things', etc. For example:

Qǐng gàosu wǒ nǐ tàitai de *qíngkuàng*.
Please tell me about your wife.

***Qíngkuàng* bù hǎo.**
Things are not good.

8 *Continuous tense particle* zài

In Chinese, the continuous tense, i.e. 'somebody *is/was doing* something', is indicated by the grammar word **zài** (or **zhèngzài**) which is placed before the verb. Depending on the context, sentences with **zài** or **zhèngzài** can refer either to something which is happening at present (habitual activity) or to something which is happening at the very moment when the sentence is uttered. For example:

Nǐ bàba hái *zài* gōngzuó ma?	Is your father still working? HABITUAL
Wǒ *zhèngzài* chī wǔfàn.	I am having my lunch. MOMENTARY

However, you must use **zài**, not **zhèngzài**, in the following two cases:

(a) when the negating word **bù** is used;
(b) when an adverb such as **hái** (still) is used.

For example:

Tā *bù* zài chī wǎnfàn.
He is *not* having his supper.

Xiǎo Wáng *hái* zài yóuyǒng ma?
Is Xiao Wang *still* there swimming?

9 *Construction* . . . bù . . . le

The construction . . . **bù** + verb + **le** conveys the meanings of '. . . no longer/not . . . any more'. Often, the verbs being negated are verbs indicating habitual behaviour. For example:

Tā tàitai *bù* gōngzuò *le.*
His wife *no longer* works.

Wǒ *bù* xiǎng qù Zhōngguó *le.*
I *don't* want to go to China *any more.*

10 *Use of* dōu

This word, always placed after the pronoun, can convey the meanings of 'both' or 'all' depending on the context. For example:

Tāmen *dōu* xiǎng xiān chī wǔfàn.
They *all* want to have lunch first.

Wǒ hé wǒ zhàngfu *dōu* tuìxūi le.
Lit. I and my husband both have been retired.
Both my husband and I are retired.

To say 'none of us . . .', or 'neither . . .', simply add the negation word before the verb:

Tāmen *dōu bù* xiǎng xiān chī wǔfàn.
None of them wants to have lunch first.

Wǒ hé wǒ zhàngfu *dōu bù* gōngzuó le.
Neither I *nor* my husband works any more.

11 *Use of the verb* shàng

The verb **shàng** (to go to) is interchangeable with **qù** (to go to) in most cases. The main difference is that **shàng** is more colloquial and informal. For example:

A: **Nǐ *shàng/qù* nǎr?**	Where are you *going*?
B: ***Shàng/Qù* cāntīng.**	Dining-room.

However, **shàng** must be used in the following:

shàng **xué**	to *go to* school (any school)
shàng **jiē**	to *go to* the town (*lit.* 'go to the street')

When **le** is used after **shàng xué** or **shàng xiǎoxué**, it means 'to have started school':

A: **Nǐde érzi *shàng (xiǎo)xué* le ma?**
Has your son *started school* yet?

B: **Méi shàng.**
Not yet.

Let us see the difference between **shàng** and **qù** in the following sentences:

Jane yǐjing *shàng* xiǎoxué *le.*
Jane *has started* primary school.

Jane yǐjing *qù* xiǎoxué *le.*
Jane *has gone to* the primary school. [She may be a pupil, a teacher there or she may have gone there for a visit.]

You may have noticed that when the words **xiǎo** (small), **zhōng** (middle/medium) and **dà** (big/large) precede **xué** (to study), we get:

xiǎoxué	primary school
zhōngxué	secondary school/middle school
dàxué	university

If we add the word **shēng** (i.e. one who studies) to **xué**, we have the noun **xuésheng** (student). If we add **xiǎo**, **zhōng** and **dà** to **xuésheng**, we have: **xiǎo xuésheng** (primary-school pupil), **zhōng xuésheng** (secondary-school student) and **dà xuésheng** (university student). Note that **shēng** has become neutral tone in the above noun phrases.

12 To negate yǒu yìsi

To negate **yǒu yìsi,** the negation word **méi** must be used. You can say either **méi yǒu yìsi** or **méi yìsi** (with **yǒu** omitted) to mean 'to be not interesting' or 'to be boring'. If adverbs such as **hěn** (very) are used, (a) they must be placed before the negation word; and (b) **yǒu** is always omitted. For example:

Zhè běn shū *méi yǒu yìsi.*	This book *is not interesting.*
Zhè ge rén *hěn méi yìsi.*	This person *is very boring.*

13 *Use of* gěi

When **gěi** is used before personal pronouns, it can mean 'for/to somebody' or 'to be for/to somebody'. If it means 'for/to somebody', the **gěi** phrase is placed before the verb. For example:

Gěi wǒ **jièshào yīxià nǐ tàitai, hǎo ma?**
Lit. To me introduce your wife, is it OK?
Will you introduce your wife *to me* please?

If it means 'to be for/to somebody', the sentence order is similar to English. For example:

Zhè bēi kāfēi *gěi nǐ.* This cup of coffee *is for you.*

To convey the meaning 'to tell somebody about something', use the construction **gěi** somebody + **jiǎngjiang** + something. For example:

Gěi nǐ yéye **jiǎngjiang nǐde qíngkuàng ba.**
Lit. To your grandpa tell your present situation
Please tell *your grandpa* about yourself.

Exercises

Exercise 1

Match the Chinese kinship terms on the left with their English equivalents on the right:

1 **jiéjie**	5 **mèimei**	(a) elder brother	(e) grandfather
2 **dìdi**	6 **āyí**	(b) elder sister	(f) grandmother
3 **gēge**	7 **nǎinai**	(c) younger sister	(g) uncle
4 **yéye**	8 **shūshu**	(d) younger brother	(h) aunt

Exercise 2

Change the following sentences into the present continuous tense using **zai** and then translate them into English:

(a) Wǒ māma hē kāfēi.
(b) Yīngméi chī zǎofàn ma?
(c) Tā bù yóuyǒng.
(d) Nǐ bàba gōngzuò ma?

Exercise 3

Fill in the blanks using **qù** or **shàng**:

(a) Nǐ àirén (*spouse*) ______________ nǎr le?
(b) Wǒménde érzi zài ______________ dàxué.
(c) Tāmen xià ge xīngqī ______________ Zhōngguó.
(d) Nǐde nǚ'ér ______________ xiǎoxué le ma?

Exercise 4

Answer the following questions in Chinese regarding Dialogue 1:

(a) Shàotáng jiéhūn le ma?
(b) Shéi shì Shàotáng de tàitai?
(c) Shàotáng de tàitai shì nǎ guó rén?
(d) Shàotáng hé ('*and*') tāde tàitai yǒu háizi ma?
(e) Tāménde háizi jiào shénme?
(f) Zhìgāng shì bù shì zhōng xuésheng?
(g) Yīngméi shì shéi?

Exercise 5

Translate the following sentences into Chinese:

(a) Lao Zhang has become the manager of the Beijing Hotel.
(b) They have two children. Both children have Chinese names.
(c) We have all retired.
(d) They no longer work.
(e) My younger brother hasn't started school yet.
(f) Going to school is very interesting.
(g) What subject do you study?
(h) Please tell me about your husband.
(i) It is my turn to speak Chinese.

Dialogue 2
Nǐ gàn shénme gōngzuò? 你干什么工作？
What do you do?

Miao Lan and Liu Xiaohong are good friends. When Miao Lan is on a business trip in Shenzhen, Liu Xiaohong, who lives in Guangzhou, makes a special trip to Shenzhen to meet Miao Lan

MIÁO LÁN: Xiǎohóng, tīngshuō nǐ huàn gōngzuò le. Nǐ xiànzài gàn shénme gōngzuò?
LIÚ XIǍOHÓNG: Dǎoyóu.
MIÁO LÁN: Zài nǎ jiā gōngsī?
LIÚ XIǍOHÓNG: Guǎngzhōu Lǚyóu Jú.
MIÁO LÁN: Tài hǎo le.
LIÚ XIǍOHÓNG: Nǐ hái zài Zhōngguó Sīchóu Màoyì Gōngsī gōngzuò ma?
MIÁO LÁN: Shì de. Wǒ hěn xǐhuān zhè ge gōngzuó.
LIÚ XIǍOHÓNG: Nǐ fùmǔ de shēntí hǎo ma?
MIÁO LÁN: Hěn hǎo, xièxie. Nǐ bàba, māma hái zhù zài Guǎngzhōu ma?
LIÚ XIǍOHÓNG: Shì de. Tāmen cháng shuōqi nǐ. Nǐ zài Shēnzhèn dāi jǐ tiān?
MIÁO LÁN: Kěxī zhǐ dāi sì tiān. Kǒngpà wǒ zhè cì méi yǒu shíjiān qù kàn tāmen. Qǐng wèn tāmen hǎo.
LIÚ XIǍOHÓNG: Wǒ huì de.

MIAO LAN: 听说你换工作了。你现在干什么工作？
LIU XIAOHONG: 导游。
MIAO LAN: 在哪家公司？
LIU XIAOHONG: 广州旅游局。
MIAO LAN: 太好了。
LIU XIAOHONG: 你还在中国丝绸贸易公司工作吗？
MIAO LAN: 是的。我很喜欢这个工作。
LIU XIAOHONG: 你父母的身体好吗？
MIAO LAN: 很好，谢谢。你爸爸，妈妈还住在广州吗？
LIU XIAOHONG: 是的。他们常说起你。你在深圳呆几天？
MIAO LAN: 可惜只呆四天。恐怕我这次没有时间去看他们。请问他们好。
LIU XIAOHONG: 我会的。

MIAO LAN: *I've heard that you've changed jobs. What are you doing now?*
LIU XIAOHONG: *Tourist guide.*
MIAO LAN: *In which company?*
LIU XIAOHONG: *Guangzhou Tourist Bureau.*
MIAO LAN: *Wonderful.*
LIU XIAOHONG: *Are you still working for China Silk Trading Company?*
MIAO LAN: *Yes, I like this job very much.*
LIU XIAOHONG: *Are your parents well?*

MIAO LAN:	*Quite well, thank you. Are your mother and father still living in Guangzhou?*
LIU XIAOHONG:	*Yes, they are. They always talk about you. How many days are you staying in Shenzhen for?*
MIAO LAN:	*Pity that I only stay for four days. I'm afraid I don't have time to go to see them this time. Please send them my regards.*
LIU XIAOHONG:	*I will.*

Vocabulary

tīngshuō	听说	to have heard [*lit.* 'hearsay']
huàn	换	to change
gàn	干	to do
dǎoyóu	导游	tourist guide
zài	在	at/in/to be at/to be in
jiā	家	[measure word]
lǚyóu	旅游	tourism/to travel
jú	局	bureau/office
sīchóu	丝绸	silk
màoyì	贸易	trading/trade
xǐhuān	喜欢	to like
fùmǔ	父母	parents
shēntǐ	身体	health
bàba	爸爸	father/dad
zhù	住	to live
dāi	呆/待	to stay
tiān	天	day
kǒngpà	恐怕	I'm afraid . . .
kěxī	可惜	pity that . . .
zhè cì	这次	this time
kàn	看	to see/to visit/to watch/to read
huì	会	will

Notes to Dialogue 2

14 Nǐ gàn shénme gōngzuò?

If you want to ask someone what job he/she is doing, you say: **Nǐ gàn shénme gōngzuò?** (*lit.* 'You do what job?'). In a context where the conversation centres around jobs, the above sentence can be translated as ‘What are you doing?’ However, if you want to know literally what someone is doing at the very moment of your speech, you say **Nǐ *zài* gàn shénme?** (What are you doing?). Look at the different answers to these questions:

A: **Nǐ *gàn shénme gōngzuò?***	What are you doing?
B: **Wǒ shì xiǎoxué lǎoshī.**	I’m a primary school teacher.
A: **Línlin, nǐ zài gàn shénme?**	What are you doing, Linlin?
B: **Wǒ zài chī wǎnfàn.**	I’m having my dinner.

15 Use of zài

In terms of character representation, this **zài** is the same as the continuous tense indicator **zài**, which must be placed before the verb (see Note 8 above). However, this **zài** can mean ‘to be at/in’ or simply ‘at/in’ and is always placed before the noun in affirmative sentences or before the question words in questions. For example:

Wǒ fùmǔ *zài* Zhōngguó. noun	My parents *are in* China.
Nǐ zhù *zài* nǎr? question word	Where do you live?

Most verbs follow prepositional phrases. Exceptions to this rule are the verbs **zhù** (to live) and **dāi** (to stay), which can be followed by or preceded by prepositional phrases:

Tā jiějie zhù *zài Xī’ān.*
verb prepositional phrase
Her elder sister lives *in Xi’an.*

Tā jiějie *zài Xī’ān* zhù.
prepositional phrase verb
Her elder sister lives *in Xi’an.*

To negate the first sentence above, put the negation word **bù** in front of the verb **zhù**, and to negate the second sentence above, put **bù** in front of **zài**:

Tā jiějie *bù* zhù zài Xī’ān.
Her elder sister *does not* live in Xi’an.

Tā jiějie *bù* zài Xī’ān zhù.
Her elder sister *does not* live in Xi’an.

In English, you say *I work for ICI*, and in Chinese, you can say:

Wǒ *zài ICI* gōngzuò.
Lit. I at ICI work.

16 More on measure words

So far, we have learnt two measure words: **gè** before people, swimming pools, restaurants, etc.; and **bēi** before drinks. In Dialogue 2, we have a new measure word, **jiā**, which is often used before companies, organizations, shops, restaurants, etc. For example:

Zhè *jiā* fàndiàn hěn hǎo.
This hotel is very good.

Wǒ bù zài zhè *jiā* gōngsī gōngzuò.
I'm not working for this company.

The noun **tiān** (day) is one of the few exceptions to the rule of using measure words between numbers and nouns. No measure word is needed between a number and **tiān**. Thus we say, for example, **sān tiān** (three days) *not* **sān gè tiān**. When **sān tiān** is used in sentences, it can mean '*for* three days'. For example:

Wǒ zài Běijīng dāi le *sān tiān*.
I stayed in Beijing *for three days*.

17 Showing concern over someone else's parents

It is very common among Chinese people to enquire about each other's parents, especially their health. The commonly used expression is **Nǐ fùmǔ de shēntǐ hǎo ma?** (*lit.* 'Your parents' health is good?'). Sometimes, **de** is omitted.

18 More on question word jǐ

We saw this question word previously in Lesson 4 when it was used to ask about the time. This question word can also be used to ask other number-related questions. However, you must remember that whenever this question word is used, the questioner expects a small number (less than twenty) in the reply. For example:

A: **Nǐ zài Běijīng dāi *jǐ* tiān?**
How many days are you staying in Beijing for?

B: **Liǎng tiān.**
Two days.

If A expects B to stay in Beijing for two years, for instance, he/she has to ask the question in a different way. Let us look at another example:

A: **Nǐménde gōngsī yǒu *jǐ* gè Měiguórén?**
How many Americans are there in your company?

B: **Jiǔ ge.**
Nine.

19 Use of yǒu shíjiān *and* méi yǒu shíjiān

The Chinese equivalent of *I have time to swim* is **Wǒ *yǒu shíjiān* yóuyǒng**. And the Chinese equivalent of *I don't have time to swim* is **Wǒ *méi yǒu shíjiān* yóuyǒng** or **Wǒ *méi shíjiān* yóuyǒng**. Let us look at some more examples:

A: **Nǐ jīntiān wǎnshang *yǒu shíjiān* ma?**
Do you have time tonight?

B: ***Yǒu (shíjiān).***
Yes, I do.

Xiǎo Wáng ràng wǒ gàosu nǐ tā *méi shíjiān* lái kàn nǐ.
Xiao Wang asks me to tell you that she doesn't have time to come to see you.

20 Verb kàn

In Chinese, for anything that is seen, we use the verb **kàn**. Thus you can say ***kàn* péngyou** (to visit/see friends), ***kàn* shū** (to read a book), ***kàn* zhàopiān** (to look at the photos), ***kàn* diànyǐng** (to see a film), ***kàn* diànshì** (to watch television) and ***kàn* zúqiú** (to watch the football).

21 Construction Qǐng wèn . . . hǎo

The phrase **Qǐng wèn** + somebody + **hǎo** literally means 'Please ask somebody good', which can be broadly translated as 'Please say hello to somebody' or 'Please give somebody my regards'. For example:

Qǐng *wèn* nǐ tàitai *hǎo*. *Please say hello* to your wife.
Qǐng *wèn* nǐ fùmú *hǎo*. *Please give* your parents *my regards*.

22 Another use of huì

The **huì** which we saw earlier in Lesson 2 means 'to be able to' or 'can'. Another meaning of **huì** is to express one's willingness to do something or to predict that something is likely to happen. When **huì** means 'will', **de** follows it in short replies or occurs at the end of the sentence. For example:

A: **Nǐ *huì* jiàndào Liú Xiǎoméi ma?**
Will you see Liu Xiaomei?

B: ***Huì de.***
Yes, I *will.*

Tā *huì* lái chī wǎnfàn *de.*
He *will* come for dinner.

Exercises

Exercise 6

Translate the following sentences into English, differentiating between **zài** ('to be at/in', or 'at/in') and **zài** (continuous tense indicator):

(a) Tā bù zhù zài Běijīng.
(b) Nǐ fùmǔ hái zài gōngzuò ma?
(c) Mǎ Lān zài chī zǎofàn.
(d) Wáng Lín zài Běijīng Fàndiàn gōngzuò.

Exercise 7

Change the following statements into questions using **jǐ** and paying particular attention to the underlined words:

Example: **Běijīng Fàndiàn yǒu sān ge cāntīng. → Běijīng Fàndiàn yǒu *jǐ* ge cāntīng?**

(a) Lǎo Wáng yǒu sān ge háizi.
(b) Wǒ zài Běijīng Fàndiàn zhù le wǔ tiān.
(c) Tā hē le liǎng bēi kāfēi.
(d) Lǐ Píng yǒu sì ge gēge.

Exercise 8

Based on what we have learnt in this lesson, what do you say on the following occasions in Chinese:

(a) You want to ask your Chinese friend if she has time to go swimming.
(b) Your Chinese friend wants to invite you to a party but unfortunately you don't have time, so you apologize, saying . . .
(c) You want to ask a Chinese person what job he does.
(d) You want to ask your Chinese friend to pass on your regards to her parents.

Exercise 9

Fill in the blanks with appropriate measure words if necessary:

(a) Wǒ zài Shànghǎi dāi le shí ________ tiān.
(b) Zhè liǎng ________ rén hěn méi yìsi.
(c) Nǐ zài nǎ ________ gōngsī gōngzuò?
(d) Wǒ ménde dàxué yǒu yī ________ yóuyǒng chí.
(e) Tā hē le sān ________ kāfēi.

Exercise 10

Translate the following into Chinese:

(a) I like my work very much.
(b) I want to go to visit my parents.
(c) Will he come to visit me?
(d) Fang Shu works for the Beijing Tourist Bureau.
(e) Where do you live?

Characters

1 Learning to write:

(a) Verb(s) kàn (to see/read/watch) and xǐhuan (to like)

kàn

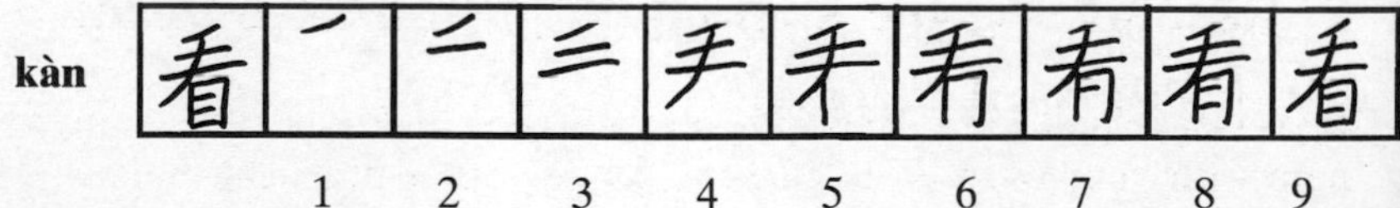

1 2 3 4 5 6 7 8 9

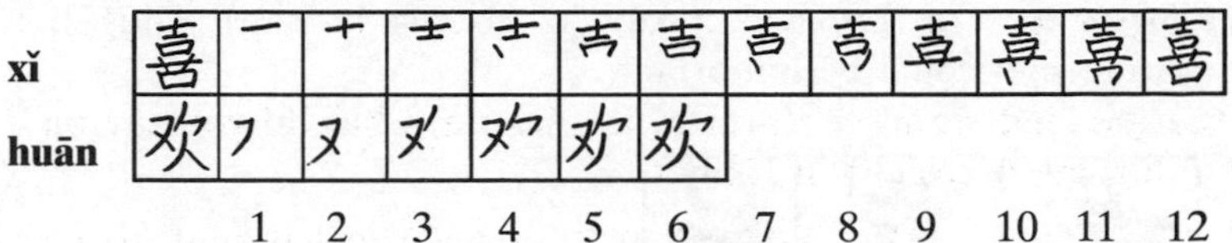

(b) Question words shénme (what) and nǎr (where)

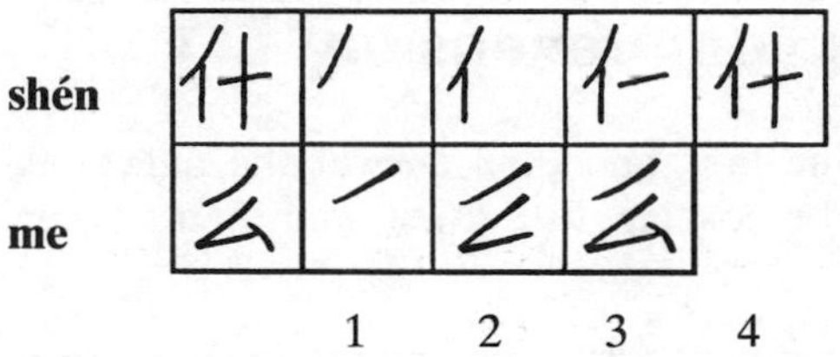

The left part of **shén** is the 'person radical' 亻 which we learnt previously, and the right part is the character for 'ten' 十 which we also learnt earlier.

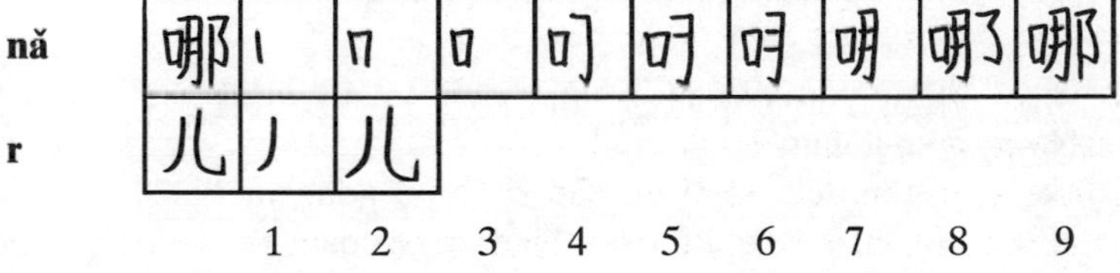

Exercise 11

Translate the following sentences into Chinese using characters:

(a) I want to go to China.
(b) Where does she want to go?

2 Recognizing the sign lǚyóu jú (tourist bureau)

If you travel in China, especially on your own, and would like some help with your rail tickets, flight tickets or other practical matters, the best place to contact is **lǚyóu jú** (tourist bureau). Thus, the following sign could be important:

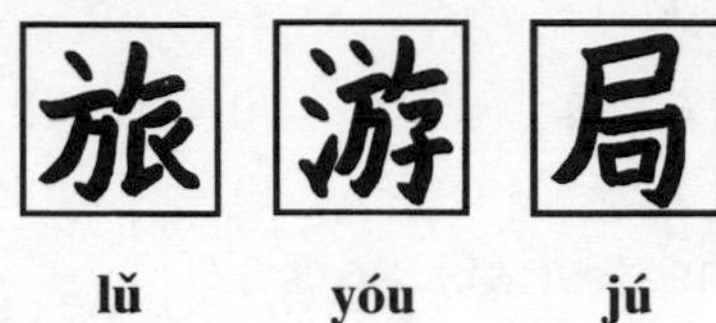

lǚ **yóu** **jú**

Reading/listening comprehension

Read the following dialogue first, and then answer the questions in English. If you have the recording, listen first, and then answer the questions:

Yang Ning and Gu Liang, who are very good friends, have not seen each other for a long time. They run into each other, and . . .

YÁNG NÍNG: Hǎo jiǔ bù jiàn, Gù Liáng. Tīngshuō nǐ huàn gōngzuò le.
GÙ LIÁNG: Shì de.
YÁNG NÍNG: Shénme gōngzuò?
GÙ LIÁNG: Zài Běijīng Sīchóu Màoyì Gōngsī dāng fānyì.
YÁNG NÍNG: Yǒu yìsi ma?
GÙ LIÁNG: Tǐng yǒu yìsi. Nǐ zěnme yàng, Yáng Níng?
YÁNG NÍNG: Wǒ jiéhūn le.
GÙ LIÁNG: Zhēn de? Nǐ àiren gàn shénme gōngzuò?
YÁNG NÍNG: Tā shì xiǎoxué lǎoshī. Nǐ xiǎng rènshi tā ma?
GÙ LIÁNG: Dāngrán xiǎng.
YÁNG NÍNG: Jīntiān wǎnshang nǐ yǒu shíjiān ma?
GÙ LIÁNG: Kǒngpà méi yǒu.
YÁNG NÍNG: Míngtiān wǎnshang ne?
GÙ LIÁNG: Míngtiān wǎnshang yǒu shíjiān.
YÁNG NÍNG: Nàme, nǐ lái wǒ men jiā chī wǎnfàn.
GÙ LIÁNG: Tài hǎo le. Xièxie.

Vocabulary

fānyì translator/interpreter
míngtiān tomorrow
àiren spouse [*lit.* 'love person']

jīntiān	today
jiā	home/family
lǎoshī	teacher [*lit.* 'old master']

Questions

A What is Gu Liang's current occupation?
B Who is Gu Liang's employer?
C What is the surprise news from Yang Ning?
D What does Yang Ning's wife do as a job?
E When and where is Gu Liang going to meet Yang Ning's wife?

6 Rìqī hé tiānqì

日期和天气

The date and the weather

By the end of this lesson, you should be able to:

- say the days of the week, dates, months of the year and years
- use time expressions appropriately
- find out information regarding dates and days
- use the question words **shénme shíhou**, **duō jiǔ** and **háishi**
- make simple comments on the weather
- recognize and write more characters

Dialogue 1

Jīntiān shì xīngqī jǐ? 今天是星期几？

What day is it today?

Below is a dialogue in a classroom between a teacher and her pupils in a primary school in China

TEACHER: Jīntiān shì xīngqī jǐ?
PUPIL A: Jīntiān shì xīngqī'èr.
TEACHER: Yī ge xīngqī yǒu jǐ tiān?
PUPIL B: Yī ge xīngqī yǒu qī tiān.
TEACHER: Yī nián yǒu jǐ ge yuè?
PUPIL C: Yī nián yǒu shí'èr ge yuè.
TEACHER: Míngtiān shì jǐ hào?
PUPIL D: Míngtiān shì yījiǔjiǔsì nián yīyuè shíbā hào.
TEACHER: Yī nián yǒu jǐ ge jìjié? Tāmen shì shénme?
PUPIL E: Sì ge jìjié. Tāmen shì chūntiān, xiàtiān, qiū tiān hé dōngtiān.

TEACHER: 今天是星期几？
PUPIL A: 今天是星期二。
TEACHER: 一个星期有几天？
PUPIL B: 一个星期有七天。
TEACHER: 一年有几个月？
PUPIL C: 一年有十二个月。
TEACHER: 明天是几号？
PUPIL D: 明天是一九九四年一月十八号。
TEACHER: 一年有几个季节？它们是什么？
PUPIL E: 四个季节。它们是春天，夏天，秋天和冬天。

Vocabulary

jīntiān	今天	today
xīngqī'èr	星期二	Tuesday
nián	年	year
yuè	月	month
míngtiān	明天	tomorrow
hào	号	date
yījiǔjiǔsì nián	一九九四年	1994
yīyuè	一月	January [*lit.* 'one month']
tāmen	它们	they (inanimate objects)
jìjié	季节	season
chūntiān	春天	spring
xiàtiān	夏天	summer
qiū tiān	秋天	autumn
hé	和	and
dōngtiān	冬天	winter

Notes to Dialogue 1

1 Days of the week

To form the words for the first six days of the week, put **xīngqī** in front of the numbers from 'one' to 'six'. The word **xīngqī** literally means 'week' when used by itself but for our purpose here we can think of it as meaning 'weekday':

Chinese	*English*
xīngqī*yī*	Monday
xīngqī'*èr*	Tuesday
xīngqī*sān*	Wednesday
xīngqī*sì*	Thursday
xīngqī*wǔ*	Friday
xīngqī*liù*	Saturday

'Sunday' is **xīngqī*rì*** or **xīngqī*tiān***, **rì** being a formal term for 'the sun' and **tiān** meaning 'day' or 'sky'.

2 Months of the year

The word for 'month' is **yuè**. Simply place numbers from 'one' to 'twelve' in front of **yuè**:

Chinese	*English*	*Chinese*	*English*
***yī*yuè**	January	***qī*yuè**	July
***èr*yuè**	February	***bā*yuè**	August
***sān*yuè**	March	***jiǔ*yuè**	September
***sì*yuè**	April	***shí*yuè**	October
***wǔ*yuè**	May	***shíyī*yuè**	November
***liù*yuè**	June	***shí'èr*yuè**	December

3 Year and date

If you want to express a particular year, simply say the numbers individually. However, remember to use the word **nián** (year) at the end to differentiate the year from other numbers. For example:

1994 **yījiǔjiǔsì *nián***   1840 **yībāsìlíng *nián***

As in English, the first two numbers of the year can be omitted. For example, '1994' can be shortened to ''94', **jiǔsì nián**. The order for a date including month and year is the reverse of that used in English. The date is thus spoken in the following order: year, month and then date. Also the term **hào** or **rì** (the former is the spoken form and the latter the written form for 'date') must be used. For example:

27 December 2001	**èrlínglíngyī nián shí'èryuè èrshíqī** ***hào/rì.***
10 February 1994	**yījiǔjiǔsì nián èryuè shí** ***hào/rì.***

4 Absence of prepositions in front of time phrases

In English, prepositions such as *at*, *in*, *on* or *for* must be put in front of the time, the month, the day, the date and expressions of duration. Whilst in Chinese, it is all very simple because such words are not needed in front of time phrases. For example:

Wǒ māma ***xīngqīsān*** **lái kàn wǒmen.**
My mother is coming to see us *on Wednesday*.

Xīnháng ***liùyuè qī hào*** **kāishǐ gōngzuò.**
Xinhang starts working *on 7 June*.

Note that in the above two sentences, both time phrases refer to a particular day or date, so they are put in front of the verb. If the time phrase refers to a period of time, it is usually put after the verb. For example:

Wǒ zài Lúndūn zhù le ***liǎng nián.***
verb
I lived in London *for two years*.

Tā zài Lancaster xué le ***bā ge yuè*** **Yīngwén.**
verb
He learnt English in Lancaster *for eight months*.

5 Use of measure word gè *before years, months and weeks*

In Note 16 of Lesson 5, we saw the omission of the measure word **gè** in between the number and the noun **tiān** (day). The same principle applies to **nián** (year), i.e. there is no need to use measure words between the number and the noun **nián**. For example:

Wǒ xué le ***sān nián*** **Yīngwén.** I learnt English for *three years*.

However, you *must* use the measure word **gè** in between the number and the noun **yuè** (month). For example: **sān *ge* yuè** (three months) as opposed to **sān yuè** (March). As for **xīngqī** (week), you can either use **gè** or drop it. Both usages are correct:

Tā zài Běijīng dāi le *sān ge xīngqī*.
or **Tā zài Běijīng dāi le *sān xīngqī*.**
He/she stayed in Beijing for *three weeks*.

6 More on the question word jǐ

When **jǐ** is used to ask the current day (or day in the near future) and the date, it means 'which' rather than 'how many'. For example:

Jīntiān shì xīngqī *jǐ*?
Lit. Today is weekday which?
What day is it today?

Jīntiān shì *jǐ* hào?
Lit. Today is which date?
What's the date today?

The question **Jīntiān shì jǐ hào?** can be replied to with a full answer specifying the year, the month and the date, or by just giving the date, depending on the context:

A: **Xià ge xīngqī'èr shì jǐ hào?**
Lit. Next Tuesday is which date?
A: What's next Tuesday's date?

B: ***Èrshíwǔ hào.*** B: *25th.*

To ask questions such as 'How many days/weeks/months/seasons . . . ?', the measure word **gè** must be used between the question word **jǐ** and those nouns which require measure word **gè** in the reply (see Note 5 above). For example:

Yī nián yǒu jǐ *ge* yuè?
Lit. A year have how many months?
How many months are there in a year?

Nǐ xué le *jǐ nián* Zhōngwén?
Lit. You learnt how many years Chinese?
For *how many years* did you learn Chinese?

7 *Use of* hé

The conjunction word **hé** (and) is never used to link two sentences. When two sentences share the same subject (e.g. 'you', 'I'), the subject is omitted in the second sentence and a comma is used. For example:

Tā jīnnián èrshí suì, shì dà xuésheng.
He is twenty this year *and* he is a university student.

The word **hé** is only used to link two or more than two nouns, pronouns or noun phrases. Even then, it can be omitted. And, if you want to say 'somebody and I', 'I' is usually mentioned first in Chinese. For example:

Wǒ yǒu liǎng ge gēge, yī ge dìdi.
I have two elder brothers and one younger brother.

***Wǒ hé Xiǎo Lǐ* xǐhuan yóuyǒng, *(hé)* pīng pāng qiú.**
Xiao Li and I like swimming and table-tennis.

Exercises

Exercise 1

Look at the following calendars and answer the questions:

(a) Jīntiān shì xīngqī jǐ?

MARCH 2000
26
SUNDAY

(b) Jīntiān shì jǐ yuè jǐ hào?

JUNE 2000
9
FRIDAY

(c) Nǐ jǐ hào qù Zhōngguó?

FEBRUARY 2000
7
MONDAY

(d) Nǐ māma xīngqī jǐ lái Táiwān?

JUNE 2000
12
MONDAY

Exercise 2

Fill in the blanks with the measure word **gè** when necessary, and then translate the sentences into English:

(a) Xiǎo Fāng zài Shēnzhèn dāi le sān ________ tiān (*three days*).
(b) Wǒ yǒu sān ________ yuè (*three months*).
(c) Wǒ zhàngfu xiǎng zài Zhōngguó lǚyóu liǎng ________ xīngqī (*two weeks*).
(d) Wǒ dìdi zài Xī'ān gōngzuò le sì ________ nián (*four years*).
(e) Wáng Dōngpíng yǒu wǔ ________ gēge (*five elder brothers*).
(f) Paul xiǎng bā ________ yuè (*August*) qù Táiwān.

Exercise 3

Translate the following sentences from English to Chinese:

(a) For how many years did Feixia live in Guangzhou?
(b) Tomorrow is Thursday.
(c) For how many months did Andrew learn Chinese?
(d) I want to go to China this March.
(e) What is next Friday's date?
(f) My husband has two younger brothers and one elder sister.

Dialogue 2
Shénme shíhou . . .? 什么时候 . . .?
When . . .?

Mick is planning to go to Beijing and he wants to find out what the weather is like. So he is chatting with Li Lü, a Chinese student who comes from Beijing

MICK: Běijīng de dōngtiān lěng ma?
LǏ LǛ: Fēicháng lěng. Cháng xiàxuě.
MICK: Xiàtiān zěnme yàng?
LǏ LǛ: Qīyuè hé bāyuè tèbié rè.

Mɪᴄᴋ: Shénme jìjié zuì hǎo?
Lǐ Lǜ: Qiū tiān, shíyuè zuǒyòu. Zěnme? Nǐ dǎsuàn qù Běijīng ma?
Mɪᴄᴋ: Shì'a.
Lǐ Lǜ: Shénme shíhou?
Mɪᴄᴋ: Jìrán nǐ shuō shíyuè zuì hǎo, wǒ jiù míng nián shíyuè qù.
Lǐ Lǜ: Nǐ qù lǚyóu háishi gōngzuò?
Mɪᴄᴋ: Lǚyóu jiā gōngzuò.
Lǐ Lǜ: Nǐ qù duō jiǔ?
Mɪᴄᴋ: Lǚyóu liǎng ge xīngqī, gōngzuò sān tiān, yígòng dàyuē sān ge xīngqī.

Mɪᴄᴋ: 北京的冬天冷吗？
Lɪ Lᴜ: 非常冷。常下雪。
Mɪᴄᴋ: 夏天怎么样？
Lɪ Lᴜ: 七月和八月特别热。
Mɪᴄᴋ: 什么季节最好？
Lɪ Lᴜ: 秋天，十月左右。怎么？你打算去北京吗？
Mɪᴄᴋ: 是啊。
Lɪ Lᴜ: 什么时候？
Mɪᴄᴋ: 既然你说十月最好，我就十月去。
Lɪ Lᴜ: 你去旅游还是工作？
Mɪᴄᴋ: 旅游加工作。
Lɪ Lᴜ: 你去多久？
Mɪᴄᴋ: 旅游两个星期，工作三天，一共大约三个星期。

Vocabulary

lěng	冷	to be cold/cold
fēicháng/tèbié	非常/特别	extremely/very
xiàxuě	下雪	to snow
qīyuè	七月	July
bāyuè	八月	August
rè	热	to be hot/hot
zuì	最	most
zuì hǎo	最好	best
shíyuè	十月	October
zěnme	怎么	why [see Note 11]
dǎsuàn	打算	to plan
shì'a	是啊	yes
shénme shíhou	什么时候	when [*lit.* 'what time?']
jìrán . . . jiù . . .	既然…就…	as . . . then
shuō	说	to say

míng nián	明年	next year
háishi	还是	or [see Note 15]
jiā	家	plus
duō jiǔ	多久	how long
yígòng	一共	altogether
dàyuē	大约	approximately/about/around

Notes to Dialogue 2

8 Use of cháng

This adverb, meaning 'often' or 'frequently', is always placed before the verb, and it is often repeated like some one-syllable words. For example:

Nǐ *cháng* yóuyǒng ma?	Do you *often* swim?
Andrew *chángchang* chūmén.	Andrew is *frequently* away.
Wǒ bù *cháng* hē kāfēi.	I don't *often* drink coffee.

9 Use of zuì

In English, the word *most* cannot be put in front of every adjective or adverb (e.g. 'the most difficult' but 'the easiest'). However, in Chinese, the word **zuì**, meaning 'most', can be placed in front of every word or verbal phrase to describe its degree. For example:

Xiǎo Wáng *zuì* niánqīng.	Xiao Wang is the young*est.*
Zhè běn shū *zuì* yǒu yìsi.	This book is *most* interesting.
Tā *zuì* bù xǐhuan zuòfàn.	He dislikes cooking *most.*

10 More on de *after adjectives*

One-syllable adjectives such as **hǎo** (good), **lǎo** (old), **dà** (big), etc. can be put before nouns without using **de**. For example:

***hǎo* péngyou**	*good* friend
***lǎo* dà xuésheng**	*old* university student
***dà* fàndiàn**	*big* hotel

Most two-syllable adjectives such as **piàoliang** (beautiful), **gāoxìng** (happy), etc., when used to modify nouns, require the use of **de** before the noun. For example:

gāoxìng *de* yī tiān	a happy day
piàoliang *de* fàndiàn	beautiful hotel

However, once these adjectives (both one-syllable and two-syllable) are modified by adverbs such as **tèbié** (extremely), **hěn** (very), **zuì** (most), etc., **de** must be used in between the adjective and the noun. For example:

***zuì* hǎo *de* péngyou**	*best* friend
***tèbié* dà *de* fàndiàn**	*extremely* big hotel
***hěn* lǎo *de* dà xuésheng**	*very* old university student
***fēicháng* piàoliang *de* dàyī**	*very* beautiful coat

11 Use of zěnme

Although **zěnme** is translated as 'why?' in this context, it is not actually seeking an answer but is used to express surprise. For example:

A: **Māma, zánmen jǐ diǎn chī fàn?**
Mum, what time are we going to eat?

B: ***Zěnme*, nǐ è le ma?**
Why? Are you already hungry?

However, **zěnme** can mean 'how come?', which is weaker than **wèishénme** (why?), which we learnt in Lesson 3. For example:

A: **Nǐ jīntiān zěnme bù gāoxìng?**
How come you aren't happy?
B: **Wǒ yě bù zhīdào.**
I don't know either.

A: **Nǐ *wèishénme* jīntiān bù shàngxué?**
Why are you not going to school today?
B: **Yīnwèi jīntiān shì xīngqītiān.**
Because it's Sunday.

12 Adding of a

In spoken Chinese, especially in southern China, **a** is frequently attached to some short expressions. It does not carry any specific meaning but merely adds a touch of informality and friendliness.

For example, if someone is knocking on your door, you can say **Shéi'*a*?** (Who is it?). Also, when you see something beautiful, you can say **Zhēn piàoliang'*a*!** (Really beautiful!).

13 Position of the question words shénme shíhou

These question words mean 'when'. They are usually placed before the verb. For example:

Nǐ érzi *shénme shíhou* qù Xiāng Gǎng gōngzuò?
When is your son going to Hong Kong to work?

Nǐ māma *shénme shíhou* lái Yīngguó?
When is your mother coming to England?

14 Construction Jìrán . . . jiù . . .

Jiù usually goes with the expression **jìrán** to mean 'as . . . (then . . .)'. It is the same word as the emphatic **jiù** in Lesson 3 but here it is used differently. The first half of the construction gives a reason, and the second half is either a suggestion or a decision. For example:

***Jìrán* nǐ tàitai shēntǐ bù hǎo, nǐ *jiù* huí jiā ba.**
As your wife is not feeling well, please go home.

***Jìrán* shíyuè shì zuì hǎo de jìjié, wǒ *jiù* shíyuè qù Běijīng.**
As October is the best season, I shall go to Beijing in October.

15 Question word háishi

Whenever you want to ask a question which gives two or more options, and you want the respondant to specify one or the other, put **háishi** in between the last two choices. Thus, **háishi** can only be used to raise questions. For example:

Nǐ shì Yīngguórén *háishi* Měiguórén?
Are you British *or* American?

Tā xiǎng xiān chī wǔfàn *háishi* xiān yóuyǒng?
Does she want to have lunch first *or* swim first?

16 Question words duō jiǔ

The question words **duō jiǔ** (how long?) are used if you have no idea at all of duration – for how long the other person is staying in Beijing, for example:

> **Nǐ dǎsuàn zài Běijīng dāi duō jiǔ?**
> How long are you staying in Beijing for?

But if you know that he/she is only staying for a couple of days, weeks, months, etc. you use the question word **jǐ**.

17 Difference between dàyuē *and* zuǒyòu

The word **zuǒyòu** (about/around) was introduced earlier, in Lesson 2. The difference between **zuǒyòu** and **dàyuē** is that they occur in different positions in the sentence. **Dàyuē** is always put in front of the phrase it modifies, whilst **zuǒyòu** always follows the phrase it modifies. For example:

A: **Nǐ dǎsuàn zài Měiguó dāi duō jiǔ?**
How long do you plan to stay in America?

B: ***Dàyuē* liǎng ge yuè.**
About two months.

Jiājiā sānshí suì *zuǒyòu*.
Jiajia is *about* thirty years old.

Exercises

Exercise 4

Translate the following expressions into Chinese paying attention to the use of **de**:

(a) my best friend
(b) extremely big swimming pool
(c) small restaurant
(d) that young and beautiful university student
(e) the oldest man

Exercise 5

Convert the following statements into questions using **shénme shíhou** (when?) or **duō jiǔ** (how long?) paying special attention to the underlined words, and then translate the sentences into English:

(a) Mick dăsuàn míng nián qù Zhōngguó.
(b) Zhāng Jūn zài Táiwān gōngzuò le wŭ nián.
(c) Láo Lĭ de nǚ'ér xià ge yuè shàngxué.
(d) Wó xiăng zài Shànghăi dāi sān tiān.

Exercise 6

Fill in the blanks using **dàyuē** or **zuŏyòu**:

(a) Wŏmen dăsuàn liù diăn ________ chī wănfàn.
(b) A: Nĭ zài Shēnzhèn gōngzuò le duō jiŭ?
B: ________ sān nián bàn.
(c) Wáng jīnglĭ sìshíwŭ suì ________.
(d) Wŏ de Yīngguó péngyou ________ liùyuè lái kàn wŏ.

Exercise 7

Translate the following sentences into Chinese:

(a) Do you want to have lunch at twelve or one o'clock?
(b) Do you often swim?
(c) Why are you unhappy?
(d) Since you are not hungry, I'll eat first.

Characters

1 Learning to write:

(a) Jīntiān shì xīngqītiān (Today is Sunday)

jīn 今
tiān 天
shì 是
xīng 星
qī 期
tiān 天
1 2 3 4 5 6 7 8 9 10 11 12

The top part of **shì** and **xīng** is very similar. It is called the 'sun radical' The vertical strokes of the 'sun radical' for **shì** are longer than the horizontal ones whilst the horizontal strokes of the 'sun radical' for **xīng** are longer than the vertical ones

(b) zài (in/at), jiā (home/family) and lǎo (old)

The word **zài** consists of six strokes:

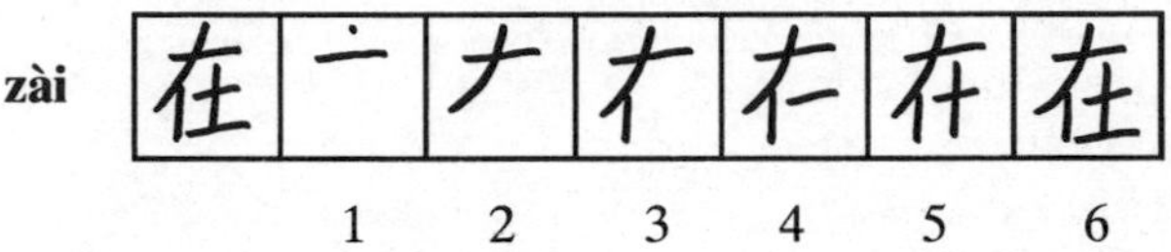

Now you know how to write, for example, **tā bù *zài*** (She is not in) in characters:

The noun **jiā** consists of ten strokes:

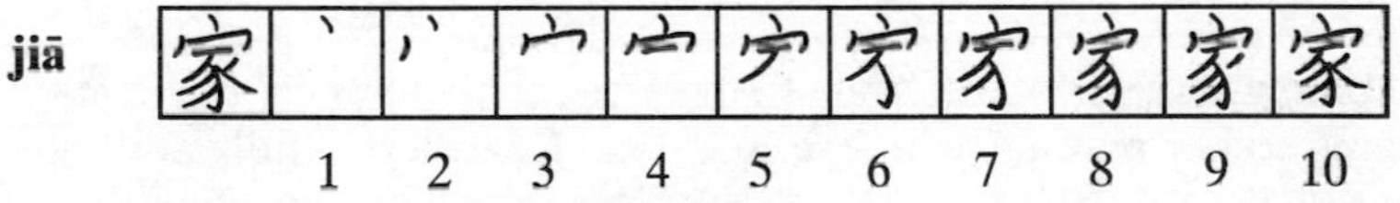

Note that the top part is the 'roof radical'. Now you know how to write, for example, **Wǒ *jiā* zài Běijīng** (My home is in Beijing) in characters:

Wǒ jiā zài Běi jīng.

The adjective **lǎo** consists of six strokes:

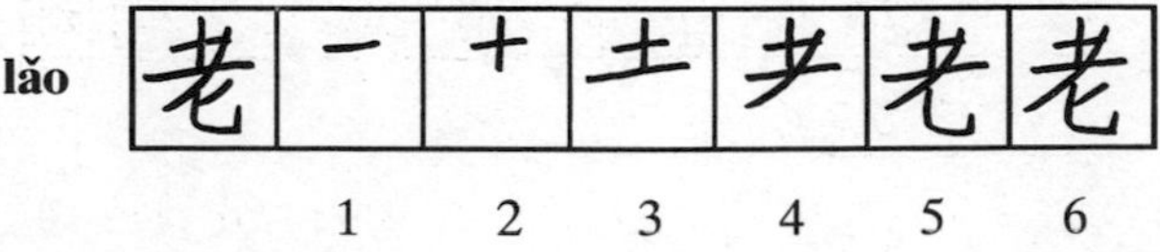

2 Recognizing some common Chinese family names

Lǐ	李	Wáng	王
Zhāng	张	Liú	刘

Exercise 8

Use the following components (as many times as you like) to form as many characters as you can:

女 口 马 子 也

Reading/listening comprehension

1 Below is a postcard from Feng Ying, who lives in the United States, to her parents, who live in China. Read it carefully and then answer the questions in Chinese. If you have the recording, listen first, and then answer the questions in Chinese.

Vocabulary

qīn'àide	dear
xiě xìn	to write a letter
Jiùjīnshān	San Francisco
xiǎng nǐménde	missing you

Qīn'àide Bàba, Māma:

Nǐmen hǎo! Nǐmen zuìjìn shēntǐ hǎo ma?

Wǒ zuìjìn cháng chūmén. Xià ge xīngqīsān, wǒ qù Jiùjīnshān gōngzuò jiā kàn péngyou, dǎsuàn dāi liǎng ge xīngqī zuǒyòu. Jiùjīnshān de xiàtiān hěn rè, búguò fēicháng yǒu yìsi.

Gēge hǎo ma? Gàosu tā gěi wǒ xiě xìn. Qǐng wèn tā hǎo.

Xiǎng nǐménde,
Yǐng
94. 6. 30

Questions

A Féng Yǐng shénme shíhou qù Jiùjīnshān?
B Féng Yǐng qù Jiùjīnshān lǚyóu ma?
C Féng Yǐng qù Jiùjīnshān gàn shénme?
D Féng Yǐng dǎsuàn zài Jiùjīnshān dāi duō jiǔ?
E Jiùjīnshān de xiàtiān zěnme yàng?
F Féng Yǐng de gēge zhù zài Měiguó ma?

2 Read aloud the following phrases or words and add on the correct tone marks. If you have the recording, listen first, and then add on the correct tone marks:

(a) **yiyue** (January)
(b) **san ge yue** (three months)
(c) **tebie da de fandian** (extremely large hotel)
(d) **xingqi'er** (Tuesday)

7 Mǎi dōngxi (I)

买东西

Shopping (I)

By the end of this lesson, you should be able to:

- tell someone the price of a product
- ask about prices
- tell the shop-assistant what and how many you want to buy
- do some bargaining
- use the question words **duō shǎo**
- write more characters and recognize more signs

Dialogue 1

Duō shǎo qián? 多少钱? How much is it?

Anne is from Canada. She is working in Chengdu, capital of Sichuan province in China. Today, she is doing her shopping. She goes into a fruit and vegetable shop where customers are served by shop-assistants

SHOP-ASSISTANT:	Nǐ hǎo. Nǐ xiǎng mǎi shénme?
ANNE:	Wǒ xiǎng mǎi yīxiē shuǐguǒ.
SHOP-ASSISTANT:	Nǐ kàn, wǒmen yǒu xīnxiān de cǎoméi, Hǎinán Dǎo xiāngjiāo, gè zhǒng píngguǒ.
ANNE:	Zhèxiē shì shénme?
SHOP-ASSISTANT:	Lìzhī.
ANNE:	Duō shǎo qián yī jīn?
SHOP-ASSISTANT:	Wǔ kuài bā máo.
ANNE:	Wǒ yào yī jīn lìzhī. Cǎoméi zěnme mài?
SHOP-ASSISTANT:	Sān kuài líng jiǔ fēn yī jīn.

ANNE:	Yào bàn jīn cǎoméi. Yǒu méi yǒu táozi?
SHOP-ASSISTANT:	Méi yǒu, duìbùqǐ. Hái yào biéde ma?
ANNE:	Bù yào, xièxie.
SHOP-ASSISTANT:	Yīgòng qī kuài sān máo liù fēn.
ANNE:	Gěi nǐ shí kuài.
SHOP-ASSISTANT:	Hǎo de. Zháo nǐ liǎng kuài liù máo sì.
ANNE:	Xièxie.

SHOP-ASSISTANT:	你好。你想买什么?
ANNE:	我想买一些水果。
SHOP-ASSISTANT:	你看，我们有新鲜的草莓，海南岛香蕉，各种苹果。
ANNE:	这些是什么?
SHOP-ASSISTANT:	荔枝。
ANNE:	多少钱一斤?
SHOP-ASSISTANT:	五块八毛。
ANNE:	我要一斤荔枝。草莓怎么卖?
SHOP-ASSISTANT:	三块零六分一斤。
ANNE:	要半斤草莓。有没有桃子?
SHOP-ASSISTANT:	没有，对不起。还要别的吗?
ANNE:	不要，谢谢。
SHOP-ASSISTANT:	一共七块三毛六分。
ANNE:	给你十块。
SHOP-ASSISTANT:	好的。找你两块六毛四。
ANNE:	谢谢。

Vocabulary

mǎi	买	to buy
yīxiē	一些	some
shuǐguǒ	水果	fruit
nǐ kàn	你看	have a look [*lit.* 'you look']
xīnxiān	新鲜	fresh
cǎoméi	草莓	strawberry
Hǎinàn Dǎo	海南岛	Hainan Island
xiāngjiāo	香蕉	banana
gè zhǒng	各种	various kinds
píngguǒ	苹果	apple
zhèxiē	这些	these
lìzhī	荔枝	lychee
duō shǎo	多少	how much/how many
qián	钱	money
Duō shǎo qián?	多少钱?	How much is it?

yī jīn 斤 half a kilo
kuài/máo/fēn 块/毛/分 [currency words, see Note 1]
yào 要 to want
mài 卖 to sell
bàn jīn 半斤 a quarter of a kilo [*lit.* 'half *jin*']
táozi 桃子 peach
biéde 别的 anything else
zhǎo 找 to return [see Note 8]

Notes to Dialogue 1

1 Currency terms

In mainland China and Taiwan, the currency word is **yuán**, for which the informal term is **kuài**. One **yuán** consists of ten **jiǎo**, the informal term for which is **máo**. And one **jiǎo** or one **máo** consists of ten **fēn**. Let us list them separately:

Informal	*Formal*
kuài	**yuán**
máo	**jiǎo**
fēn	**fēn**

The sign for Chinese yuan is ¥. Let us look at the following prices expressed with informal currency terms:

¥ 0.05 **wǔ** ***fēn***
¥ 0.80 **bā** ***máo***

¥ 0.23	**liǎng *máo* sān *fēn***
¥ 1.50	**yī *kuài* wǔ *máo***
¥ 2.95	**liǎng *kuài* jiǔ *máo* wǔ *fēn***
¥ 12.30	**shí'èr *kuài* sān *máo***
¥ 6.05	**liù *kuài* líng wǔ *fēn***

Note that if there is more than one currency term involved in a price, the last one can always be omitted. Thus, it is correct to express four of the above prices in the following way:

¥ 1.50	**yī *kuài* wǔ**
¥ 2.95	**liǎng *kuài* jiǔ *máo* wǔ**
¥ 12.30	**shí'èr *kuài* sān**
¥ 6.05	**liù *kuài* líng wǔ**

Since most currencies have only two terms (e.g. pounds and pence; dollars and cents), it is very easy to make the mistake of saying **bāshí fēn** (eighty fen) for ¥ 0.80, for example. You must remember to say **bā máo** or **bā jiǎo**.

2 Unit of weight

The official unit of weight is **gōngjīn** (kilogram). However, **jīn** (half a kilo) is most commonly used in dealing with small quantities of goods, especially in shops. As **jīn** itself is a unit of weight, measure words are not needed in between a number and **jīn**. For example:

A: **Nǐ yào jǐ *jīn* píngguǒ?**
How many *half-kilos* of apples do you want?
B: **Wǒ yào liǎng *jīn* píngguǒ.**
I want a *kilo* of apples.

3 Use of place names

Place names (e.g. names of cities and countries) can be used as adjectives in front of nouns. For example:

***Zhōngguó* fàn**	*Chinese* food
***Yīngguó* gōngsī**	*British* company
***Měiguó* péngyou**	*American* friends
***Hǎinán Dǎo* xiāngjiāo**	*Hainan* bananas

4 Asking the price

The most important phrase to remember is **Duō shǎo qián?** You can specify the goods and the quantity. For example:

Píngguǒ *duō shǎo* *qián* yī jīn?
Lit. Apple how much money one jin?
How much is a half-kilo of apples?

***Duō shǎo* *qián* yī jīn píngguǒ?**
Lit. How much money one jin apple?
How much is a half-kilo of apples?

If the context makes it clear that you are talking about – for example, bananas – you can simply say:

Duō shǎo qián? *or* **Duō shǎo qián yī jīn?**

Another common way of asking the price is **Zěnme mài?**, which can be broadly translated as 'How is it sold?' If you want to specify the goods, they should always be placed at the beginning of the question. For example:

Lìzhī *zěnme mài?* *How* are lychees *sold*?
Lit. Lychee how sell?

5 Difference between duō shǎo *and* jǐ

As we learnt before, when the question word **jǐ** (how many?) is used, the questioner expects a small quantity (fewer than twenty) in the reply. Another thing to remember about **jǐ** is that in most cases either a measure word or unit word must be used. **Duō shǎo** (how many?/how much?) does not have such restrictions. For example:

Nǐ yào *jǐ jīn* xiāngjiāo?
How many jins of bananas do you want?

Nǐ yào *duō shǎo* xiāngjiāo?
What quantity of bananas do you want?

6 Difference between yào *and* xiǎng

Look at the these three sentences:

Wǒ *yào* kāfēi.
Lit. I want coffee.

Wǒ *yào* hē kāfēi.
Lit. I want drink coffee.

Wǒ *xiǎng* hē kāfēi.
Lit. I want drink coffee.

The verb **yào** can be followed by nouns or verbs whilst **xiǎng** must be followed by another verb if the meaning 'to want' is intended. When **xiǎng** is followed by a noun or a sentence, it means 'to miss' or 'to think'. For example:

Wǒ *xiǎng* kāfēi.	I *miss* coffee.
Wǒ *xiǎng*, tā èrshí zuǒyòu.	I *think* he's about twenty.

There is also a subtle difference in meaning between **yào** and **xiǎng**. **Xiǎng** is more like the English 'would like' when followed by another verb whilst **yào** is a straightforward 'to want' showing a certain degree of determination. For example:

Wǒ *xiǎng* mǎi yīxiē shuíguǒ.	I'd *like* to buy some fruit.
Wǒ *yào* mǎi yīxiē shuíguǒ.	I *want* to buy some fruit.

7 Verbs mǎi *and* mài

Although **mǎi** (to buy) and **mài** (to sell) share the same pronunciation, they differ in tones and character representation. Do not worry if you cannot get the tone right, because the context will always help.

8 Use of zhǎo

This verb has several meanings. The meaning 'to return' is only restricted to situations where someone gives someone else the change. For example:

A: **Gěi nǐ wǔ kuài.**
Here is five kuai.

B: ***Zhǎo* nǐ yī kuài bā máo.**
Here is one kuai and eight mao change.

(A being the customer, and B the shop-assistant.) Remember that **zhǎo** cannot be used to mean 'to return' other things (e.g. books).

9 Extra vocabulary on fruit

You may find the following words useful:

lízi	pear	**júzi**	tangerine
xìngzi	apricot	**bōluó**	pineapple
chénzi	orange	**xīguā**	water melon

10 Construction yǒu méi yǒu

Like **. . . shì bù shì . . .?** (see Note 6 of Lesson 5), **. . . yǒu méi yǒu . . .?** is an alternative pattern to **. . . yǒu . . . ma?** For example:

Nǐ *yǒu* Zhōngguó chá *ma*?
becomes **Nǐ *yǒu méi yǒu* Zhōngguó chá?**
Do you have any Chinese tea?

Exercises

Exercise 1

Look at the following drawings, paying attention to the price next to each drawing, and answer the questions using complete sentences:

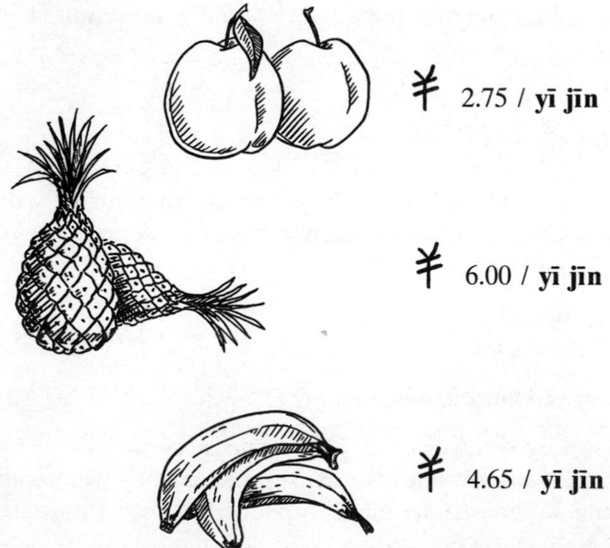

¥ 2.75 / **yī jīn**

¥ 6.00 / **yī jīn**

¥ 4.65 / **yī jīn**

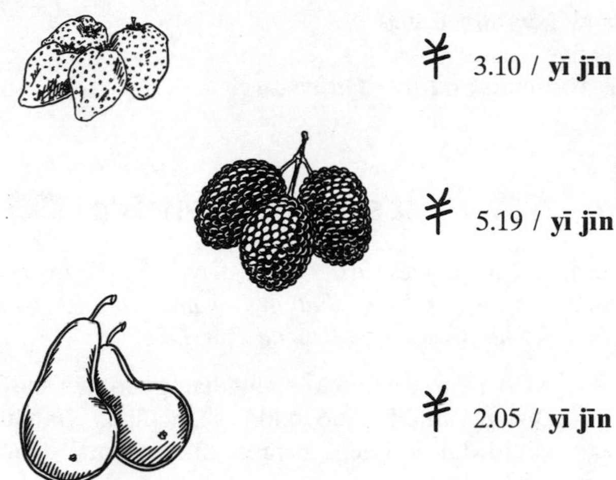

(a) Píngguǒ duō shǎo qián yī jīn?
(b) Shénme liù kuài yī jīn?
(c) Xiāngjiāo zěnme mài?
(d) Cǎoméi duō shǎo qián yī jīn?
(e) Shénme liǎng kuài líng wǔ yī jīn?
(f) Duō shǎo qián yī jīn lìzhī?

Exercise 2

Fill in the blanks using **yào** or **xiǎng**, and in some cases either can be used:

(a) (When asked what David wants to drink, his mum says:) David _______ yī bēi júzi zhī (**júzi zhī** means 'orange juice').
(b) Wǒ bù _______ hē kāfēi.
(c) (In a shop) Wǒ _______ sān jīn cǎoméi.
(d) Tā _______ xiān chī wǔfàn.

Exercise 3

Translate the following sentences into Chinese:

(a) I'd like to buy some Hainan Island bananas.
(b) He doesn't want strawberries.
(c) I bought a kilo of apples
(d) Do you want anything else?

(e) I don't know how much it is.
(f) A: Here is five kuai.
B: Here is two mao and five fen change.

Dialogue 2
Tài guì le 太贵了 It's too expensive

Dale is in Taiwan on a business trip. After a week's tough negotiation, he suddenly remembers that he wants to do some shopping. So he asks his Chinese colleague Fan Ting

DALE:	Xiǎo Fàn, xīngqītiān shāngdiàn guānmén ma?
FÀN TÍNG:	Bù guānmén. Suóyǒude shāngdiàn, yínháng, yóujú dōu kāimén. Zěnme, nǐ xiǎng mǎi dōngxi ma?
DALE:	Shì de. Wǒ xiǎng gěi wǒ tàitai mǎi jǐ tiáo zhēn sī wéijīn, gěi xiǎohái hē péngyou mǎi yīxiē lǐwù.
FÀN TÍNG:	Nà bù nán. Wǒ kěyǐ dài nǐ qù bǎihuò shāngdiàn.
DALE:	Nǐ tài hǎo le. Duō xiè.

(*as they could not find everything Dale would like to buy in the big department stores, they decide to go to a nearby market where bargains are to be found. Dale sees a nice silk tie*)

DALE:	Xiǎojie, zhè tiáo lǐngdài zěnme mài?
STREET-VENDOR:	Liǎng bái wǔshí kuài yī tiáo.
DALE:	Tài guì le.
STREET-VENDOR:	Liǎng bǎi kuài, xíng ma?
DALE:	Sān bái wǔshí kuài mǎi liǎng tiáo, zěnme yàng?
STREET-VENDOR:	Hǎo ba, hǎo ba.
DALE:	Wǒ yào le.

DALE:	小范，星期天商店关门吗？
FAN TING:	不关门。所有的商店，银行，邮局都开门。怎么，你想买东西吗？
DALE:	是的。我想给我太太买几条真丝围巾，给小孩和朋友买一些礼物。
FAN TING:	那不难。我可以带你去百货商店。
DALE:	你太好了。多谢。

DALE:	小姐，这条领带怎么卖？
STREET-VENDOR:	两百五十块一条。
DALE:	太贵了。

Street-vendor:	两百块，行吗？
Dale:	三百五十块买两条，怎么样？
Street-vendor:	好吧，好吧。
Dale:	我要了。

Vocabulary

xīngqītiān	星期天	Sunday
shāngdiàn	商店	shop
guānmén	关门	to be closed/to close
suóyǒude	所有的	all
yínháng	银行	bank
yóujú	邮局	post-office
dōngxi	东西	things
mǎi dōngxi	买东西	to go shopping/to do shopping [*lit.* 'buy things']
jǐ	几	several
tiáo	条	[measure word, see Note 14]
zhēn sī	真丝	pure silk [*lit.* 'real silk']
wéijīn	围巾	scarf
xiǎohái	小孩	small children
lǐwù	礼物	presents/gifts
nán	难	to be difficult/difficult
dài	带	to take
bǎihuò shāngdiàn	百货商店	department store [*lit.* 'hundred goods shop']
duō xiè	多谢	many thanks
xiǎojie	小姐	Miss [*lit.* 'little sister']
lǐngdài	领带	tie
guì	贵	to be expensive
bǎi	百	hundred

Notes to Dialogue 2

11 Use of suóyǒude . . . dōu . . .

Back in Lesson 5, we learnt the word **dōu**, which means 'all' in the sense of 'all those who have been mentioned before'. However, if you want to say 'all the banks' inclusively, use **suóyǒude** and **dōu** at the same time. Put **suóyǒude** in front of nouns and **dōu** in front of verbs. For example:

Zài Yīngguó, *suóyǒude* yínháng xīngqītiān *dōu* guānmén.
In Britain, *all* the banks are closed on Sunday.

Suóyǒude dōngxi *dōu* hěn guì.
All the things are very expensive.

12 Verbal phrase mǎi dōngxi

Literally, **mǎi dōngxi** means 'to buy things'; idiomatically, it means 'to do shopping'. If you want to say 'to go shopping', the verb **qù** (to go) must be used before **mǎi dōngxi**. Phrases such as **yīxiē** (some), **yīdiǎn** (a little) are inserted in between **mǎi** and **dōngxi**. For example:

Wǒ xiānsheng bù xǐhuan *mǎi dōngxi.*
My husband does not like *going shopping.*

Māma qù *mǎi dōngxi* le.
Mum has *gone shopping.*

Tā *mǎi* le yīxiē *dōngxi.*
He *did* some *shopping.*

13 Construction gěi . . . mǎi . . .

In English, you say *I buy something for somebody*; in Chinese, you say 'for somebody I buy something'. For example:

	Tā	**xiǎng**	***gěi***	**tāde**	**xiǎohái**	***mǎi***	**yīxiē**	**lǐwù.**
Lit.	She	want	for	her	children	buy	some	presents.
	She wants to buy some presents for her children.							

	Wǒ	***gěi***	**wǒde**	**tàitai**	***mǎi***	**le**	**yī tiáo**	**wéijīn.**
Lit.	I	for	my	wife	bought		a	scarf.
	I bought a scarf for my wife.							

14 Measure word tiáo

This measure word is used in between a number or pronouns **zhè/nà** (this/that) and certain nouns (e.g. scarf, tie, trousers). For example:

Zhè *tiáo* lǐngdài hěn piàoliang.
This tie is very beautiful.

Tā mǎi le sān *tiáo* zhēn sī wéijīn.
She bought three pure silk scarves.

15 *Adjective* jǐ

This is the same **jǐ** as the question word **jǐ** (how many?/which?). However, in this context, it means 'several' and is used to refer to any number that is more than one but less than ten. Let us compare **jǐ** as a question word to **jǐ** as an adjective in the following two sentences:

A: **Māma, wǒ yǒu *jǐ tiáo* lǐngdài?**
Mum, *how many* ties do I have?
B: **Wǒ zěnme zhīdào?**
How could I know?

A: **Nǐ qù nǎr?**
Where are you going?
B: **Mǎi dōngxi. Wǒ xiǎng mǎi *jǐ* jīn shuíguǒ.**
Going shopping. I'd like to buy *several* jins of fruit.

16 *Construction* dài . . . qù/lái

If you want to take someone from where you are to somewhere else, you use the verb **dài** with **qù** (to take); and if you want to bring someone from somewhere else to where you are, you use the verb **dài** with **lái** (to bring). The words **qù** and **lái**, originally meaning 'to go' and 'to come' respectively, are directional words in this context. There is always a person's name or a personal pronoun in between **dài** and **qù/lái**. Let us look at some examples:

Fàn Tíng *dài* Dale *qù* mǎi dōngxi.
Fan Ting *takes* Dale to do the shopping.

Nǐ kěyi *dài* wǒ *qù* yínháng ma?
Could you *take* me to the bank?

Tā bù xiǎng *dài* tāde xiǎohái *lái*.
She doesn't want to *bring* her children along.

17 Nǐ tài hǎo le

The phrase **Nǐ tài hǎo le**, literally meaning 'You are extremely good', is equivalent to the English expressions *It's very kind of you* or *You are too kind.*

18 Use of Xiǎojie

As China opens to the west, the term **xiǎojie** (which is like the French word *mademoiselle*) is becoming more and more popular to address, for example, female shop-assistants instead of the term **tóngzhì** (comrade). It is also a way of attracting someone's attention. **Xiǎojie** can also be used as a title to mean 'Miss'. For example:

> Customer: ***Xiǎojie*, nǐmen yóu cǎoméi ma?**
> *Miss*, do you have strawberries?
>
> (On the phone) **Wáng *xiǎojie* zài ma?**
> Is *Miss* Wang in?

19 Wǒ yào le

This is a commonly used phrase in shops when you have decided that you want to buy something, which can be broadly translated as 'I'll take it'.

Exercises

Exercise 4

You tell the shop-assistant that you would like to buy

(a) a pure silk tie
(b) one kilo of bananas
(c) two scarves

Exercise 5

You ask your Chinese friend if he/she can take you to

(a) a department store
(b) a bank
(c) a post-office

Exercise 6

What would you say on the following occasions based on what we have learnt:

(a) A street-vendor approaches you and asks you if you would like a silk scarf; you see the price tag and you think it is too expensive.
(b) After some bargaining, you have decided to make a purchase.
(c) You are in a fruit shop, but the shop-assistant is not aware of your presence. You want to attract her attention and also ask her if they have lychees.
(d) You are new in a city and a colleague of yours has offered to take you shopping; you want to express your gratitude using a more sophisticated expression.

Exercise 7

Complete the following sentences using the expressions in the brackets, and then translate them into English:

(a) Tā ______ (*for his girl-friend*) mǎi le yì tiáo zhēn sī wéijīn.
(b) Wǒ yīnggāi qù bǎihuò shāngdiàn ______ (*do some shopping*).
(c) Xīngqītiān (*all banks*) ______ kāimén.
(d) Xiǎo Wáng hē le ______ (*several cups of*) kāfēi.
(e) Wǒ gēge huì ______ (*bring my mother*) kàn wǒmen.

Characters

1 Learning to write:
(a) Mǎi dōngxi (to go shopping)

		1	2	3	4	5	6
mǎi	买						买
dōng	东	一				东	
xi	西	一					西

(b) Verbs yào (to want/to take) and zǒu (to walk/to leave)

The upper part of **yào** 西 which is pronounced **xī**, means 'west' in isolation; and we have learnt the lower part of **yào** 女 in Lesson 1. It is the 'woman radical' except that here, it is not as thin as it is in **hǎo** 好.

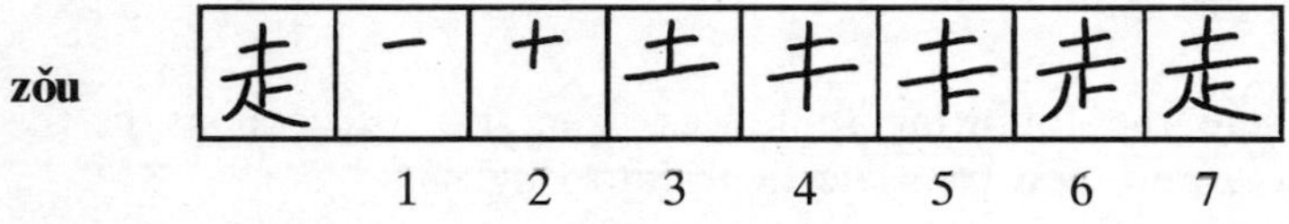

2 Recognizing important signs:

Reading/listening comprehension

Read the following dialogue, and then answer the questions in English below. If you have the recording, listen first, and then answer the questions in English.

Bill is going back to Toronto after working in Beijing for a couple of weeks, and he has just done some shopping. A Chinese friend of his, Yang Wen, has come to see him and asks about his shopping

YÁNG WÉN: Nǐ mǎi le yīxiē shénme?
BILL: Hěnduō dōngxi. Wǒ gěi wǒ tàitai mǎi le yī jiàn shuìyī.
YÁNG WÉN: Zhēn piàoliang. Shì zhēn sī ma?
BILL: Shì de.
YÁNG WÉN: Duō shǎo qián?
BILL: Yī bǎi bāshí wǔ kuài. Guì ma?
YÁNG WÉN: Zhēnde bù guì. Zhèxiē shì shénme?
BILL: Jǐ tiáo zhuōbù.
YÁNG WÉN: Wǒ kěyi kànkan ma?
BILL: Dāngrán kěyi.
YÁNG WÉN: Tài piàoliang le.

Vocabulary

hěnduō a lot of/many
jiàn [measure word for clothes]
shuìyī night gown [*lit.* 'sleep clothes']
zhuōbù table-cloth
kànkan to take a look

Questions

A What did Bill buy for his wife?
B How much is it?
C What does Yang Wen think of the present Bill has bought for his wife?
D What else did Bill buy?

8 Mǎi dōngxi (II)

买东西

Shopping (II)

By the end of this lesson, you should be able to:

- say some colour words
- make simple comparisons
- ask to borrow things from somebody
- ask someone's opinion about two things
- use phrases containing percentages
- write more characters

Dialogue 1

Nǎ jiàn hǎo? 哪件好？ Which is better?

Paul is studying Chinese at a university in Beijing. Today, he is going shopping with his flatmate Liu Hong. They are looking at some sweaters

PAUL: Xiǎo Liú, nǐ shuō zhè liǎng jiàn máoyī, nǎ jiàn hǎo?
LIÚ HÓNG: Wǒ juéde lǜ de bǐ huáng de hǎo. Nǐ chuān lǜ yánsè bǐjiào hǎo.
PAUL: Hǎo ba, wǒ tīng nǐde.

(*Paul has decided to take the green sweater and as he is reaching for his wallet . . .*)

PAUL: Zāogāo! Wǒ wàng le dài qiánbāo. Xiǎo Liú, nǐ kěyi jiè gěi wǒ yīxiē qián ma?
LIÚ HÓNG: Méi wèntí. Nǐ yào duō shǎo?
PAUL: Sānshí kuài, xíng ma?
LIÚ HÓNG: Xíng. Gòu ma?
PAUL: Gòu le.
LIÚ HÓNG: Gěi nǐ.
PAUL: Tài xièxie nǐ le. Míngtiān wǒ yīdìng huán gěi nǐ qián.
LIÚ HÓNG: Bù jí. Zánmen qù shūdiàn kànkan, hǎo ma? Wǒ xiǎng mǎi jǐ běn shū
PAUL: Hǎo de.

PAUL: 小刘，你说这两件毛衣，哪件好？
LIU HONG: 我觉得绿的比黄的好。你穿绿颜色比较好。
PAUL: 好吧，我听你的。

PAUL: 糟糕！我忘了带钱包。小刘，你可以借给我一些钱吗？
LIU HONG: 没问题。你要多少？
PAUL: 三十块，行吗？
LIU HONG: 行。够吗？
PAUL: 够了。
LIU HONG: 给你。
PAUL: 太谢谢你了。明天我一定还给你钱。
LIU HONG: 不急。咱们去书店看看，好吗？我想买几本书。
PAUL: 好的。

Vocabulary

jiàn	件	[measure word for clothes]
máoyī	毛衣	sweater/jumper
juéde	觉得	to think/to feel
lǜ	绿	green
bǐ	比	to be compared with
huáng	黄	yellow
chuān	穿	to wear

yánsè	颜色	colour
bǐjiào	比较	quite/rather/relatively
tīng	听	to listen to
zāogāo	糟糕	Damn it!
wàng	忘	to forget
dài	带	to bring/to take
qiánbāo	钱包	wallet/purse
jiè	借	to lend
méi wèntí	没问题	no problem
gòu	够	to be enough
gěi nǐ	给你	here you are [*lit.* 'for you']
yīdìng	一定	definitely/must
huán	还	to return
jí	急	hurry/to be urgent/urgent
shū	书	book
shū diàn	书店	bookshop
běn	本	[measure word for books]

Notes to Dialogue 1

1 Nǐ shuō . . .

This is one of the ways to ask someone's advice. Literally, **nǐ shuō** means 'you say' or 'you speak', which can be broadly translated as 'What do you think . . .?' or 'What would you say . . .?'. For example:

	Nǐ	***shuō***	**zánmen**	**jǐ diǎn**	**qù yóuyǒng?**
Lit.	You	say	we	what time	go swimming?
	What time *do you think* we shall go swimming?				

	Nǐ	***shuō***	**Běijīng**	**dà**	**háishì**	**Lúndūn dà?**
Lit.	You	say	Beijing	big	or	London big?
	What would you say? Is Beijing bigger or is London bigger?					

2 Colours

Below are some commonly used colour words:

Chinese	*English*	*Chinese*	*English*
hóng	red	**bái**	white
hēi	black	**lán**	blue

Chinese	*English*	*Chinese*	*English*
huī	grey	**jīnhuáng**	golden
júhuáng	orange	**hè**	brown
zǐ	purple	**fěn**	pink

The above colour words are adjectives. If you want to say 'the red' or 'the blue one', simply add **de** (see Note 14, Lesson 3) to the appropriate colour adjective. If you want to say 'the white colour', add **yánsè** (colour) or **sè** (the same **sè** as in **yánsè)** to the adjective **bái** (white). For example:

A: **Nǐ yào nǎ zhǒng yánsè?**	A: Which colour do you want?
B: **Hóng** ***de.***	B: The red.
A: **Nǐ xǐhuan shénme yánsè?**	A: What colour do you like?
B: **Lán** ***yánsè.*****/Lán** ***sè.***	B: The blue colour.

If you want to say, for example, 'dark blue' or 'light blue', place **shēn** (dark) or **qiǎn** (light) in front of **lán** (blue). Thus we have **shēn lán** or **qiǎn lán**.

3 Comparing two things

If you compare A with B and want to say 'A is better than B', or 'A is more beautiful than B', in Chinese you say:

A ***bǐ*** B ***hǎo.*** A ***bǐ*** B ***piàoliang.***

For example:

Lìzhī ***bǐ*** **píngguǒ guì.**
Lychees are *more* expensive *than* apples.

Dōngtiān, **Běijīng** ***bǐ*** **Lúndūn lěng.**
In winter, Beijing is cold*er than* London.

Zhè jiàn lǜ máoyī ***bǐ*** **hēi de hǎo.**
This green jumper is *better than* the black one.

When asking someone's opinion about two things, you list the two things first, and then ask the question in the usual order. For example:

Lǜ máoyī ***hé*** **hēi máoyī, nǎ jiàn hǎo?**
Lit. Green jumper and black jumper, which [measure word] be good?
Which is better, the green jumper or the black jumper?

Nǐ ***hé*** **nǐ gēge, shéi gāo?**
Lit. You and your elder brother who be tall?
Who is taller, you or your elder brother?

4 Use of bǐjiào

This adverb is very often used in front of adjectives to modify them. It can mean 'relatively', 'quite' or 'rather'. It is one of those favourite words people use when they express their opinions or give advice to somebody so that it does not sound too aggressive or bossy. For example:

Wǒ juéde nǐ chuān hēi yánsè ***bǐjiào*** **hǎo.**
Lit. I think you wear black colour quite well.
I think black suits you *quite* well.

Zhōngwén ***bǐjiào*** **nán.**
The Chinese language is *rather* difficult.

5 Verb tīng

The verb **tīng** (to listen to) can be followed by a noun, a phrase or a sentence. For example:

John xǐhuan ***tīng*** **Zhōngguó yīnyuè.**
John likes *to listen to* Chinese music.

Qǐng ***tīng*** **tā shuō.**
Please *listen to* what he says.

The expression **Wǒ tīng nǐde** (*lit.* 'I listen to yours'), which occurs in Dialogue 1, can be taken to mean 'I'll take your advice'.

6 Verb wàng

This is a very useful word to remember. It is often used together with the past indicator **le** to mean 'to forgot' or 'to have forgotten'. For example:

Wǒ ***wàng le*** **gěi xiǎohái mái lǐwù.**
I *forgot* to buy presents for the children.

A: **Zhōngwén zěnme shuō 'lychee'?**
How do you say 'lychee' in Chinese?

B: **Duìbùqǐ, wǒ** ***wàng le.***
Sorry, I *forgot*.

7 *More on the verb* dài

In Note 16 of Lesson 7, we came across this verb. In that context, it meant 'to bring' or 'to take' *somebody* to somewhere. Here, it means 'to bring' or 'to take' *something*. For example:

Wǒ wàng le *dài* qiánbāo.	I forgot to *bring* the wallet.
Nǐ *dài* qián le ma?	*Have you got* some money on you?

When the verb **dài** is used without any directional words, it is ambiguous. For example, the sentence **Wǒ mèimei *dài* le yīxiē shuíguǒ** can mean 'My younger sister *brought* some fruit' or 'My younger sister took some fruit'. To make it clear that it means 'to bring', you can use the directional word **lái** either after the verb **dài** or after the object. For example:

Tā fùmǔ *dài lái* le yīxiē Zhōngguó chá.
Her parents *brought* some Chinese tea.

or **Tā fùmǔ *dài* le yīxiē Zhōngguó chá *lái*.**
Her parents *brought* some Chinese tea.

Note the position of the past indicator **le** in the above two sentences.

8 *Verb* jiè

When **jiè** is used to mean 'to lend', it is almost always used together with the prepositional phrase **gěi** + somebody (to somebody). For example:

Liú Hóng *jiè gěi* le *Paul* sānshí kuài qián.
Liu Hong *lent* thirty yuan to *Paul*.

Nǐ kěyi *jiè gěi wǒ* yīxiē qián ma?
Could you *lend me* some money?

Note that the past particle **le** is placed after the preposition **gěi**.

9 *Verb* huán

The verb **huán**, meaning 'to return' or 'to give . . . back' can only be followed by things or money which you have borrowed. It cannot be used to mean 'to return home', for example. If you want to say 'to return something to somebody' or 'to return somebody something', use the phrase **gěi** + somebody after the verb **huán**. For example:

Nǐ shénme shíhou ***huán gěi wǒ*** **qián?**
Lit. You when return to me money?
When are you going to *give me* the money *back*?

When the preposition **gěi** is used in a statement, the past indicator **le** is usually placed after **gěi** instead of after the verb; when **gěi** occurs in a yes/no question, **le** is placed immediately before the question word **ma**. For example:

Tā huán ***gěi le wǒ*** **yī běn shū.**	She has *returned* one book to me.
Tā huán ***gěi*** **nǐ shū** ***le*** **ma?**	Has she *returned* any books to you?

The preposition **gěi** is sometimes omitted in the spoken language. For example:

Wǒ wàng le ***huán*** **tā qián.**
I forgot to *return* the money to him.

10 Use of gòu

This is a very useful phrase, especially at the dinner table. Until you say **Gòu le** (That's enough) food will be offered to you again and again. The phrase tends to be repeated to show that it is the truth, not out of politeness. For example:

A: **Gòu ma?**	A: Is it enough?
B: ***Gòu le, gòu le.***	B: Yes, it's enough.

Remember that although **le** has no significant meaning, it must be used together with **gòu** to mean 'Yes, it's enough'. However, when the negation word **bù** is used, **le** is usually omitted. For example:

A: **Gòu ma?**	A: Is it enough?
B: ***Bù gòu.***	B: *No, it's not.*

11 Omission of yǒu *in* méi wèntí

The verb **yǒu** (to have) is usually omitted when it is negated by **méi** in phrases or sentences. For example

Méi ***yǒu*** **wèntí**	*becomes*	**Méi wèntí**	No problem.
Méi ***yǒu*** **guānxi**	*becomes*	**Méi guānxi**	It doesn't matter.
Wǒ méi yǒu kāfēi.	*becomes*	**Wǒ méi kāfēi.**	I don't have coffee.

Exercises

Exercise 1

Compare the following two things or people in each drawing and make up sentences using **bǐ**:

(a)

(b)

(c)

(d)

(e)

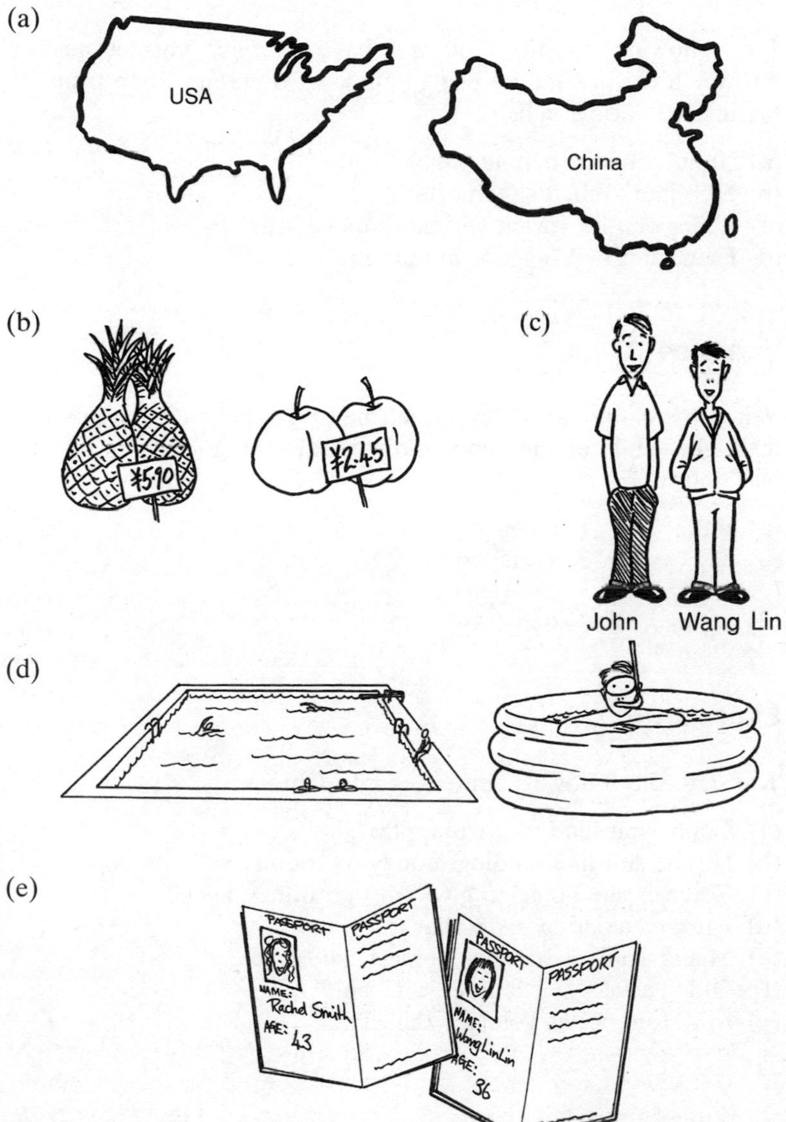

Some adjectives you may need in making comparisons:

gāo	tall	**dà**	old (age only)
ǎi	short	**xiǎo**	young (age only)

Exercise 2

The following questions do not have a *single* correct answer. Answer them in Chinese using your own opinions. Then translate the answers into English:

(a) Nǐ zuì xǐhuan shénme yánsè?
(b) Nǐ bǐjiào xǐhuan shénme fàn?
(c) Zhōngwén hé Fǎwén (French), nǎ ge nán?
(d) Fǎguó fàn bǐ Yīngguó fàn hǎo ma?

Exercise 3

Match the colour words in the left-hand column with the nouns in the right-hand column (one colour word may go with more than one noun):

(a) lán	1 píngguǒ
(b) lǜ	2 xiāngjiāo
(c) huáng	3 chá (tea)
(d) hóng	4 tiān (sky)

Exercise 4

Translate the following sentences into Chinese:

(a) Could you lend me two apples?
(b) He doesn't like lending money to friends.
(c) When is she going to give me the money back?
(d) I forgot to bring my wallet.
(e) Thank you for bringing some Chinese tea.
(f) Did she take her jumper with her?
(g) Liu Hong looks younger than Paul.

Dialogue 2
Zhēn hésuàn 真合算 It's a bargain

Jane and Yuan Yi work for a joint-venture company in Guangzhou and they have become very good friends. Yuan Yi speaks a little English. Jane has invited Yuan Yi to her place for a meal. When Jane arrives, she finds Yuan Yi waiting outside her flat

JANE: Duìbùqǐ. Wǒ chí dào le.
YUÁN YÌ: Méi guānxi. Wǒ gāng lái.
JANE: Jīntiān xià bān zǎo. Wǒ qù guàng le guàng zìyóu shìchǎng.
YUÁN YÌ: Yǒu shénme hǎo dōngxi ma?
JANE: Yǒu hěnduō. Kěxī wǒ méi dài zúgòu de qián. Wǒ mǎi le yī jiàn . . . Zhōngwén zěnme shuō 'jumper'?
YUÁN YÌ: 'Máoyī'.
JANE: Duì. Wǒ mǎi le jiàn máoyī.
YUÁN YÌ: Ràng wǒ kànkan. (*after she has had a look and felt it*) Zhēn bù cuò. Shì chún máo ma?
JANE: Bù shì. Hán bǎifēnzhī bāshí de máo.
YUÁN YÌ: Mōshangqu hěn shūfu. Duō shǎo qián?
JANE: Wǔshí duō kuài.
YUÁN YÌ: Zhème piányi! Zhēn hésuàn. Wǒ hěn xǐhuan zhè zhǒng yánsè. Hái yǒu ma?
JANE: Shēn hóng sè de mài guāng le. Zhè shì zuìhòu yī jiàn. Búguò, hái yǒu hěnduō qítā hǎokàn de yánsè.
YUÁN YÌ: Wǒ míngtiān bú shàng bān, chōu kòng qù kànkan.

JANE: 对不起。我迟到了。
YUAN YI: 没关系。我刚来。
JANE: 今天下班早。我去逛了逛自由市场。
YUAN YI: 有什么好东西吗?
JANE: 有很多。可惜我没带足够的钱。我买了一件...
中文怎么说 'JUMPER'?
YUAN YI: '毛衣'。
JANE: 对。我买了件毛衣。
YUAN YI: 让我看看。(...)真不错。是纯毛的吗?
JANE: 不是。含百分之八十的毛。
YUAN YI: 摸上去很舒服。多少钱?
JANE: 五十多块。
YUAN YI: 这么便宜!真合算。我很喜欢这种颜色。还有吗?

JANE: 深红色的卖光了。这是最后一件。不过，还有其它好看的颜色。
YUAN YI: 我明天不上班，抽空去看看。

Vocabulary

chí	迟	late/to be late
dào	到	to arrive/to get there
gāng	刚	just
lái	来	to arrive
xià bān	下班	to finish work
zǎo	早	early
guàng	逛	to look around
zìyóu	自由	free/freedom/to be free
shìchǎng	市场	market
shénme	什么	any/anything
zúgòu de	足够的	enough
chún máo	纯毛	pure wool
hán	含	to contain
bǎifēnzhī	百分之	per cent
mōshangqu	摸上去	it feels . . .
shūfu	舒服	nice/comfortable/to be comfortable
duō	多	more than/over
zhème	这么	so
piányi	便宜	to be cheap/cheap
hésuàn	合算	good bargain
hěn	很	very much
zhǒng	种	kind
shēn	深	dark/deep/to be dark/to be deep
mài guāng le	卖光了	to be sold out
zuìhòu	最后	the last
qítā	其它	other
hǎokàn	好看	to be good-looking/to be nice/ good-looking/nice [*lit.* 'good see']
shàng bān	上班	go to work/be at work
chōu kòng	抽空	to make time/to find time

Notes to Dialogue 2

12 Verbs lái *and* dào

The verb **lái** can mean both 'to come' or 'to arrive', whilst the verb **dào** can only mean 'to arrive'. They are interchangeable when the meaning of 'to arrive' is intended. For example:

Wǒ gāng *lái*.	I've just *arrived*.
Wǒ gāng *dào*.	I've just *arrived*.

Note that when the word **gāng** (just) is used, **le** is not needed.

13 Adverbs chí *and* zǎo

Regarding the verb **lái** (to arrive/come), **chí** (late) and **zǎo** (early) are placed *after* it. For example:

Xiǎo Wáng lái *chí* le wǔ fēnzhōng.
Xiao Wang arrived five minutes *late*.

Wǒ lái *zǎo* le.
I arrived *earlier*.

However, **chí** must be placed *before* **dào** in **Wǒ *chí* dào le** (*lit.* 'I *late* arrived'). The expression **Wǒ chí dào le** is used more frequently than **Wǒ lái chí le** if the meaning of 'I'm late' is intended. An alternative to **chí** is **wǎn**, which is often used after the verb.

14 Verb guàng

The verb **guàng** can be broadly translated as 'look around' (usually followed by shopping places). The phrase **guàng shāngdiàn** has slightly different implications from **mǎi dōngxi**. When you **guàng shāngdiàn**, there is nothing specific you want to buy, whereas the phrase **mǎi dōngxi** suggests that you know what you want to buy. For example:

Wǒ xǐhuan *guàng* zìyóu shìchǎng.
I like to *look around* free markets.

Tā bù xǐhuan *guàng* shāngdiàn.
She doesn't like to *look around* shops.

15 Zìyóu shìchǎng

In mainland China, **zìyóu shìchǎng**, meaning 'free market', are places where prices are not controlled by the government. Thus bargains are expected in those 'free markets'.

16 Repetition of some one-syllable verbs

When some one-syllable verbs are repeated, a touch of informality is added to the expression. For example:

Wǒ qù kàn*kan*.
I'll go and have a look.

Nǐ xiǎng guàng*guang* zìyóu shìchǎng ma?
Would you like to have a look around the market?

Note that the repeated syllable (i.e. the second syllable) is toneless.

If the past indicator **le** is used when the verb is repeated, it is placed between the two verbs *not* after the second verb. For example:

Wǒ kàn *le* kàn nà běn shū, méi yìsi.
I had a read of that book. Not interesting.

Wǒ tīng *le* tīng tāde Zhōngwén, hái bù cuò.
I had a listen to her Chinese. Not bad.

Note that because **le** is toneless, the repeated verb following it must keep its original tone.

17 Phrases shàng bān *and* xià bān

The verb **shàng** in **shàng bān** is the same **shàng** as in **shàng xué** (to go to school) (see Note 11 of Lesson 5). The verb **xià** in **xià bān** can also be used to form the expression **xià xué** (to finish school). **Shàng bān** means 'to go to work' and **xià bān** means 'to finish work':

Míngtiān nǐ *shàng bān* zǎo ma?
Are you *going to work* early tomorrow?

Nǐ jīntiān jǐ diǎn *xià bān*?
What time do you *finish work* today?

When adverbs **chí** (late) and **zǎo** (early) are used to modify the verbal phrases **shàng bān** and **xià bān** (usually to describe the past action), (a) they are placed after **shàng bān** and **xià bān**; and (b) if no other expressions such as 'five minute', 'half an hour', etc. follow **chí** and **zǎo**, the past particle **le** is omitted. For example:

Wǒ jīntiān shàng bān *chí le* yí kè zhōng.
I was fifteen minutes *late* for work today.

Wǒmen jīntiān xià bān hěn *zǎo*.
We finished work very early today.

18 Use of shénme

Shénme can also be used in front of nouns in questions and negative sentences to mean 'any'. For example:

Zìyóu shìchǎng yǒu *shénme* hǎo dōngxi ma?
Is there *any* good stuff in the market?

Tā méi yǒu *shénme* péngyou.
He doesn't have *any* friends.

19 More on the question word zěnme

We saw this word previously in **Zěnme yàng?**, **Zěnme mài?**, etc. Let us see how it is used in asking more complex questions. For example:

Zhōngwén (nǐ) zěnme shuō 'TV'?
How do you say 'TV' in Chinese?

Nǐde míngzi (nǐ) zěnme xiě?
How do you write your name?

Zhōngguórén zěnme guò xīnnián?
How do Chinese people spend the New Year?

Note that the pronoun **nǐ** in the above first two sentences can be omitted.

20 Omission of yī *before measure words*

The number **yī** (one) is usually omitted before measure words that precede nouns. However, if the noun following the measure word is omitted, the number word **yī** must remain. For example:

	Wǒménde dàxué	**yǒu**	*ge*	**Fǎguórén.**
Lit.	Our university	have	[measure word]	France person.

There is a French person at our university.

Xiǎo Wáng mǎi le liǎng jiàn máoyī. Wó mǎi le *yī jiàn.*
Xiao Wang bought two jumpers and I bought one.

21 Use of bǎifēnzhī

In English, the number comes before the expression *per cent*. In Chinese, the opposite is so: the number comes after **bǎifēnzhī** (per cent). For example:

***bǎifēnzhī* shí**
10 per cent

***bǎifēnzhī* líng diǎn wǔ**
0.5 per cent ('point' is pronounced **diǎn**)

***bǎifēnzhī* bǎi**
100 per cent (**bái** as in **yī bái**)

If phrases with **bǎifēnzhī** occur before nouns, the word **de** should be used to link them:

Zhè jiàn máoyī hán bǎifēnzhī bāshí *de* máo.
This jumper contains 80 per cent wool.

22 Use of duō

The word **duō** is used after a number to mean 'more than' or 'over'. If there is a measure word in the sentence, **duō** must be placed before the measure word. For example:

Wǒde Zhōngwén lǎoshī sānshí *duō* suì.
My Chinese teacher is *over* thirty.

Tā yǒu èrshí *duō ge* shūshu hé ā'yí.
He has *more than* twenty uncles and aunts.

23 Use of hěn *before the verb*

When **hěn** is used before the adjective, it means 'very' (see Lesson 1). Here, it is used before the verb and it means 'very much'. Let us compare the following two sentences:

Tā *hěn* hǎokàn. — She is very good-looking.
(**hǎokàn**: adjective)

Wǒ *hěn* xǐhuan Zhōngguó fàn. I like Chinese food very much.
verb

24 Verbal phrase chōu kòng

The verb **chōu** literally means 'to draw/pull'. When it is used together with **kòng** (*lit.* 'space/vacancy'), we have the phrase **chōu kòng** meaning 'to make time'. For example:

Wǒ yīdìng *chōu kòng* qù kàn nǐ.
I'll definitely *make time* to go to see you.

Nǐ kěyi *chōu kòng* qù mǎi dōngxi ma?
Could you *make time* to go shopping?

Another expression which also means 'to make time' is **chōu shíjiān**. For example:

Nǐ *chōu shíjiān* gěi wǒ jiǎngjiang nǐde qíngkuàng, hǎo ma?
Will you *make some time* to tell me about yourself?

25 Difference between gòu *and* zúgòu de

The word **gòu** (followed by **le** in affirmative sentences) is used *after* nouns to mean 'there is enough . . .' or 'be enough' whereas **zúgòu de** is used *before* nouns to mean 'enough'. For example:

A: **Qián *gòu* ma?**	A: Is there *enough* money?
B: ***Gòu le.***	B: *It's enough.*
Tā yǒu *zúgòu de* qián.	He has *enough* money.

Exercises

Exercise 5

Fill in the blanks with **qù**, **shàng**, or **guàng**:

(a) Wǒ jīntiān bù ________ bān.
(b) Nǐ xiǎng qù ________ zìyóu shìchǎng ma?
(c) Zhū Mǐn xià ge yuè ________ Zhōngguó.
(d) Nǐde érzi ______ xiǎoxué le ma?

Exercise 6

Based on what we have learnt so far, what do you say in the following situations:

(a) You are late for your appointment and you apologize.
(b) You want to assure your friend that there is absolutely no problem if he wants to borrow some money from you.
(c) You do not know how to say the phrase 'good bargain' in Chinese and you ask your Chinese teacher.
(d) You have just borrowed some money from your friend, and you want to assure her that you will definitely give it back to her tomorrow.

Exercise 7

Re-arrange the word order of the following so that each set of words becomes a meaningful sentence. Then translate the sentences into English:

(a) hán, zhè tiáo lǐngdài, wǔshí, bǎifēnzhī, sī, de
(b) shāngdiàn, wǒ, le, guàng, guàng
(c) gěi le wǒ, Tāng Bīn, èrshí kuài qián, jiè
(d) dào, tā, jīntiān zǎoshang, chí, èrshí fēnzhōng, le

Exercise 8

Fill in the blanks with **gòu** or **zúgòu de**:

(a) Sìshí kuài ________ ma?
(b) Wǒ méi yǒu ________ shíjiān qù yóuyǒng.
(c) A: Bàn jīn cǎoméi ________ ma?
    B: ________ le.
(d) Tāmen yǒu ________ qián qù Zhōngguó lǚyou.

Exercise 9

Translate the following sentences into Chinese:

1 She doesn't have any good friends.
2 I'm not working tomorrow. I can find some time to go swimming.
3 I guess he is over fifty.
4 I'm sorry. The dark blue jumpers are sold out. Will black do?
5 It's a real good bargain. Any more of these?

Characters

Exercise 10

Choose the right character to fill in the blanks and then translate the sentence into English:

(a) **我妈妈明_____来看我。**

i) 夫 ii) 大 iii) 天

(b) **他不想_____买东西。**

i) 丢 ii) 去 iii) 共

Exercise 11

Convert the following sentence in pinyin into characters:

Wǒ xǐhuan xué Zhōngwén.

Reading/listening comprehension

Below are seven Chinese sentences. Underneath each sentence are three English sentences. Read or listen to (if you have the recording) the Chinese sentence first and tick one English sentence which is closest in meaning to the original Chinese sentence.

A **Duìbùqǐ. Yìdàlì kāfēi mài guāng le. Hǎinán Dǎo kāfēi xíng ma?**
(a) There is plenty of Italian coffee.
(b) Coffee from Hainan Island is available.
(c) Coffee is sold out.

B **Míngtiān, wǒ qī diǎn shàng bān.**
(a) I am not working tomorrow.
(b) I finish work at seven tomorrow.
(c) I start work at seven tomorrow.

C **Xiǎo Fāng jiè gěi le David wǔshí kuài qián.**
(a) David borrowed fifty yuan from Xiao Fang.
(b) David lent Xiao Fang fifty yuan.
(c) Xiao Fang has got fifty yuan with her.

D **Zāogāo! Wǒ wàng le huán Línlin qián.**
(a) I forgot to buy Linlin a present.
(b) I forgot to give Linlin her money back.
(c) I forgot how old Linlin is.

E **Wǒ mèimei bǐ wǒ hǎokàn.**
(a) I think that my younger sister is good-looking.
(b) I think that I am better-looking than my younger sister.
(c) I think that my younger sister is better-looking than me.

F **David bù zhīdao Zhōngwén zěnme shuō 'toilet'.**
(a) David knows how to say 'toilet' in Chinese.
(b) David does not know how to say 'toilet' in Chinese.
(c) David wants to know how to say 'toilet' in Chinese.

G **Chén Lìli chuān huáng sè bǐjiào hǎo.**
(a) Chen Lili looks nice in yellow.
(b) Chen Lili looks nice in blue.
(c) Chen Lili likes the colour yellow.

9 Zài cānguǎn 在餐馆

At the restaurant

By the end of this lesson, you should be able to:

- name a few Chinese dishes
- order some food and drinks in a restaurant
- use two more measure words
- use **guò** to describe a past experience
- use **rúguǒ** in conditional sentences
- position some adverbs correctly by using **de**
- write and recognize more characters

Dialogue 1

Diǎn cài ma? 点菜吗? Ready to order?

Li Youde had previously met Daniel and Janet whilst on a business trip in Australia. Now, Daniel and Janet are visiting Taiwan and Li Youde is their host. Today, he is taking them out for dinner. They have just entered a restaurant

WAITER: Wǎnshang hǎo. Jǐ wèi?
LǏ YŌUDÉ: Sān wèi.
WAITER: Qǐng gēn wǒ lái.
(*they follow the waiter to a table*)
WAITER: Qǐng zuò. Nǐmen xiǎng xiān hē yīdiǎn shénme?
DANIEL: Wǒ yào yī píng Qīngdǎo píjiǔ.
LǏ YŌUDÉ: Wǒ yě yīyàng.
WAITER: Xiǎojie xiǎng hē shénme?
JANET: Yī bēi chénzi zhī.
WAITER: Hǎo de. Qǐng kàn càidān.

(*the waiter hands out a menu to each of them. After leaving them enough time to decide what they want, the waiter returns*)

WAITER: Diǎn cài ma?
LǏ YŌUDÉ: Diǎn. Wǒ xiān diǎn. Yī ge hǎixiān tāng hé yī ge niúròu chǎo miàntiáo.
WAITER: Nǐn ne, xiānsheng?
DANIEL: Yī ge suānlà dòufu tāng, yī ge jī dīng chǎo shícài, èr liǎng xiǎo lóng bāozi. Wǒ è sǐ le.
WAITER: Xiǎojie?
JANET: Wǒ yào yī xiǎo pán zhá dàxiā, yī ge tángcù yú, hái yào yī ge bái mǐfàn.
WAITER: Hǎo de. Qǐng shāo děng.

WAITER: 晚上好。几位?
LI YOUDE: 三位。
WAITER: 请跟我来。

WAITER: 请坐。你们想先喝一点什么?
DANIEL: 我要一瓶青岛啤酒。
LI YOUDE: 我也一样。
WAITER: 小姐想喝什么?
JANET: 一杯橙子汁。
WAITER: 好的。请看菜单。

WAITER: 点菜吗?
LI YOUDE: 点。我先点。一个海鲜汤和一个牛肉炒面条。
WAITER: 您呢,先生?

DANIEL: 一个酸辣豆腐汤，一个鸡丁炒时菜，二两小龙包子。我饿死了。
WAITER: 小姐？
JANET: 我要一小盘炸大虾，一个糖醋鱼，还要一个白米饭。
WAITER: 好的。请稍等。

Vocabulary

wèi	位	[measure word, see Note 1]
gēn	跟	to follow
zuò	坐	to sit/to sit down
píng	瓶	[measure word]
píjiǔ	啤酒	beer
yīyàng	一样	to be the same/same
chénzi zhī	橙子汁	orange juice
càidān	菜单	menu [*lit.* 'dish list']
diǎn cài	点菜	to order [+ food]
hǎixiān	海鲜	seafood
tāng	汤	soup
niúròu	牛肉	beef
chǎo	炒	to stir-fry
miàntiáo	面条	noodles
nín	您	you [the polite form]
Nín ne?	您呢？	What about you?/And you?
suānlà	酸辣	hot and sour
dòufu	豆腐	tofu [made of soya beans]
jī	鸡	chicken
jī dīng	鸡丁	diced chicken [*lit.* 'chicken dice']
shícài	时菜	seasonal vegetables
liǎng	两	[unit of weight, see Note 7]
xiǎo lóng	小笼	small steam-container
bāozi	包子	steamed bread with fillings
è sǐ le	饿死了	to be starving [*lit.* 'hungry died']
yī xiǎo pán	一小盘	a small plate
zhá	炸	to deep fry
dàxiā	大虾	king prawn [*lit.* 'big shrimp']
tángcù	糖醋	sweet and sour [*lit.* 'sugar vinegar']
yú	鱼	fish
bái mǐfàn	白米饭	boiled rice [*lit.* 'white rice food']
shāo děng	稍等	just a second [*lit.* 'a while wait']

Notes to Dialogue 1

1 Measure words wèi *and* píng

Wèi is only used in front of people. It is a polite form of the measure word **gè**. For example:

Zhōngwén Xì yǒu liǎng *wèi* jiàoshòu.
There are two professors in the Chinese Department.

Waiter: **Jǐ wèi?**	Waiter: How many of you?
Customer: **Sì wèi.**	Customer: Four.

Píng is used to indicate bottles and jars. For example:

Wǒ mǎi le sān *píng* píjiǔ.
I bought three bottles of beer.

2 Use of gēn

In English, you say *Follow me*; in Chinese, you must say 'Follow me walk', 'Follow me read', 'Follow me come', etc. depending on the activity. For example:

Qǐng *gēn* wǒ *lái*.
Lit. Please follow me come.
Please follow me./This way, please.

Qǐng *gēn* tā *dú*.
Lit. Please follow him read.
Please follow him./Please read after him.

3 Wǒ yě yīyàng

This phrase can be used if you wish to show that you agree with someone else's choice or opinion of a kind of drink, a film, etc. It can be broadly translated as 'Same for me, please', 'I think the same' or 'Me too', depending on the context. For example:

A: **Wǒ yào yī bēi chénzi zhī.**
I'd like a glass of orange juice.
B: ***Wǒ yě yīyàng.***
Same for me, please.

A: **Wǒ hěn xǐhuan Zhōngguó fàn.**
I like Chinese food very much.
B: ***Wǒ yě yīyàng.***
Me too.

4 *Phrase* diǎn cài

The phrase **diǎn cài**, literally meaning 'point dish', can only be used in restaurant situations. For example:

Waiter:	**Xiānsheng, diǎn cài ma?**	Ready to order, sir?
Customer:	**Diǎn.**	Yes, please.

The verb **diǎn** can be followed by dish names. For example:

A: **Nǐ *diǎn* le shénme cài?**
What have you ordered?

B: **Wǒ *diǎn* le yī ge tángcù yú.**
I've ordered sweet and sour fish.

Note that the word **cài** can be omitted from A's utterance above.

5 *Chinese dishes*

Chinese dishes usually have imaginative names such as 'Beef in Bird Nest', 'Aunts Climbing the Tree', which may be named according to the presentation, shape or the way it is cooked. There are fixed expressions for dishes: for example, the Chinese word for 'sweet' is **tián**, but you must say **tángcù** (*lit.* 'sugar vinegar') for 'sweet and sour' and **suānlà** (*lit.* 'sour chilli') for 'hot and sour'.

There is also a difference between 'rice' and 'cooked rice' in Chinese. The word for 'rice' is **dàmǐ.** (*lit.* 'large rice'). The word **mǐfàn** (*lit.* 'rice food') is 'cooked rice'. Then we have **bái mǐfàn** (boiled or steamed rice), **cháo mǐfàn** (fried rice), etc. You can also say **bái fàn** or **chǎo fàn** with **mǐ** omitted.

Xiǎo lóng bāozi is a real treat. It is steamed bread with a variety of fillings inside (e.g. minced pork, minced beef, shrimps with vegetables, or simply mixed vegetables).

The word **niúròu** (beef) literally means 'cattle meat'. The word **ròu** can be added to some animal names: for example, if we add **ròu** to **zhū** (pig) and **yáng** (sheep), we have **zhūròu** (pork) and **yángròu** (lamb).

6 *More dish names and vegetarian dishes*

jiǎozi	dumpling	**sùcān**	vegetarian meal
chūnjuǎn	spring rolls	**chǎo dòuyá**	stir-fried bean-sprouts
dàn chǎo fàn	egg fried rice	**sù jiǎozi**	vegetarian dumpling
húntun tāng	won ton soup	**sù chūnjuǎn**	vegetarian spring rolls

7 Unit of weight liǎng

In Lesson 7, the word **jīn** (half a kilo) was introduced. A smaller unit of measure is **liǎng**: 1 ***jīn*** = 10 ***liǎng***.

8 Common drinks

Below are the names for some common drinks which you may wish to order:

shuǐ	water	**kuàngquán shuǐ**	mineral water
chá	tea	**píngguǒ zhī**	apple juice
bōluó zhī	pineapple juice	**yēzi zhī**	coconut juice
kékóu kělè	Coca Cola	**pútao jiǔ**	wine

(You can add **hóng** or **bái** in front of **pútáo jiǔ** to make it 'red wine' or white wine'.)

mí jiǔ	rice wine	**bái jiǔ**	spirits (*lit.* 'white alcohol')

9 Verb–adjectives + sǐ le

This is a very useful combination to remember. It can be used whenever you want to exaggerate things. Literally, **sǐ le** means 'to have died' or 'died'. For example:

Wǒ gāoxìng ***sǐ le.***
Lit. I be happy died.
I'm so happy.

Wǒ è ***sǐ le.***
Lit. I be hungry died.
I'm starving.

10 Verb děng

The expression **Qǐng shāo děng** (*lit.* 'Please a while wait') is a more formal way of saying 'Just a second'. When it is used in restaurant situations, it is almost equivalent to 'Thank you' in English. On more casual occasions, you can say ***Děng*** **yīxià** (*lit.* 'Wait a second') or ***Děngdeng***. (*lit.* 'Wait wait').

Exercises

Exercise 1

What do you say if you want to order the following?

(a) a glass of orange juice
(b) a bottle of beer
(c) two glasses of white wine
(d) some Chinese tea

Exercise 2

Look at the menu below and say what you would like to order:

CÀIDĀN

		JIÀGÉ
TĀNG		
Suānlà dòufu tāng		¥ 4.56
Hǎixiān tāng		¥ 6.00
Húntun tāng		¥ 5.20
ZHÈNGCĀN		
Tángcù zhūròu		¥ 8.60
Jī dīng chǎo shícài		¥ 10.80
Niúròu chǎo qīngjiāo		¥ 11.50
Zhá dàxiā		¥ 20.90
Hóng shāo yú		¥ 18.70
Yú tóu shāo dòufu		¥ 16.30
Chǎo shícài		¥ 7.50
Jīdàn chǎo mǐfàn		¥ 1.80
Bái mǐfàn		¥ 1.00
Xiǎo lóng bāozi	(1 liǎng)	¥ 1.20
Jī sī chǎo miàntiáo		¥ 3.50

New words in the menu above:

jiàgé	price	**zhèngcān**	main course
jīdàn	egg (*lit.* 'chicken egg')	**yú tóu**	fish head
hóng shāo	stewed in soya sauce (*lit.* 'red stew')	**qīngjiāo**	green pepper
		jī sī	shredded chicken

Exercise 3

Translate the following phrases and sentences into Chinese:

(a) Please sit down.
(b) I'd like to have a look at the menu.
(c) This way, please. (uttered by a waiter in a restaurant)
(d) I'm starving.
(e) Just a second.

Dialogue 2
Nǐ chī guo kǎo yā ma? 你吃过烤鸭吗？
Have you ever had roast duck?

Gao Xiaohua lives in Taiwan. This is her first visit to mainland China since she left in the early 1940s. She is now visiting some of her school friends in Beijing and Liu Qingqing is one of them. They are discussing which restaurant to go to

QĪNGQING: Nǐ chī guo Běijīng kǎo yā ma, Xiǎohuá?
XIǍOHUÁ: Méi yǒu.
QĪNGQING: Shì ma? Nà, nǐ yīdìng děi chángchang. Nǐ jīntiān wǎnshang yǒu kòng ma?
XIǍOHUÁ: Yǒu kòng.
QĪNGQING: Nà, wǒ jīnwǎn qíng nǐ chī kǎo yā, zěnme yàng?
XIǍOHUÁ: Tài hǎo le. Zánmen qù nǎ jiā cānguǎn?
QĪNGQING: Běijīng Kǎo Yā Diàn, hǎo bù hǎo?
XIǍOHUÁ: Tài hǎo le.

(*later that evening, Xiaohua and Qingqing are enjoying their meal at the Beijing Roast Duck Restaurant*)

XIǍOHUÁ: Nǐ tài duì le. Zhēn haǒchī.
QĪNGQING: Wǒ zhēn gāoxìng ní xǐhuan kǎo yā. Duō chī yīxiē.

XIǍOHUÁ:	Hǎo de. Qǐng dì gěi wǒ jiàng.
QĪNGQING:	Bǐng gòu ma?
XIǍOHUÁ:	Wǒ gòu le. Wǒ kuài chī bǎo le. Nǐ rúguǒ xiǎng dehuà, jiù zài yào yīxiē.
QĪNGQING:	Wǒ qíshí yǐjing chī bǎo le. Wǒ bǐ nǐ chī de kuài.

QINGQING:	你吃过北京烤鸭吗？
XIAOHUA:	没有。
QINGQING:	是吗？那，你一定得尝尝。你今天晚上有空吗？
XIAOHUA:	有空。
QINGQING:	那，我今晚请你吃烤鸭，怎么样？
XIAOHUA:	太好了。咱们去哪家餐馆？
QINGQING:	北京烤鸭店，好不好？
XIAOHUA:	太好了。

XIAOHUA:	你太对了。真好吃。
QINGQING:	我真高兴你喜欢烤鸭。多吃一些。
XIAOHUA:	好的。请递给我酱。
QINGQING:	饼够吗？
XIAOHUA:	我够了。我快吃饱了。你如果想的话，就再要一些。
QINGQING:	我其实已经吃饱了。我比你吃得快。

Vocabulary

guo	过	[see Note 10]
kǎo	烤	to roast
yā	鸭	duck
Shì ma?	是吗？	Is that so?
nà	那	in that case
děi	得	to have got to/must
cháng	尝	to taste
jīntiān wǎnshang	今天晚上	this evening/tonight
yǒu kòng	有空	to have time/to be free
qǐng	请	to invite
cānguǎn	餐馆	restaurant
diàn	店	restaurant/snack-bar/shop
Nǐ tài duì le.	你太对了	You are so right.
haǒchī	好吃	tasty [*lit.* 'good eat']
duō	多	more
dì	递	to pass
jiàng	酱	sauce

bǐng	饼	pancake
kuài	快	nearly
bǎo	饱	to be full
rúguǒ	如果	if
zài	再	once again
qíshí	其实	in fact
de	得	[see Note 21]

Notes to Dialogue 2

11 Use of guo

Guo is inserted after some verbs to indicate that something happened in the definite past. The emphasis is on the past experience as opposed to when it happened. Expressions denoting past times (e.g. last year, yesterday) are usually not used together with **guo**. A verb plus **guo** is the equivalent of the English expressions *to have been to . . .* or *to have done something*. For example:

Nǐ qù *guo* Zhōngguó ma?	Have you ever been to China?
Wǒ chī *guo* Yìdàlì fàn.	I have had Italian food.

To negate verbs with **guo** following them, use **méi yǒu** or **méi**. For example:

Xiǎohuá *méi yǒu* chī guo Běijīng kǎo yā.
Xiaohua hasn't had Beijing roast duck before.

12 Use of děi

Děi is a colloquial word meaning 'to have to' or 'must'. If you want to be very persistent, the adverb **yídìng** (definitely/must) can be placed before **děi**. For example:

Wǒ *děi* zǒu le.	I'*ve got to* leave.
Nǐ yīdìng *děi* lái wǒmen jiā chī fàn.	You'*ve got to* come to ours for a meal.

The negation of **děi** is **bú yòng** or **bú bì** *not* **bú děi**. For example:

Nǐ *bù yòng* lái.	You *don't have to* come.
Nǐ *bù bì* mǎi píjiǔ.	You *don't have to* buy any beer.

13 Forming time expressions with jīntiān

In English, you say *this morning*, *this afternoon* and *this evening*; whilst in Chinese, you put **jīntiān** (today) in front of **zǎoshang**, **xiàwǔ** and **wǎnshang**. Thus we have:

jīntiān zǎoshang	this morning
jīntiān xiàwǔ	this afternoon
jīntiān wǎnshang	this evening

Note that **jīntiān zǎoshang** and **jīntiān wǎnshang** can be shortened to **jīnzǎo** and **jīnwǎn**.

14 Use of yǒu kòng

The word **kòng** is the same **kòng** as in **chōu kòng** (to make time) which appeared in Lesson 8. **Yǒu kòng** means 'to have time' or 'to be free'. To negate **yǒu kòng**, put **méi yǒu** or **méi** in front of **kóng**. For example:

A: **Nǐ míngtiān wǎnshang *yǒu kòng* ma?**
Will you *be free* tomorrow evening?

B: **Kǒngpà *méi* kòng.**
I'm afraid *not*.

15 Verb qǐng

We learnt this word back in Lesson 1, where it meant 'please'. When **qǐng** is used as a verb, it means 'to invite' or 'to treat someone to something'. If you want to say 'to invite someone to dinner', you must say 'to invite someone eat dinner'. For example:

Wǒ xiǎng *qǐng* nǐ *chī* wǎnfàn. I'd like to invite you to dinner.

If it is a past event, put the past indicator **le** after **chī** *not* **qǐng**. For example:

Zuówǎn Lǎo Lǐ *qǐng* wǒ chī *le* kǎo yā.
Lao Li treated me to some roast duck last night.

16 Duō chī yīxiē

This expression is usually used in situations where a host/hostess insists that a guest has some more to eat or a parent asks the child to eat more. **Duō chī yīxiē** literally means 'more eat some'. Here the word **duō** is an adverb which describes the verb **chī**. It is put before the verb in sentences which make suggestions or give orders. For example:

Qǐng *duō* mǎi yīxiē shuǐguǒ.	Please buy some *more* fruit.
***Duō* chī yīxiē dàxiā.**	Have some *more* prawns.
***Duō* hē yīxiē píjiǔ.**	Have some *more* beer.

17 Verb dì

This verb is usually used together with the preposition **gěi** to mean 'to pass something to somebody'. For example:

Nǐ kěyi *dì gěi* wǒ táng ma?	Could you *pass* me the sugar?
Qǐng *dì géi* wǒ bǐng.	Please *pass* me the pancakes.

18 Wǒ gòu le

Grammatically, this is not a correct sentence because it means 'I'm enough'. However, this has become an accepted expression to mean 'I've got enough' or 'It's enough for me'.

19 Chī bǎo le

This is another very popular phrase at the dinner table. If you are already full and do not wish to have any more food put into your bowl, you can say one of these:

Wǒ chī bǎo le.
Chī bǎo le.
Wǒ bǎo le.
} I'm full./I've had enough to eat.

20 Conditional word rúguǒ . . . dehuà

The word **rúguǒ**, meaning 'if', is used either at the very beginning of a sentence or after the subject so that it makes the sentence conditional. For example:

***Rúguǒ* nǐ bù rènshi Xiǎo Wáng, wǒ gěi nǐ jièshào.**
If you don't know Xiao Wang, I'll introduce you to her.

Nǐ *rúguǒ* méi yǒu qián, wǒ kěyi jiè gěi nǐ yīxiē.
If you don't have any money, I can lend you some.

Rúguǒ is often used together with **dehuà** (it has no specific meaning and the first syllable carries no tones) in the first half of a conditional sentence. For example:

***Rúguǒ* nǐ méi kòng *dehuà*, wǒ zìjǐ qù mǎi dōngxi.**
If you don't have the time, I'll go shopping myself.

Sometimes, the emphatic word **jiù** is used in the second half of the sentence. For example:

Rúguǒ nǐ xiǎng dehuà, *jiù* zài yào yīxiē.
If you want, order some more.

21 Use of de *to link verbs or verb–adjectives with their adverbs*

The particle **de**, which is a different **de** from the **de** in **wǒde** (my/mine), for example, is used to link verbs or verb–adjectives with adverbs if you wish to describe the degree of something. Adverbs such as **kuài** (fast), **duō** (more), **zhǎo** (early), **chí** (late), **hǎo** (well), etc. are usually used for this purpose. Thus, the pattern is:

verb/verb–adjective + **de** + adverb

For example:

(a) **Lǎo Zhāng chī *de* hěn duō.**
chī = verb; duō = adverb
Lao Zhang eats a lot.

(b) **Wǒ chī *de* bǐ nǐ kuài.**
chī = verb; kuài = adverb
Lit. I eat compared with you fast.
I eat faster than you do.

With verb–adjectives, it does not matter whether the adverb is placed before the verb–adjective or after it. For example:

Běijīng de dōngtiān lěng *de* hěn.
lěng = verb–adj.; hěn = adverb
Beijing's winter is very cold.

Běijīng de dōngtiān hěn lěng.
hěn = adverb; lěng = verb–adj.
Beijing's winter is very cold.

With verbs, the position of **kuài** depends on whether it is an order or describes one's manner. For example:

Qǐng *kuài* chī.	Please eat quickly.
Tā chī *de kuài*.	He eats fast.

To negate sentences (a) and (b) above, place **bù** *after* **de**. For example:

Lǎo Zhāng chī de *bù* hěn duō.
Lao Zhang does*n't* eat much.

Wǒ chī de *bù* bǐ nǐ kuài.
I'm not eating faster than you are.

To negate verb–adjectives plus **de**, use the normal negation order, i.e. put **bù** before the verb–adjective and omit both **de** and the adverb. Alternatively, move the adverb before the verb–adjective and put **bù** before the adverb. For example:

Běijīng de dōngtiān *bù* lěng.	Beijing's winter is*n't* cold.
Běijīng de dōngtiān *bù* hěn lěng.	Beijing's winter is*n't* very cold.

Another thing to remember is that when this structure is used to describe a past event, do not use **le** nor **guo** with **de**. In most situations, the context makes it clear if it was a past event. For example:

Jīntiān zǎoshang, tā lái *de* hěn zǎo.
She arrived very early this morning.

Exercises

Exercise 4

Translate the following sentences into Chinese using either **guo** or **le**:

(a) Has Alan ever been to China?
(b) Linda went to London yesterday.
(c) He has not had Chinese food before.
(d) A: Have you had your breakfast?
B: Not yet.

Exercise 5

What do you say in the following situations:

(a) You want to let your host know that you have had enough to eat.

(b) You would like to have some more pancakes.
(c) You want one of the people at the table to pass you the sauce.
(e) You stop the waiter and ask for another bottle of beer.
(d) At the dinner table, you want to invite your guests to have some more food.

Exercise 6

Complete the following sentences with the phrases provided in the brackets:

(a) ________ (*If you have time*), zánmen qù chī kǎo yā, hǎo ma?
(b) ________ (*you've got to*) lái kàn wǒmen.
(c) ________ (*This morning*) wǒ shàng bān chí dào le èrshí fēnzhōng.
(d) Rúguǒ nǐ è dehuà, ________ (*let's have lunch first*), hǎo bu hǎo?
(e) Xiǎo Zhāng bù xiǎng ________ (*invite Lao Wang*).

Exercise 7

Translate the following sentences into Chinese using **de** to link verbs or verb–adjectives with adverbs where appropriate:

(a) The swimming pool opened very early this morning.
(b) Please come early.
(c) I came in very late this morning.
(d) John speaks very quickly.

Exercise 8

Negate the following sentences:

(a) Nǐ shuō de duì.
(b) Wǒ mèimei lái de hěn zǎo.
(c) Yīngguó de xiàtiān rè de hěn.
(d) Tāde fùmǔ tuìxiū de hěn zǎo.
(e) Xiǎohuá gāoxìng de hěn.

Characters

1 Learning to write méi yǒu kòng (do not have time)

The left part of **méi** 氵 is called the 'water radical', and it is a very commonly used radical. The character **kòng** consists of a top part and bottom part. The top part 宀 is called the 'roof radical', and it is frequently used.

2 Learning to write the verbs chī (to eat) and hē (to drink)

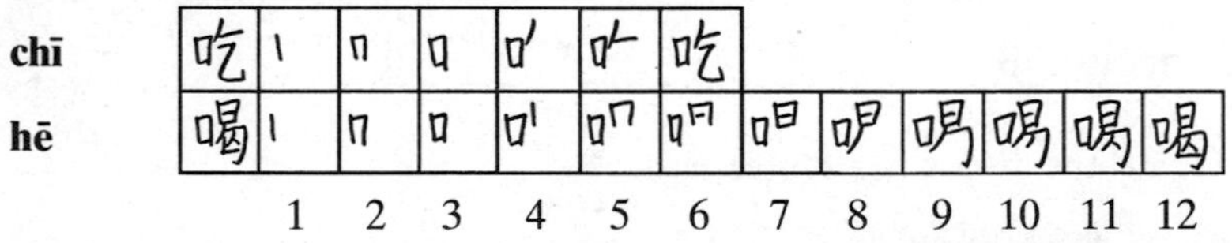

Both **chī** and **hē** share the same 'mouth radical' which we learnt earlier in Lesson 8. This is another frequently used radical. Most words that have something to do with the mouth have the 'mouth radical'.

3 Recognizing two signs:

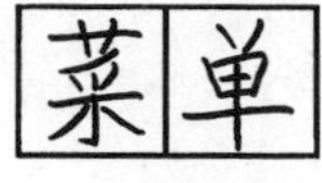

cài dān menu

cān guǎn restaurant

Cān in **cānguǎn** (restaurant) is the same **cān** as appears in **cāntīng** (dining-room/restaurant) which we learnt in Lesson 4. **Cān** is a very formal word for 'meal'.

Exercise 9

Convert the following sentences in *pinyin* into characters:

(a) **Wǒ māma shì Zhōngguórén.**
My mother is Chinese.

(b) **Tā méi yǒu kòng.**
She doesn't have time.

(c) A: **Nǐ qù mǎi dōngxi ma?**
Are you going to go shopping?
B: **Shì de.**
Yes.

Reading comprehension

There is a menu on page 176. First read it and then read the dialogue between the waitress, who speaks a little English, and Charles. Answer the questions in Chinese afterwards:

Dialogue

WAITRESS: Zǎoshang hǎo, xiānsheng.
CHARLES: Zǎoshang hǎo.
WAITRESS: Nín xiǎng yòng zǎocān ma?
CHARLES: Xiǎng.
WAITRESS: Qǐng zuò. Zhè shì zǎocān de càidān.

CÀIDĀN (zǎocan)

dàmǐ xīfàn
dòushā bāozi
jiān jī dàn
xiān yā dàn

* * *

chénzi zhī
niúnǎi
kāfēi
kǎo miànbāo
xiánròu
mógū & xīhóngshì

CHARLES:	Xièxie. Wǒ xiān yào yì bēi kāfēi, xíng ma?
WAITRESS:	Dāngrán xíng.
(*when the waitress leaves, Charles looks at the menu*)	
WAITRESS:	Zhè shì nínde kāfēi. Hái yào biéde ma?
CHARLES:	Shì de. Xiánròu. (*pointing at* xián yā dàn) Zhè shì shénme?
WAITRESS:	Zhè shì 'duck egg', 'boiled', 'salted'. Yào ma?
CHARLES:	Bù yào, bù yào. Wǒ yào jiān jī dàn.
WAITRESS:	Hǎo de. Yào mógū hé xīhóngshì ma?
CHARLES:	Yào yīdiǎn mógū.
WAITRESS:	Qǐng shāo děng.

Vocabulary

yòng	to have [polite expression]
zǎocān	formal word for 'breakfast'
xī fàn	porridge
dòushā	red-bean paste
jiān	fried/to fry
xián yā dàn	salted duck-egg
niúnǎi	milk
kǎo miànbāo	toast [*lit.* 'baked bread']

xiánròu	bacon
mógū	mushroom
xīhóngshì	tomato

Questions

A Zhōngwén zěnme shuō 'milk'?
B Charles chī guò xián yā dàn ma?
C Charles hē le niúnǎi háishì kāfēi?
D Tā hái chī le shénme?

10 Wèn lù 问路

Asking for directions

By the end of this lesson, you should be able to:

- ask how to get to certain destinations
- understand some expressions regarding directions
- distinguish between **kàn**, **kàn jiàn** and **kàn de jiàn**
- distinguish between the use of **kàn bú jiàn** and **méi yǒu kàn jiàn**
- say ordinal numbers (e.g. first, second, etc.)
- write and recognize more characters

Dialogue 1

Cèsuǒ zài nǎr? 厕所在哪儿? Where's the toilet?

Imagine that you are in a place where Chinese is spoken and you do not know your way around very well. Below are three situations you may find yourself in

(a) *Inside a hotel*

You:	Qǐng wèn, cèsuǒ zài nǎr?
Chinese speaker:	Zài cāntīng de zuǒ biān.

(b) *In the street*

You:	Qǐng wèn, fùjìn yǒu gōngyòng diànhuà ma?
Chinese speaker:	Kǒngpà méi yǒu. Nǐ kàn de jiàn qiánmian hónglǜ dēng ma?
You:	Kàn de jiàn.

CHINESE SPEAKER: Zǒu dào hónglǜ dēng, wǎng yòu guǎi. Wǒ jìde nàr yǒu.

(c) *In the street*

YOU: Nǐ néng gàosu wǒ zuò jǐ lù chē qù huǒchē zhàn ma?
CHINESE SPEAKER: Bù yòng zuò chē. Zǒulù shí fēnzhōng jiù dào le.
YOU: Zěnme zǒu?
CHINESE SPEAKER: Dì yī ge lùkǒu wǎng dōng guǎi.

(a) *Inside a hotel*

YOU: 请问，厕所在哪儿？
CHINESE SPEAKER: 在餐厅的左边。

(b) *In the street*

YOU: 请问，附近有公用电话吗？
CHINESE SPEAKER: 恐怕没有。你看得见前面红绿灯吗？
YOU: 看得见。
CHINESE SPEAKER: 走到红绿灯，往右拐。我记得那儿有。

(c) *In the street*

YOU: 你能告诉我坐几路车去火车站吗？
CHINESE SPEAKER: 不用坐车。走路十分钟就到了。
YOU: 怎么走？
CHINESE SPEAKER: 第一个路口往东拐。

Vocabulary

cèsuǒ	厕所	toilet
zuǒ	左	left
biān	边	side
fùjìn	附近	near by/close by
gōngyòng	公用	public [*lit.* 'public use']
diànhuà	电话	telephone [*lit.* 'electric talk']
kàn jiàn	看见	to see/to have seen
kàn de jiàn	看得见	to be able to see
qiánmiàn	前面	ahead
hónglǜ dēng	红绿灯	traffic light [*lit.* 'red green light']
zǒu	走	to walk
dào	到	until/up to
wǎng yòu guǎi	往右拐	to turn right [*lit.* 'towards right turn']
jìde	记得	to remember
nàr	那儿	there
néng	能	can/could
zuò	坐	to take/to catch [*lit.* 'to sit']
lù	路	route/road
chē	车	car/bus
huǒchē zhàn	火车站	railway station [*lit.* 'fire car stop']
bù yòng	不用	no need/do not need
zǒulù	走路	to walk [*lit.* 'walk road']
jiù . . . le	就...了	[see Note 12]
Zěnme zǒu?	怎么走?	How do I get there?/How do I get to . . .? [*lit.* 'How to walk?']
dìyī	第一	first
lùkǒu	路口	crossroads/junction
dōng	东	east

Notes to Dialogue 1

1 Zuǒ *and* yòu

Do you remember the term **zuǒyòu** we learnt in Lesson 2, which means 'approximately'? On its own, **zuǒ** means 'left' and **yòu** right. If you want to say 'A is on the left/right', you must use the word **biān** and say **A zài zuǒ/yòu biān**. For example:

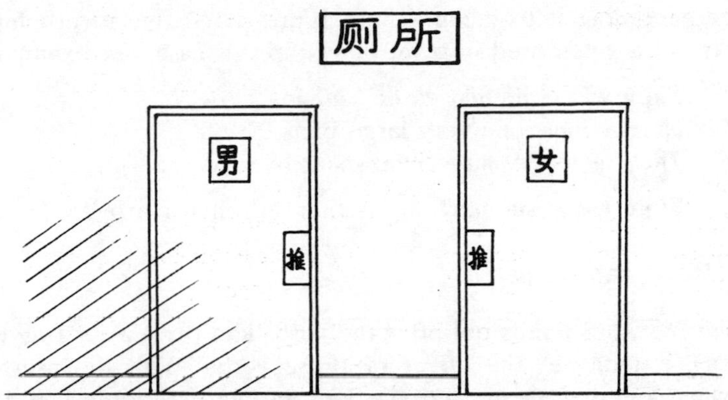

Nán cèsuǒ zài ***zuǒ biān.*** **Nǚ cèsuǒ zài** ***yòu biān.***
The men's toilet is *on the left* and the women's is *on the right.*

If you want to say 'A is on B's left/right' or 'A is to the left/right of B', you must say **A zài B de zuǒ/yòu biān**. For example:

Yóujú zài cāntīng de ***yòu biān.***
The post-office is *to the right* of the dining-room.
(Looking at a photograph)
Wǒ mèimei zài wǒde ***zuǒ biān.*** My sister is *on my left.*

2 Other direction words

Whilst **zuǒ** and **yòu** in Note 1 above can be used to describe both human beings and objects, **dōng, nán, xī, běi** (east, south, west, north) can only be used to describe objects. The usage is the same as **zuǒ/yòu**. For example:

Bǎihuò shāngdiàn ***zài*** **Běijīng Fàndiàn** ***de dōng biān.***
The department store is *to the east* of the Beijing Hotel.

The combinations of these direction words are different in order from English. See below:

dōngběi	northeast	**dōngnán**	southeast
xīběi	northwest	**xīnán**	southwest

3 *More on* yǒu

We learnt **yǒu** (to have) in Lesson 4 in saying, for example, **Běijīng Fàndiàn yǒu yí ge yóuyǒng chí**. **Yǒu** can also be used without a noun preceding it to mean 'There is/are . . .'. The adverb **fùjìn** (near by) is often used in front of **yǒu** in this case. For example:

Fùjìn *yǒu* yī jiā hěn dà de yínháng.
Lit. Nearby have one very large bank.
There is a very large bank near by.

Fùjìn *yǒu* cèsuǒ ma? Is there a toilet nearby?

4 *Use of* kàn de jiàn

When the word **jiàn** is put after the verbs **kàn** (to see) or **tīng** (to listen), it indicates the effect of those verbs. With **de** inserted between **kàn** or **tīng** and **jiàn**, i.e. **kàn de jiàn** or **tīng de jiàn**, the emphasis is on whether one is able, for example, to see or hear. For example:

A: **Nǐ *kàn de jiàn* ma?** A: Can you see?
B: ***Kàn de jiàn.*** B: Yes, I can.

To negate, replace **de** with **bù.** For example:

Wǒ kàn *bù* jiàn hónglǜ dēng. I ca*n't* see the traffic lights.

(On the phone)
Wǒ tīng bù jiàn nǐ shuō shénme. I can't hear what you are saying.

If you want to say 'to have seen/heard', there is no need to use **de**, simply say **kàn jiàn *le*** or **tīng jiàn *le***, which again is different from **kàn le** and **tīng le** because the latter means 'looked at' or 'listened' respectively. For example:

Wǒ *kàn jiàn le* cèsuǒ. I've seen the toilet./I saw the toilet.
Wǒ *kàn le* cèsuǒ. I looked at the toilet.

Note that to negate the above, place **méi** or **méi yǒu** in front of the verb. Let us compare the two negations:

Wǒ *méi yǒu* kàn jiàn cèsuǒ. I *didn't* see the toilet.
Wǒ kàn *bù* jiàn cèsuǒ. I *can't* see the toilet.

5 *Use of* wǎng . . . guǎi

The Chinese equivalent of 'to turn left' is **wáng zuó guǎi**. Simply put the direction words (see Notes 1 and 2 above) between **wǎng** and **guǎi**. For example:

Zǒu dào hónglǜ dēng, *wǎng* dōng *guǎi*.
Walk as far as the traffic lights, then *turn* east.

6 *Use of* jìde

The verb **jìde** is used to indicate things that you now remember or have remembered. For example:

Nǐ *jìde* tā tàitai de míngzi ma?	Do you *remember* his wife's name?
Wǒ *jìde* nǐ.	I *remember* you.

To negate, use **bù** in front of the verb. For example:

Wǒ *bù* jìde tā duō dà le.	I *don't remember* how old he is.

Note that the verb **jìde** cannot be used to express a notion of future time. For example, it cannot be used to say 'Please remember something' or 'I will remember something'.

7 *Position of* nàr *and* zhèr

Do you remember the two pronouns **nà** (that) and **zhè** (this)? Once **ér** is added to them, we have **nàr** (there) and **zhèr** (here), which are always placed either before the verb or after **zài** (to be at/to be in). For example:

***Nàr* yǒu yī ge gōngyòng diànhuà.**
There's a public telephone there.

(Looking at a map)
Wǒde dàxué zài *zhèr*.
My university is *here*.

8 *Difference between* huì *and* néng

In Lesson 2 we learnt the auxiliary verb **huì** which means 'can' or 'to be able to'. **Huì** emphasizes ability whereas **néng** emphasizes willingness. For example:

Wǒ gēge bù *huì* yóuyǒng.
My elder brother *cannot* swim.

Nǐ *néng* jiè gěi wǒ yīxiē qián ma?
Could you lend me some money?

9 *Shortening of* gōnggòng qìchē *to* chē

Anything that has got wheels is a **chē**. Thus we have:

zìxíng*chē*	bicycle (**zìxíng** means 'self-pedalling')
xiǎo*chē*	car (**xiǎo** means 'small')
huǒchē	train (**huǒ** means 'fire')
chūzū*chē*	taxi (**chūzū** means 'on rent')
mǎ*chē*	horse-drawn carriage (**mǎ** means 'horse')

However, **gōnggòng qìchē (gōnggòng** means 'public together' and **qìchē** means 'vehicle') is often shortened to **chē** in mainland China. For example:

Nǐ kěyi zuò shí lù *chē* qù Tiān'ānmén.
You can take *Bus* No. 10 to go to Tian'anmen.

10 *More on the question word* jǐ

This question word has appeared earlier in various questions that have to do with numbers. **Jǐ** is also used to ask which number bus to take. For example:

Qǐng wèn, zuò *jǐ* lù chē qù huǒchē zhàn?
Could you tell me please *which* number bus to catch to get to the railway station?
Zhè shì *jǐ* lù chē? — *Which* number bus is this?

11 *Use of* bù yòng

In Note 12 of Lesson 9, it was mentioned that the negative form of **děi** (to have to) is **bù yòng.** Basically, **bù yòng** means 'there is no need to' or 'do not need'. For example:

Nǐ *bù yòng* gěi wǒ mǎi lǐwù.
You *don't need* to buy me any presents.

Bù yòng xiè. Zánmen shì hǎo péngyou.
Lit. No need to thank. We are good friends.
Don't mention it. We're good friends.

12 *Construction* jiù . . . le

One usage of this construction is to emphasize the verb or verb–adjective which is inserted between **jiù** and **le**. It is very difficult to find a direct English equivalent of this construction. Let us look at some examples:

Zǒulù shí fēnzhōng *jiù* dào *le.*
Lit. Walk ten minutes get there.
It's only ten minutes' walk, and you'll be there.

Shí kuài qián *jiù* gòu *le.*
Ten yuan will be enough.

13 Zěnme zǒu?

This is a very common way of asking how to get to somewhere, although literally the phrase means 'How to walk?' You can put your desired destination in front of **zěnme zǒu**. For example:

Huǒchē zhàn *zěnme zǒu*?
How do I get to the railway station?

You can also place the verb **qù** (to go) before the destination. For example:

***Qù* nǐménde dàxué *zěnme zǒu*?**
How do I get to your university?

14 Ordinal numbers (e.g. first, second, etc.)

It is very easy to form ordinal numbers in Chinese. Simply put **dì** in front of a numeral (e.g. **yī**, **èr**, **sān**, etc.). For example:

dì yī	first	***dì* èr**	second
***dì* shíyī**	eleventh	***dì* èrshísān**	twenty-third

If you want to say, for example, 'the first junction', the measure word **gè** needs to be inserted between the ordinal number and the noun. Thus we have **dì yī *ge* lùkǒu**.

Exercises

Exercise 1

You want to find out the following from a Chinese speaker:

(a) Where the toilet is.
(b) If there is a public telephone nearby.

(c) Where the No. 10 bus is.
(d) How to get to the railway station.
(c) Which number bus to catch to go to the Beijing Hotel.

Exercise 2

Look at the picture below and then complete the sentences describing the position of each person in relation to someone else in the picture:

(a) Lǎo Zhāng ______________________.
(b) Maria ______________________.
(c) Linda ______________________.

Exercise 3

Look at the following two pictures and answer the questions (see page 193 for new signs):

I A plan of a corner of the ground floor of a hotel (facing page)

(a) Cèsuǒ zài nǎr?
(b) Gōngyòng diànhuà zài nǎr?
(c) Cāntīng zài nǎr?

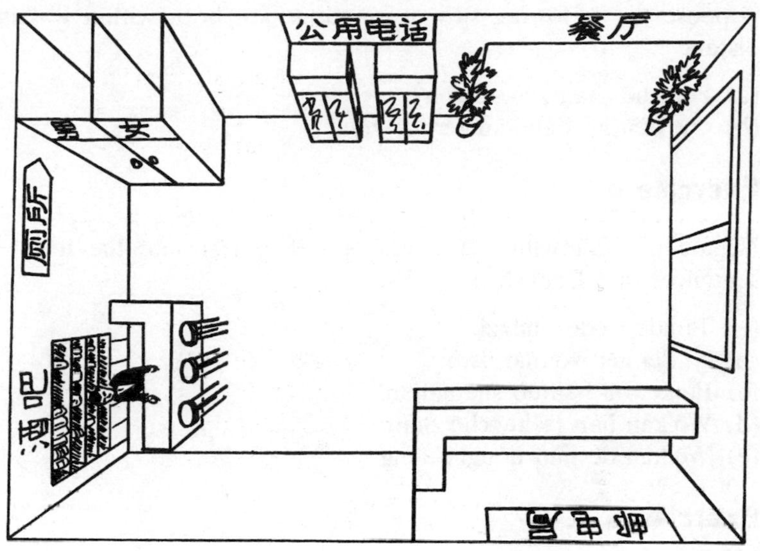

II A map of a corner of Beijing

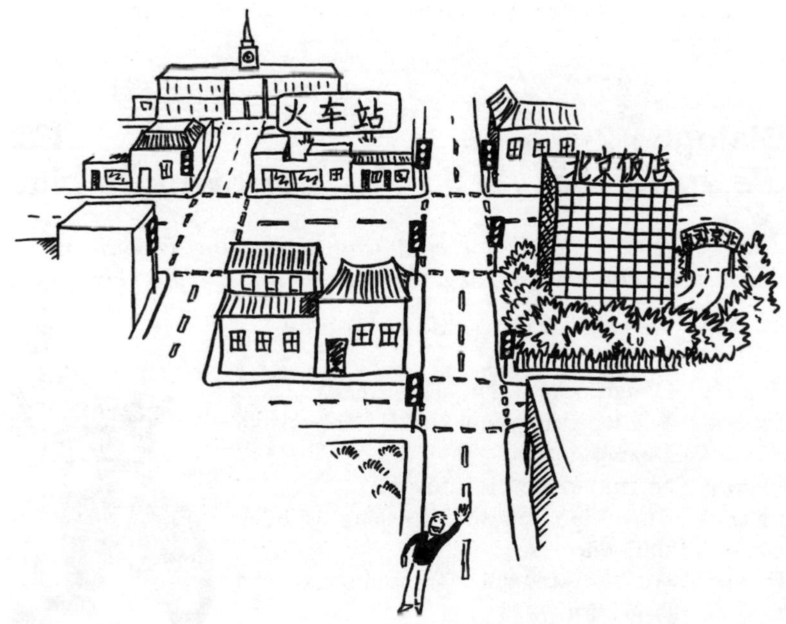

Suppose the following two destinations are both within walking distance:

(a) Huǒchē zhàn zěnme zǒu?
(b) Qù Běijīng Fàndiàn zěnme zǒu?

Exercise 4

Negate the following sentences and then translate the negated sentences into English:

(a) Tā jìde wǒde míngzi.
(b) Nǐ děi gěi wǒ mǎi lǐwù.
(c) Fùjìn yǒu bǎihuò shāngdiàn.
(d) Wǒ kàn jiàn le huǒchē zhàn.
(e) Wǒ kàn de jiàn hónglǜ dēng.

Exercise 5

Translate the following sentences into Chinese:

1 There is a post-office there.
2 She can speak Chinese.
3 I can't tell you about him.
4 Turn right at the first junction. You'll get there in about 15 minutes.

Dialogue 2
Jiè zìxíngchē 借自行车 Borrowing a bike

This dialogue is between Frank, who is teaching English at the Guangzhou Foreign Language Institute, and his friend Feixia.

FRANK: Wǒ kěyi jiè yīxià nǐde zìxíngchē ma?
FĒIXIÁ: Dāngrán kěyi. Nǐ yào qù nǎr?
FRANK: Yéxǔ xīngqītiān qù Zhōngshān Dàxué.
FĒIXIÁ: Nǐ zhīdao zěnme zǒu ma?
FRANK: Bù zhīdao. Dànshì, wǒ xiǎng wǒ néng zhǎo dào.
FĒIXIÁ: Wǒ bù xiāngxìn. Nǐ zuìhǎo xiān chá yīxià dìtú.

FRANK: Hǎo zhǔyi. Qí chē dàyuē xūyào duō jiǔ?
FĒIXIÁ: Yī ge bàn xiǎoshí zuǒyòu.

FRANK: 我可以借一下你的自行车吗？
FEIXIA: 当然可以。你要去哪儿？
FRANK: 也许星期天去中山大学。
FEIXIA: 你知道怎么走吗？
FRANK: 不知道。但是，我想我能找到。
FEIXIA: 我不相信。你最好先查一下地图。
FRANK: 好主意。骑车大约需要多久？
FEIXIA: 一个半小时左右。

Vocabulary

jiè	借	to borrow
zìxíngchē	自行车	bicycle
yào	要	to be going to/will
yéxǔ	也许	perhaps
dàxué	大学	university
dànshì	但是	but
wǒ xiǎng	我想	I think . . .
zhǎo dào	找到	to succeed in finding something
xiāngxìn	相信	to believe
nǐ zuìhǎo	你最好	you'd better
chá	查	to check
dìtú	地图	map
hǎo zhǔyi	好主意	good idea
qí	骑	to ride
xūyào	需要	to require/to need
xiǎoshí	小时	hour

Notes to Dialogue 2

15 Use of jiè

In Chinese, the word for 'to borrow' is the same as the word for 'to lend', which we learnt earlier in Lesson 8. The only difference lies in its usage. Let us compare **jiè** (to borrow) with **jiè** (to lend):

> **Wǒ xiǎng *jiè* yīxià nǐde zìxíngchē.**
> I'd like to *borrow* your bike.

Wǒ *jiè* gěi le Xiǎo Lǐ wǒde zìxíngchē.
I *lent* my bike to Xiao Li.

Note that **yīxià** here does not have any specific meaning except reducing the abruptness of the tone. **Yīxià** usually follows **jiè** when it means 'to borrow'; and **gěi** always follows **jiè** when it means 'to lend'. For example:

Wǒ kěyi *jiè yixià* nǐde dìtú ma?
Could I *borrow* your map for a while?

Nǐ kěyi *jiè gěi* wǒ nǐde dìtú ma?
Could you *lend* me your map?

16 Use of yào

In addition to the meaning of 'to want' which we learnt in Lesson 7, **yào** can also be used in front of verbs to indicate that something, often a planned action, is happening in the near future. For example:

Susan *yào* qù Zhōngguó lǚyóu.
Susan is going to China to travel.

Wǒ fùmǔ liùyuè *yào* lái Yīngguó.
My parents are coming to England in June.

17 Zhōngshān Dàxué

Zhongshan University (**Zhōngshān Dàxué**) was named after Sun Yat-sen, the founder of the first Chinese republic, whose given name was **Zhōngshān** (literally meaning 'middle mountain'). **Yat-sen** was his other given name.

18 Verb phrase zhǎo dào

When the phrase **zhǎo dào** is preceded by **néng** or **kěyi**, it means 'to be able to find'. If you cannot find something, put **bù** between **zhǎo** and **dào**. For example:

A: **Nǐ *néng zhǎo dào* huǒchē zhàn ma?**
Can you find the railway station?
B: **Zhǎo *bù* dào.**
I *can't*.

When **zhǎo dào** is followed by **le**, it means 'to have found' or 'found', and if you have not or did not find something, put the negation word **méi(yǒu)** in front of **zhǎo dào**. For example:

A: **Nǐ *zhǎo dào* nǐde qiánbāo *le* ma?**
Have you found your wallet?

B: ***Méi yǒu* zhǎo dào.**
No, I *haven't* found it.

19 Verb xiāngxìn

If you want to say 'I don't believe it', you can either say **Wǒ bù *xiāngxìn*** or **Wǒ bù *xìn***. In spoken Chinese, **xiāng** is often omitted from **xiāngxìn**. For example:

A: **Wǒ jīnnián sānshíwǔ suì.** A: I'm thirty-five this year.
B: **Wǒ bù *xìn*.** B: I don't believe it.

20 Use of qí

When **qí** is followed by **zìxíngchē**, it means 'to ride a bike', 'by bike' or 'go cycling'. For example:

Nǐ huì *qí* zìxíngchē ma?
Can you ride a bike?

Zuótiān, wǒ *qí zìxíngchē* qù le Tiān'ānmén.
I *went* to Tian'anmen *by bike* yesterday.

Ní xǐhuan *qí zìxíngchē* ma?
Do you like *cycling*?

21 Use of xūyào

The verb **xūyào** means 'to require' or 'to need'. It can also be translated as 'It takes . . .' in certain contexts. For example:

Tā *xūyào* yí jiàn máoyī.
He *needs* a jumper.

Qí zìxíngchē qù Zhōngshān Dàxué *xūyào* èrshí fēnzhōng.
It *takes* twenty minutes to get to Zhongshan University by bike.

22 Xiǎoshí *as opposed to* diǎn

Xiǎoshí (hour) is used for the duration of time and **diǎn** is used to tell the time. For example:

A: **Cāntīng jǐ *diǎn* kāimén?**
What *time* does the restaurant open?

B: **Hái yǒu yī ge *xiǎoshí*.**
Still an *hour* to go.

Let us compare the use of **bàn** (half) in combination with **diǎn** and **xiǎoshí**:

yī diǎn *bàn*	half past one
yī ge *bàn* xiǎoshí	one hour and a half
***bàn* ge xiǎoshí**	half an hour

Exercises

Exercise 6

What do you say if you want to know how long it takes to:

(a) cycle to Zhongshan University
(b) walk to the railway station
(c) get to Tian'anmen Square by bus?

Exercise 7

What does the verb **jiè** mean in the following sentences? Write 'borrow' or 'lend':

(a) Wǒ xiǎng jiè yīxià nǐde zìxíngchē.
(b) Nǐ kěyi jiè gěi wǒ yīxiē qián ma?
(c) Wǒ bù xiǎng jiè wǒ fùmǔ de qián.
(d) Xiǎo Fāng jiè gěi le Lǎo Wáng wǔshí kuài qián.

Exercise 8

Translate the following sentences into Chinese:

(a) I don't believe that you don't have a bike.
(b) I'm going to Shanghai next Saturday.

(c) Frank didn't find Zhongshan University.
(d) You'd better check the map.
(e) It takes more than an hour to cycle to my university.
(f) This is a good idea.

Characters

Recognizing three signs

cè suǒ
toilet

gōng yòng diàn huà
public telephone

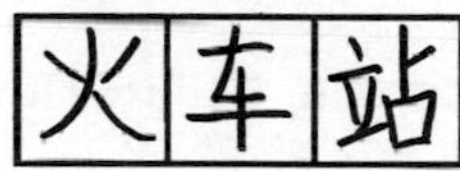

huǒ chē zhàn
railway station

Exercise 9

Match the following signs on the left with the English equivalent on the right:

1 **餐馆**	(a) hotel
2 **旅游局**	(b) tourist bureau
3 **邮局**	(c) bank
4 **银行**	(d) post-office
5 **饭店**	(e) shop
6 **商店**	(f) restaurant

Reading/listening comprehension (multiple choice)

1 Below are five Chinese sentences. Underneath each sentence are three English sentences. Read or listen to (if you have the

recording) the Chinese sentence first and tick the English sentence which is closest in meaning to the original Chinese sentence:

A **Gōngyòng diànhuà zài shí lù gōnggòng qìchē zhàn de zuǒ biān.**

(a) There is no public telephone nearby.
(b) The number 10 bus stop is on the left of the public telephone.
(c) The public telephone is on the left of the number 10 bus stop.

B **Nǐ zuìhǎo zuò èrshí lù chē qù huǒchē zhàn.**

(a) You should walk to the bus station.
(b) You'd better go to the station by bus.
(c) You'd better go to the station by bike.

C **Qí zìxíngchē dào Běijīng Fàndiàn xūyào yī ge bàn xiǎoshí zuǒyòu.**

(a) It takes about an hour and a half to get to the Beijing Hotel by bike.
(b) It takes half an hour to get to the Beijing Hotel by bus.
(c) It takes an hour to get to the Beijing Hotel by bike.

D **Wǒ méi zhǎo dào wǒde qiánbāo.**

(a) I found my wallet.
(b) I failed to find my wallet.
(c) I can't find my wallet.

E **Tā bù jìde qù Zhōngshān Dàxué zěnme zǒu.**

(a) She cannot remember Zhongshan University.
(b) She remembers Zhongshan University.
(c) She cannot remember how to get to Zhongshan University.

2 Read the following phrases and add the correct tone marks. If you have the recording, listen first, and then add the correct tone marks:

(a) **Qing zuo.** Sit down, please.
(b) **E si le.** Starving.
(c) **you kong** to be free
(d) **chi de kuai** to eat quickly
(e) **nar** there
(f) **Wo bu xin.** I don't believe it.

11 Mǎi qìchē piào hé huǒchē piào

买汽车票和火车票

Buying bus and train tickets

By the end of this lesson, you should be able to:

- buy bus and train tickets
- say which train you wish to take
- use more sophisticated phrases to modify nouns by using **de**
- make more sophisticated comparisons
- write and recognize more characters

Dialogue 1
Yǒu rén mǎi piào ma? 有人买票吗？
Fares, please!

Andrew, a sales manager for a publishing company, is travelling in China. Today, he wants to try to find his way around without a tourist guide. At the moment he is on a bus

BUS CONDUCTOR: Yǒu rén mǎi piào ma?
ANDREW: Yǒu. Wǒ mǎi yī zhāng qù dòngwùyuán de piào.
BUS CONDUCTOR: Zhè liàng chē bù qù dòngwùyuán.
ANDREW: Shénme? Wǒ zuò cuò chē le ma?
BUS CONDUCTOR: Bié jí. Nǐ xià yī zhàn xià chē, huàn shíbā lù diànchē.
ANDREW: Duìbùqǐ, wǒ méi tīng qīng. Qǐng màn yīdiǎn shuō.
BUS CONDUCTOR: (*repeats slowly*) Nǐ xià yī zhàn xià chē, huàn shíbā lù diànchē.
ANDREW: Xièxie. Nà, wǒ mǎi yī zhāng piào. Duōshǎo qián?
BUS CONDUCTOR: Yī máo.

PASSENGER: Wǒ gānghǎo yě qù huàn shíbā lù. Nǐ gēn wó zǒu ba.
ANDREW: Tài xièxie nǐ le.

BUS CONDUCTOR: 有人买票吗？
ANDREW: 有。我买一张去动物园的票。
BUS CONDUCTOR: 这辆车不去动物园。
ANDREW: 什么？我坐错车了吗？
BUS CONDUCTOR: 别急。你下一站下车，换十八路电车。
ANDREW: 对不起，我没听清。请慢一点说。
BUS CONDUCTOR: 你下一站下车，换十八路电车。
ANDREW: 谢谢。那，我买一张票。多少钱？
BUS CONDUCTOR: 一毛。
PASSENGER: 我刚好也去换十八路。你跟我走吧。
ANDREW: 太谢谢你了。

Vocabulary

yǒu rén 有人 anybody/somebody [*lit.* 'have people']
piào 票 ticket
zhāng 张 [measure word, see Note 3]
dòngwùyuán 动物园 the zoo [*lit.* 'animal park']
liàng 辆 [measure word, see Note 3]
cuò 错 wrongly/to be wrong
bié 别 do not
xià yī zhàn 下一站 next stop
xià chē 下车 to get off
diànchē 电车 tram/streetcar [*lit.* 'electric vehicle']

méi tīng qīng	没听清	did not hear clearly
màn	慢	slowly/slow/to be slow
gānghǎo	刚好	to happen to/by chance/just as well

Notes to Dialogue 1

1 On a Chinese bus

Buses in mainland China always have a conductor who sells tickets and ensures that everyone has one. The bus driver's job is only to drive.

2 Use of Yǒu rén

When **Yǒu rén** is used in a yes/no question, it means 'Is there anybody who . . .?' or simply 'Anybody . . .?' For example:

> ***Yǒu rén*** **xiǎng hē kāfēi ma?**
> *Is there anybody* who'd like to have coffee?
>
> **Zhèr, *yǒu rén* jiào Liú Xiá ma?**
> *Anybody* called Liu Xia here?

When **Yǒu rén** is used in affirmative sentences, it means 'someone/somebody'. For example:

> ***Yǒu rén*** **gěi nǐ mǎi le yī tiáo lǐngdài.**
> *Someone* has bought you a tie.

3 Measure words zhāng *and* liàng

The measure word **zhāng** is used before nouns such as **piào** (ticket), **bàozhǐ** (newspaper), **zhǐ** (sheets), etc. whenever required. For example:

> **liǎng *zhāng* gōnggòng chìchē piào** two bus tickets
> **yī *zhāng* huǒchē piào** one train ticket

The measure word **liàng** is used before nouns such as **gōnggòng qìchē** (bus), **huǒchē** (train), **fēijí** (plane), **zìxíngchē** (bike), etc. For example:

> **sān *liàng* diànchē** three trams
> **yī *liàng* zìxíngchē** one bike

4 *Using* de *to link a verbal phrase with a noun*

In English, prepositions such as 'in', 'to', etc. are used to specify nouns (e.g. a woman *in* a red jumper; a ticket *to* London). Also, in English, these modifying phrases or clauses come after the noun. This situation is very different in Chinese. Verbal phrases, not prepositions, are used to specify or modify nouns and they come before nouns. They are linked by **de**. For example:

Wǒ mǎi yī zhāng qù dòngwùyuán *de* piào.
Lit. I buy one go to zoo ticket.
A ticket to the zoo, please.

Nà ge chuān hóng máoyī *de* rén shì wǒ jiějie.
Lit. That wear red jumper person is my elder sister.
The one in the red jumper is my elder sister.

5 *Use of* cuò

When **cuò** is used to mean 'to be wrong', it must be followed by **le**. For example:

Duìbùqǐ, wǒ *cuò le*. Sorry, *I'm wrong*.

Cuò can also be used as an adverb to modify verbs. For instance, in English the sentence *I got it wrong* can be used to refer to things one has said, seen, heard, etc. However, in Chinese, you must say **Wǒ shuō cuò le** (*lit.* 'I spoke wrong.'), **Wǒ kàn cuò le** (*lit.* 'I saw wrong'), **Wǒ tīng cuò le** (*lit.* 'I heard wrong'), etc. depending on the context. For example:

(A to C): **Wǒmen xīngqīsì qù Shànghǎi.**
We are going to Shanghai on Thursday.

(B interrupts): **Nǐ *shuō cuò le*. Shì xīngqīsān.**
You *got it wrong*. It's Wednesday.

When a verb takes an object (e.g. 'to take the bus' – 'the bus' being the object of 'to take'), **cuò** is placed after the verb but before the object. **Le** can be put either after **cuò** or after the object providing that the object that follows the verb is not a very long phrase. For example:

Zāogāo, wǒ diǎn *cuò le* cài. Damn it! I ordered the *wrong* dish.
object

Wǒ zuò *cuò* chē *le* ma? Have I taken the *wrong* bus?
object

6 *Use of* bié

The word **bié**, meaning ‘do not’, is only used in imperative sentences (e.g. ‘Don’t smoke’). It is always placed before the verb. For example:

***Bié* jí. Hái yǒu shíjiān.**	*Don’t* worry. There’s still time.
***Bié* gàosu Sàisai wǒ zài zhèr.**	*Don’t* tell Saisai that I’m here.

7 Xià ge *and* xià yī . . .

In Lesson 3, we learnt the phrase **xià ge** when it was used in **xià ge xīngqī** (next week) with **yī** omitted. The complete form is **xià yī ge xīngqī**. **Yī** is usually omitted when it is followed by the measure word **gè**. Numbers other than **yī** cannot be omitted. For example:

xià *liǎng* ge xīngqī	next *two* weeks
xià *sān* ge yuè	next *three* months

We have also learnt that some nouns require measure words other than **gè**. In these cases, you must use **xià** + number + that measure word to mean ‘next’. For example:

yī *liàng* zìxíngchē one bike → ***xià yī liàng* zìxíngchē** *next* bike
sān *zhāng* piào three tickets → ***xià sān zhāng* piào** *next* three tickets

There are a couple of nouns such as **zhàn** (stop), **bù** (step), etc., which can be used as measure words. In this case, you must use **xià** + number + noun to mean ‘next’. For example:

yī zhàn one stop → ***xià yī zhàn*** next stop
liǎng bù two steps → ***xià liǎng bù*** next two steps

8 *Use of* gānghǎo

This phrase is always placed before verbs. For example:

Wǒ *gānghǎo* yào qù huǒchē zhàn. Wǒ dài nǐ qù.
I happen to be going to the railway station. I’ll take you there.

Wǒ wàng le Zhōngwén zěnme shuō ‘toilet’. *Gāngháo* nà ge rén huì shuō yīdiǎn Yīngwén.
I forgot how to say ‘toilet’ in Chinese. Just as well that chap could speak a little bit of English.

Exercises

Exercise 1

Use **de** to form one complete sentence from the pairs of sentences below. Then translate them into English:

Example: **Chuān hóng máoyī** (wear red jumper).
Nà ge rén shì wǒde gēge.
Change to: **Nà ge chuān hóng máoyī *de* rén shì wǒde gēge.**

(a) Qù dòngwùyuán (*go to the zoo*). Wǒ mǎi sān zhāng piào.
(b) Gāng dào (*just arrived*). Nà ge nánhái shì Lǎo Liú de érzi.
(c) Chángchang chí dào (*always be late*).
Wáng jīnglǐ bù xǐhuan nàxiē rén (nàxiē *means 'those'*).

Exercise 2

Fill in the blanks with appropriate measure words:

(a) Tā mǎi le liǎng ________ zhēnsī lǐngdài.
(b) Yī ________ qù huǒchē zhàn de piào duō shǎo qián?
(c) Nǐ zuò cuò chē le. Zhè ________ chē bù qù huǒchē zhàn.
(d) Tā mǎi le wǔ ________ Qīngdǎo píjiǔ.

Exercise 3

What do you say to yourself when you realize that:

(a) you have taken the wrong bus
(b) you have ordered the wrong dish
(c) you have called someone the wrong name
(d) you have bought the wrong coffee

Exercise 4

You tell your friend not to:

(a) worry
(b) take a bus
(c) tell Lao Wang how old you are
(d) speak English
(e) lend his bike to Liu Hong

Exercise 5

Translate the following sentences into Chinese:

(a) Next stop is the zoo.
(b) I didn't know that you were going away for the next two weeks.
(c) You need to get off at the next stop and change to bus number 12.
(d) Is there anybody called Kan Jiā in this hotel?
(e) Sorry, I didn't hear it clearly.
(f) Please speak slowly.

Dialogue 2
Māi huǒchē piào 买火车票 Buying train tickets

Chen Xiaojuan, who is an American Chinese born in Taiwan, is travelling in China by herself. She wants to take a train journey from Chendu to Guilin

CHÉN XIǍOJUĀN:	Qǐng wèn, zhè shì shòupiào chù ma?
TICKET ASSISTANT:	Shì de.
CHÉN XIǍOJUĀN:	Wǒ xiǎng mǎi yī zhāng qù Guìlín de huǒchē piào.
TICKET ASSISTANT:	Shénme shíhou zǒu?
CHÉN XIǍOJUĀN:	Xià ge xīngqīsān, jiù shì liùyuè sì hào.
TICKET ASSISTANT:	Nǐ dǎsuàn chéng nǎ cì lièchē?
CHÉN XIǍOJUĀN:	Wǒ bù qīngchu. Zuìhǎo shì wǎnshang liù dián zuǒyòu.

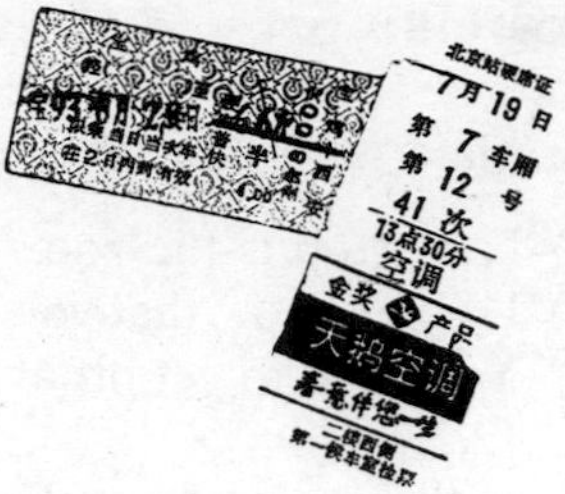

Ticket assistant: Bāshīyī cì zěnme yàng? Shíjiǔ diǎn sìshíwǔ fāchē.
Chén Xiǎojuān: Shénme shíhou dào Guìlín?
Ticket assistant: Dì èr tiān shíliù diǎn èrshí fēn dào.
Chén Xiǎojuān: Shíjiān bù cuò. Wǒ jiù mǎi zhè cì chē de piào.
Ticket assistant: Nǐ yào yìngwò háishi ruǎnwò?
Chén Xiǎojuān: Wǒ bù dǒng.
Ticket assistant: Yìngwò bǐ ruǎnwò piányi wǔshí kuài, dànshì yìngwò méi ruǎnwò shūfu.
Chén Xiǎojuān: Wǒ yào yī zhāng yìngwò.

Chen Xiaojuan: 请问，这是售票处吗？
Ticket assistant: 是的。
Chen Xiaojuan: 我想买一张去桂林的火车票。
Ticket assistant: 什么时候走？
Chen Xiaojuan: 下个星期三，就是六月四号。
Ticket assistant: 你打算乘哪次列车？
Chen Xiaojuan: 我不清楚。最好是晚上六点左右。
Ticket assistant: 八十一次怎么样？十九点四十五发车。
Chen Xiaojuan: 什么时候到桂林？
Ticket assistant: 第二天十六点二十分到。
Chen Xiaojuan: 时间不错。我就买这次车的票。
Ticket assistant: 你要硬卧还是软卧？
Chen Xiaojuan: 我不懂。
Ticket assistant: 硬卧比软卧便宜五十块，但是硬卧没软卧舒服。
Chen Xiaojuan: 我要一张硬卧。

Vocabulary

shòupiào chù	售票处	ticket office [*lit.* 'sell ticket place']
Guìlín	桂林	[a city in the southwest of China]
huǒchē piào	火车票	train ticket
zǒu	走	to leave
jiù shì	就是	that is
chéng	乘	to take/to catch [train, bus, plane, etc.]
cì	次	number
lièchē	列车	train
qīngchu	清楚	to be clear/clearly

zuìhǎo	最好	ideally
fāchē	发车	to depart/departure
dì èr tiān	第二天	the following day [*lit.* 'the second day']
bù cuò	不错	quite good/quite well [*lit.* 'not wrong']
yìngwò	硬卧	hard-sleeper
ruǎnwò	软卧	soft-sleeper
dǒng	懂	to understand

Notes to Dialogue 2

9 Use of the verb zǒu

The verb **zǒu** has several meanings. In Dialogue 2, it means 'to leave'. However, it can also mean 'to get there', 'to walk', etc. depending on the context. For example:

Nǐ māma shénme shíhou *zǒu*?
When is your mother *leaving*?

Nǐ xiǎng *zǒu*lù háishi zuò ché?
Do you want to *walk* or take the bus?

Qù nǐménde dàxué, zěnme *zǒu*?
How *do you get* to your university?

***Zǒu* dào dì yī ge lùkǒu, wǎng dōng guǎi.**
Walk to the first junction, then turn east.

10 Use of jiù shì

This phrase is always used to explain things further and sometimes to reinforce a certain piece of information. It can be broadly translated as 'that is . . .'. For example:

A: **Nǐ qīzi shénme shíhou dào?**
When is your wife arriving?

B: **Xià ge xīngqīliù, *jiù shì* sānyuè sān hào.**
Next Saturday, that is, 3 March.

Sometimes, there is no need to translate **jiù shì** into English. For example:

Tiějūn, *jiù shì* Xiǎoméi de jiějie, jiè gěi le wǒ tāde zìxíngchē.
Tiejun, Xiaomei's elder sister, lent me her bike.

11 Use of cì

All the passenger trains in China are numbered. **Cì**, meaning 'number', is used between a number and that train in the same way as **lù** is used between a number and a bus or tram. For example:

jiǔ *cì* lièchē *no.* 9 train **shíbā *cì* lièchē** *no.* 18 train

12 Difference between huǒchē *and* lièchē

Huǒchē is a general term for trains whilst **lièchē** usually refers to a specific train. For example:

Wǒ bù xǐhuan zuò *huǒchē*.
I don't like taking *trains*.

Shíyī cì *lièchē* shísì diǎn líng wǔ fāchē.
Train no. 11 departs at 14:05.

It is inappropriate rather than wrong to use **huǒchē** for a specific train. The term **lièchē** is often shortened to **chē**. For example:

Shíyī cì *chē* dào le ma? Has the number 9 *train* arrived?
Zhè shì qù Guìlín de *chē* ma? Is this the *train* to Guilin?

13 Difference between chéng *and* zuò

There is no difference in meaning between these two terms. Both **chéng** and **zuò** can be followed by road vehicles, planes and ships when the meaning 'to take' or 'to catch' is intended. The only difference is that **chéng** is more formal than **zuò**. For example:

(A train-conductor says to a customer)
Huānyíng nín *chéng* èrshíyī cì lièchē.
Welcome to [travel with] no. 21 train.

When the phrase **chéng/zuò** + means of transportation precedes the verb **qù** (to go), it means 'to go by train/bus, etc.'. For example:

Xiǎojuān *zuò* huǒchē *qù* Guìlín.
Xiaojuan *is going* to Guilin *by train.*

14 *Use of* bù cuò

Literally, **bù cuò** means 'not bad'. However, the Chinese **bù cuò** actually means 'quite good' or 'quite well'. For example:

Zhè ge fàndiàn *bù cuò*.
This hotel is *quite good*.

A: **Nǐ fùmǔ zuìjìn zěnme yàng?**
How are your parents these days?

B: ***Bù cuò*, xièxie.**
Quite well, thank you.

15 More on making comparisons

In Lesson 8, we learnt to make simple comparisons. For example, we learnt how to say 'A is older than B', but we did not learn how to say 'A is five years older than B', 'B is not as old as A' or 'B is less expensive than A'. Let us compare these three sentences:

Pattern: A + **bǐ** + B + adjective

Dǒng Mín *bǐ* Gù Liáng dà.
Dong Min is older than Gu Liang.

Pattern: A + **bǐ** + B + adjective + *specifics*

Dǒng Mín bǐ Gù Liáng dà *wǔ suì*.
Dong Min is five years older than Gu Liang.

Pattern: B + **méi** or **méi yǒu** + A + adjective

Gù Liáng *méi* Dǒng Mín dà.
Gu Liang is not as old as Dong Min.

Let us see some more examples:

Yìngwò bǐ ruǎnwò guì *wǔshí kuài*.
Hard-sleepers are fifty yuan more expensive than soft-sleepers.

Xīn Qín bǐ Miáo Lán kuài *yī fēnzhōng*.
Xin Qin is one minute faster than Miao Lan.

Yìngwò *méi* ruǎnwò guì.
Hard-sleepers are less expensive than soft-sleepers.

Jīntiān *méi yǒu* zuótiān lěng.
Today is not as cold as yesterday.

Exercises

Exercise 6

You want to tell the railway ticket-assistant that you want to buy:

(a) two tickets to Beijing
(b) one ticket to Shanghai on 8 March
(c) three hard-sleepers to Guilin
(d) two tickets for the number 26 train

Exercise 7

Make as many comparative sentences as possible based on the two sentences in each group:

Example: Yìngwò piào wǔshí wǔ kuài. Ruǎnwò piào yì bǎi kuài.

Yìngwò piào bǐ ruǎnwò piào piányì sìshíwǔ kuài.

or Ruǎnwò piào bǐ yìngwò piào guì sìshíwǔ kuài.

or Yìngwò méi yóu ruǎnwò guì.

(a) Qīngdǎo píjiǔ yī kuài qī máo yī píng.
Běijīng píjiǔ yī kuài yī máo yī píng.
(b) Xiǎoméi sānshíyī suì.
Andrew sānshí suì.
(c) Lǎo Wáng juéde Zhōngguó fàn hǎochī.
Lǎo Wáng juéde xīcān ('western food') bù tài hǎochī.
(d) Běijīng de xiàtiān hěn rè.
Lúndūn (London) de xiàtiān bù tài rè.

Exercise 8

Translate the following sentences into Chinese:

(a) The train arrives in Guilin at 13:05 the following day.
(b) I leave on Friday, that is, 25 March.
(c) My parents are quite well healthwise.
(d) What time does the number 67 train depart?

Characters

Recognizing two signs

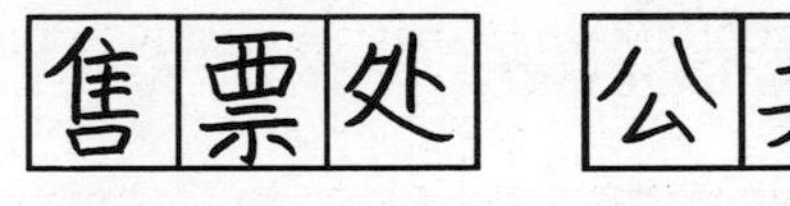

公共汽车站

shòu piào chù — ticket office

gōng gòng qì chē zhàn — bus stop

Exercise 9

Use the following characters (as many times as you wish) to form as many phrases as you can:

买　　好　　票　　看　　吃　　人

Reading/listening comprehension

1 Below is a departure timetable for some trains. Use it to answer the following questions in Chinese:

CHE CI	MUDIDI	FACHE SHIJIAN
10	Kūnmíng	9:50
36	Xiàmén	20:10
69	Wūlǔmùqí	17:05
121	Lánzhōu	7:45

Vocabulary

chē cì train number
mùdìdì destination

Questions

A **Nă cì chē qù Kūnmíng?**
B **Liùshíjiŭ cì chē jĭ diăn fāchē?**
C **Qù Xiàmén de lièchē jĭ diăn fāchē?**
D **Qù Lánzhōu de chē shíqī diăn fāchē ma?**
E **Liùshíjiŭ cì chē qù năr?**

2 Below are four sentences. Read each sentence first and then decide if the interpretation below is correct or not by writing 'true' or 'false'. If you have the recording, listen to the sentence first, and then decide if the interpretation is 'true' or 'false':

(a) **Wó xiŏng măi sān zhāng qù Yúnnán de huŏchē piào.**
I'd like to buy three train tickets to Yunnan.
(b) **Wŏ māma bù xiăng zuò wănshang fāchē de huŏchē.**
My mother doesn't like taking trains.
(c) **Rúguŏ méi yìngwò dehuà, wŏ jiù măi míngtiān de ruănwò.**
If there aren't any hard-sleepers, I'm not going.
(d) **Qĭng zuò shí lù chē qù Bĕijīng Fàndiàn.**
Please take the number 10 bus to get to the Beijing Hotel.

12 Zài fàndiàn 在饭店

At the hotel

By the end of this lesson, you should be able to:

- ask about the availability of hotel rooms
- describe the kind of room you would like to have
- use ordinal numbers with appropriate measure words
- make some complaints
- recognize more characters

Dialogue 1
Yǒu kòng fángjiān ma? 有空房间吗？
Any vacancies?

Jonathan has just finished a conference in Beijing, and he would like to stay on for a couple of days in a hotel near the centre of the city. So he has checked out of the conference hotel and goes into a downtown hotel

JONATHAN: Qǐng wèn, nǐmen yǒu kòng fángjiān ma?
RECEPTIONIST: Yào kàn qíngkuàng. Nǐ yào dānrén fángjiān háishi shuāngrén fángjiān?
JONATHAN: Dān jiān.
RECEPTIONIST: Zhù jǐ tiān?
JONATHAN: Sān tiān.
RECEPTIONIST: Ràng wǒ chácha. (*after checking the computer*) Zhēn qiǎo! Yǒu yī jiān kòng fángjiān.
JONATHAN: Dān jiān dài wèishēng jiān ma?
RECEPTIONIST: Dài.
JONATHAN: Duō shǎo qián yī tiān?

RECEPTIONIST: Liǎng bǎi sān shí yuán.
JONATHAN: Wǒ yào le.

(*after Jonathan has filled in all the necessary forms . . .*)

RECEPTIONIST: Zhè shì nǐde fángjiān yàoshi. Fángjiān zài dì sān céng.

JONATHAN: 请问，你们有空房间吗？
RECEPTIONIST: 要看情况。你要单人房间还是双人房间？
JONATHAN: 单间。
RECEPTIONIST: 住几天？
JONATHAN: 三天。
RECEPTIONIST: 让我查查。(...) 真巧！有一间空房间。
JONATHAN: 单间带卫生间吗？
RECEPTIONIST: 带。
JONATHAN: 多少钱一天？
RECEPTIONIST: 两百三十元。
JONATHAN: 我要了。

RECEPTIONIST: 这是你的钥匙。房间在第三层。

Vocabulary

kòng	空	vacant/free
fángjiān	房间	room
Yào kàn qíngkuàng	要看情况	It depends [*lit.* 'will see situation']
dānrén	单人	single [*lit.* 'single person']
shuāngrén	双人	double [*lit.* 'double people']
chácha	查查	to check
zhēn qiǎo	真巧	What a coincidence!/coincidentally
jiān	间	[measure word for rooms, see Note 6]
dài	带	to include/to have/with
wèishēng jiān	卫生间	bathroom [*lit.* 'hygiene room']
yàoshi	钥匙	key
céng	层	floor/layer

Notes to Dialogue 1

1 Use of kòng fángjiān

Literally, **kòng fángjiān** means 'empty room'. The word **kòng** used here is the same **kòng** as in **yǒu kòng** (to have time) in Lesson 9.

In the context of booking into a hotel, **kòng fángjiān** can mean 'vacancy' or 'rooms available'. For example:

Duìbùqǐ. Wǒmen méi yǒu *kòng fángjiān*.
Sorry. We don't have any *vacancies*.

Nǐ zhīdao Běijīng Fàndiàn yǒu *kòng fángjiān* ma?
Do you know if there are any *rooms* available in the Beijing Hotel?

2 *Phrase* kàn qíngkuàng

This is a very useful phrase. We actually learnt the term **qíngkuàng** in Lesson 5 in sentences such as **Gàosu wǒ nǐde *qíngkuàng*** (Tell me about yourself). The phrase **Kàn qíngkuàng** or **Yào kàn qíngkuàng** means 'It depends'. For example:

A: **Nǐ míngtiān qù yóuyǒng ma?**
Are you going swimming tomorrow?

B: ***Kàn qíngkuàng.***
It depends.

If you want to say 'It depends on something', you must say **Yào kàn** + something. For example:

A: **Nǐ xiǎng mǎi zhēnsī lǐngdài ma?**
Do you want to buy some silk ties?
B: ***Yào kàn jiàgé.***
It depends on the price.

A: **Nǐ qí zìxíngchē shàngbān ma?**
Do you go to work by bike?
B: ***Yào kàn tiānqì.***
It depends on the weather.

3 Shortening of noun phrases

Some noun phrases or proper nouns sometimes get shortened by omitting certain parts. Unfortunately, there are no rules to follow. Below are a few phrases we have already learnt which can be shortened:

dān*rén fáng*jiān	→	***dān jiān***	single room
shuāng*rén fáng*jiān	→	***shuāng jiān***	double room
***Běi*jīng *Dà*xué**	→	***Běi Dà***	Beijing University

4 *Use of* dài

In Lesson 7, **dài** was used as a verb to mean 'to take' or 'to bring'. Here it is also used as a verb but to mean 'to include' or 'to have' (in the sense 'to come with' as opposed to 'to possess'). For example:

> **Nǐde fángjiān *dài* wèishēng jiān ma?**
> Does your room *include* a bathroom?
>
> **Liùshíqī cì lièchē *dài* kōngtiáo ma?**
> Does the no. 67 train *have* air-conditioning?

Dài can also be used as a preposition to mean 'with'. It is always placed after the noun phrase. For example:

> **Shuāng jiān *dài* wèishēng jiān duōshǎo qián?**
> How much is it for a double room *with* bathroom?
>
> **Wǒ xǐhuan kāfēi *dài* niúnǎi.**
> I like coffee *with* milk.

5 Duō shǎo qián yī tiān?

When you ask about the hotel tariff in English, you say *How much is it per night?* In Chinese, you say 'How much is it per day?' For example:

> **Dān jiān *duō shǎo qián yī tiān*?**
> *How much is it per night* for a single room?
>
> **Běijīng Fàndiàn de shuāng jiān sān bǎi yuán *yī tiān*.**
> Double rooms in the Beijing Hotel cost three hundred yuan *per night*.

In the west, the price is per person. In mainland China, the price quoted for a double room is usually for two people. However, if you choose to have a double room and you are the only customer, you still have to pay the double room price.

6 *Use of ordinal numbers with measure words*

In Lesson 10, we learnt how to say ordinal numbers, i.e. **dì yī** (first), **dì èr** (second). When ordinal numbers precede nouns that require the measure word **gè**, you must put **gè** after the ordinal number if you want to refer to any one of them. For example:

liǎng *ge* cāntīng	two dining-rooms	***dì èr ge***	the second one
wǔ *ge* dà xuésheng	five university students	***dì wǔ ge***	the fifth one

If the noun used requires a measure word other than **ge**, you must put that measure word after the ordinal number. For example:

sān *liàng* zìxíngchē	three bikes	→	**dì sān *liàng***	the third bike
liǎng *jiān* fāngjiān	two rooms	→	**dì èr *jiān***	the second room
liù *céng*	six floors	→	**dì liù *céng***	the sixth floor

Note that the word **céng** is only used to refer to different floors in a building. It cannot be used to mean the 'floor' in, for example, 'wooden floor'.

Nouns such as **tiān** (day), **nián** (year), etc., which do not require measure words, must follow the ordinal number. For example:

yī *tiān*	one *day*	→	**dì yī *tiān***	the first *day*
sì *nián*	four *years*	→	**dì sì *nián***	the fourth *year*

Exercises

Exercise 1

Below is the price information in a hotel brochure. Read it first and then answer the questions in Chinese:

Fángjiān zhǒnglèi	Jiàgé (měi tiān)
dānrén fángjiān (bù dài wèishēng jiān)	¥55.00
dānrén fángjiān (dài wèishēng jiān)	¥85.00
shuāngrén fángjiān (bù dài wèishēng jiān)	¥122.00
shuāngrén fángjiān (dài wèishēng jiān)	¥185.00

zhǒnglèi	type
měi tiān	each day/everyday

(a) Dān jiān dài wèishēng jiān duō shǎo qián yī tiān?
(b) Shuāng jiān dài wèishēng jiān duō shǎo qián yī tiān?
(c) Shénme fángjiān wǔshíwǔ yuán yī tiān?

Exercise 2

You tell the receptionist at a hotel that you would like:

(a) a single room with bathroom
(b) a double room with bathroom
(c) a single room for three nights

Exercise 3

Translate the following sentences into Chinese:

(a) Do you have any rooms available?
(b) My room does not have a telephone.
(c) Your room is on the fourth floor.
(d) The third bike on the left is mine.

Dialogue 2
Diàndēng huài le 电灯坏了 The light is not working

The following morning, Jonathan bumps into the duty manager of the hotel

DUTY MANAGER:	Zǎoshang hǎo. Nín zuówǎn shuì de hǎo ma?
JONATHAN:	Lǎoshí shuō, shuì de bù hǎo.
DUTY MANAGER:	Zěnme huí shì?
JONATHAN:	Zuótiān wǎnshang, gébì fángjiān hěn chǎo. Chǎo dào bànyè liǎng diǎn.
DUTY MANAGER:	Zhēn bàoqiàn. Wǒ huì chǔlǐ zhè jiàn shì.
JONATHAN:	Xièxie. Ò, duì le. Wǒde fángjiān lǐ yǒu ge diàndēng huài le.
DUTY MANAGER:	Shì ma? Wǒ yīdìng ràng rén qù xiū. Hái yǒu biéde wèntí ma?
JONATHAN:	Zànshí méi yǒu. Huí jiàn.

DUTY MANAGER:	早上好。您昨晚睡得好吗？
JONATHAN:	老实说，睡得不好。
DUTY MANAGER:	怎么回事？
JONATHAN:	昨天晚上，隔壁房间很吵。吵到半夜两点。
DUTY MANAGER:	真抱歉。我会处理这件事。

JONATHAN:	谢谢。噢，对了。我的房间里有个电灯坏了。
DUTY MANAGER:	是吗？我一定让人去修。还有别的问题吗？
JONATHAN:	暂时没有。回见。

Vocabulary

lǎoshí shuō	老实说	frankly speaking/to be honest
shì	事	thing/matter
Zěnme huí shì?	怎么回事？	What's the matter?
gébì	隔壁	next door
chǎo	吵	to be noisy
bànyè	半夜	early hours of the morning
zhēn bàoqiàn	真抱歉	many apologies
chǔlǐ	处理	to see to/to handle
zhè jiàn shì	这件事	this matter
jiàn	件	[measure word, see Note 10]
duì le	对了	right/by the way
lǐ	里	inside
diàndēng	电灯	light [*lit.* 'electric light']
huài le	坏了	to have broken/does not work
ràng rén	让人	to send for someone
xiū	修	to repair
wèntí	问题	problem
zànshí	暂时	at the moment/temporarily

Notes to Dialogue 2

7 Zěnme húi shì?

This is a very colloquial phrase. The complete phrase should be **Zěnme yī huí shì?** (*lit.* 'How one thing?' – **huí** is another measure word for matters). This phrase is usually used if something has gone wrong and you want to find out about it. It means 'What's the matter?', 'What's the problem?' or 'What happened?' The word **shì**, which is a different word from **shì** (be), is a general term used to refer to abstract things. For example:

> **Wǒ míngtiān yǒu *shì*.**
> I've got *things* to do tomorrow.

> **Shénme *shì*?**
> What is it?

Wǒ yǒu liǎng jiàn *shì* gàosu nǐ.
I've got two *things* to tell you.

8 More on the past tense

So far, we have learnt two different ways to indicate a past event or an event which is related to the past by using **le** or **guo** together with some verbs. However, you must not use either of the above two devices in sentences which describe a stable state of affairs in the past as opposed to momentary action. In the former case, the past tense is indicated by time-related phrases such as **zuótiān** (yesterday), **shàng ge xīngqī** (last week), etc. In particular, **le** or **guo** must not be used in the following four sentence types:

(a) Sentences with static verbs such as **shì** (to be), **yǒu** (to have), **xiǎng** (to want), **xǐhuan** (to like), **zhīdao** (to know), etc. For example:

***Liǎng nián qián*, tā *yǒu* yī liàng zìxíngchē.**
He *had* a bike *two years ago*.

***Qù nián*, tā *shì* dǎoyóu.**
She *was* a tourist guide *last year*.

***Zuówǎn*, wǒ bù *xiǎng* chī fàn.**
I *didn't* want to eat *last night*.

(b) Sentences with verb–adjectives or the word **zài** (to be at/in). For example:

***Zuówǎn*, gébì hěn *chǎo*.**
Next door *was* very noisy *last night*.

***Zuótiān*, wǒ bàba bù *zài* jiā.**
My father *was*n't *at* home *yesterday*.

(c) Sentences with verbal phrases followed by **de**. For example:

Zuówǎn, wǒ shuì de hěn hǎo.
I slept very well last night.

(d) Sentences negated with **méi** or **méi yǒu** (see Note 17 of Lesson 3)

You may have noticed that verbs used in the above sentences cannot be negated by **méi yǒu** or **méi**.

9 Use of dào

Dào (until) can be used after a verbal phrase, verb or verb–adjective to describe the duration of an event. For example:

Wǒ děng tā *dào* shí'èr diǎn.
I waited for him *until* twelve o'clock.

Tāmen chǎo *dào* hěn wǎn.
They were noisy all night.

Usually, if the verb is a two-syllable word, put **dào** after the first syllable and omit the second syllable. Let us take **kāimén** (to open) as an example:

Cāntīng *kāi* dào wǎnshang shí diǎn.
The restaurant *is open* until ten o'clock.

10 Measure word jiàn

This is the same **jiàn** as in **yī *jiàn* máoyī** (one jumper) in Lesson 8, but it is different from the **jiān** as in **yī *jiān* fángjiān** (one room). Let us see how these two measure words differ in the following phrases:

	Tone	*Character*	*English*
yī *jiàn* shì	fourth tone	件	one matter
liǎng *jiàn* máoyī	fourth tone	件	two jumpers
sān *jiān* fángjiān	first tone	间	one room

11 Use of Duì le

This is used when the current topic of conversation reminds you of something. It has the same effect as *Oh, yes/right* in English when used in those circumstances. For example:

A: **Xiǎo Lǐ qǐng wǒ chī wǎnfàn.**
Xiao Li has invited me to dinner.

B: ***Duì le.* Wǒ wàng le gàosu nǐ . . .**
Oh, right. I forgot to tell you . . .

A: **Wǒ mǎi le yī zhāng qù Shànghǎi de huǒchē piào.**
I bought a train ticket for Shanghai.

B: ***Duì le.* Lǐ Bīng shuō tā yě qù Shànghǎi.**
Oh, yes. Li Bing says she is going to Shanghai as well.

12 Use of lǐ

The word **lǐ**, meaning 'inside' or 'in', indicates the position of an object. It is always placed *after* the noun. For example:

Nǐménde fángjiān *lǐ* yǒu wèishēng jiān ma?
Lit. Your room inside have bathroom [question word]?
Is there a bathroom *in* your room?

Wǒde qiánbāo *lǐ* méi yǒu qián.
Lit. My wallet inside not have money.
There is no money in my wallet.

Note that **lǐ** usually changes to neutral tone when used in the middle of sentences.

13 Something + huài le

Literally, **huài** means 'bad'. So we can say **huài rén** (bad person), **huài zhǔyi** (bad idea), etc. When **huài le** follows a noun, it means something 'does not work', 'is broken' or 'has gone bad'. For example:

Tāde fángjiān lǐ yǒu ge diàndēng *huài le*.
One of the lights in his room *is not working*.

Wǒde zìxíngchē *huài le*.
My bike *is broken*.

Māma, wǒ juéde kǎo yā *huài le*.
Mum, I think the roast duck *has gone off*.

14 Construction ràng *+ somebody + do something*

In this context, the verb **ràng** means 'to ask' (see **ràng** in Lesson 3). For example:

Lǎo Wáng *ràng* wǒ dài nǐ qù yínháng.
Lao Wang *asked* me to take you to the bank.

Andrew *ràng* wǒ wèn nǐde fùmú hǎo.
Andrew *asked* me to say hello to your parents.

When **rén** (person) follows **ràng**, **rén** in this context means 'somebody'. Thus **ràng rén** can mean 'to send for somebody' or 'to ask someone'. For example:

Wǒ yīdìng *ràng rén* qù xiū nǐde dēng.
I'll definitely *send someone* to fix your light.

Mù Yīng huì *ràng rén* géi wǒ mǎi yī zhāng huǒchē piào de.
Mu Ying will *ask somebody* to buy me a train ticket.

Exercises

Exercise 4

Which is the odd word out in each group below?

(a) hē kāfēi chī kǎo yā chī zǎofàn diàndēng
(b) chúlǐ dān jiān shuāng jiān wèishēng jiān
(c) Yīngguórén Zhōngguórén Měiguórén fàndiàn
(d) Wèishénme? Zěnme huí shì? Shénme shíhou?

Exercise 5

Pair off the verbs on the left with nouns on the right:

(a) xiū	1 zhè jiān shì
(b) chúlǐ	2 lǐwù
(c) yǒu	3 diàndēng
(d) mǎi	4 gōnggòng qìchē
(e) kàn	5 kòng fángjiān
(f) děng	6 péngyou

Exercise 6

You complain to the duty manager in your hotel that:

(a) the light in your room is not working
(b) people next door are very noisy
(c) your room is too cold

Exercise 7

Translate the following into Chinese:

(a) Many apologies.
(b) Frankly speaking, . . .
(c) Did you sleep well?
(d) It depends.
(e) Sifang asked me to tell you that she is leaving next Thursday.
(f) There is no money inside my wallet.
(g) A: Any other problems?
B: Not for the moment.

Exercise 8

Describe the following in the past tense:

(a) your room's temperature yesterday
(b) you were not in a going-out mood last night
(c) your neighbour being noisy last night
(d) the room you had did not have a bathroom

Reading comprehension

There are a few odd things in the following dialogue. Pick out the strange words or phrases. Then you need to decide whether to cross them out or to replace them with more suitable words or phrases.

Emily Brown has walked into a hotel in Taiwan. She wants to find out if there are any rooms available

RECEPTIONIST:	Nǐ hǎo.
EMILY:	Xièxie. Nǐmen yǒu kòng fángjiān ma?
RECEPTIONIST:	Yào kàn qíngkuàng. Nǐ yào wèishēng jiān háishi shuāng jiān?
EMILY:	Yào dān jiān. Dān jiān dài yóuyǒng chí ma?
RECEPTIONIST:	Dāngrán dài. Nǐ dǎsuàn zhù jǐ tiān?
EMILY:	Liǎng ge tiān.
RECEPTIONIST:	Ràng nǐ chácha. Yǒu kòng fángjiān.
EMILY:	Duō shǎo qián yī tiān?
RECEPTIONIST:	Yī bǎi bāshí yuán. Xíng ma?
EMILY:	Xíng. Wǒ yào le.

13 Dǎ diànhuà 打电话

Making telephone calls

By the end of this lesson, you should be able to:

- use some appropriate expressions on the telephone
- use the **shì . . . de** construction to express the time or manner of a past action
- indicate that you have completed an action by using **wán . . . le**
- distinguish the usage between **yī** and **yāo**
- recognize more characters

Dialogue 1

Wèi 喂 Hello

Alan is doing his doctorate in Buddhism. He is now in Beijing to do some research. Alan is going to call his old friend Li Man, whom he met in England two years ago

ALAN: Wèi, qǐng zhǎo yīxià Lǐ Màn.
LǏ MÀN: Wǒ jiù shì. Nǐ shì shéi'a?
ALAN: Wǒ shì Alan. Cóng Yīngguó lái de Alan.
LǏ MÀN: Zhēn de! Nǐ shì shénme shíhou lái de? Wǒ zěnme bù zhīdao?
ALAN: Shàng ge xīngqīsì lái de. Shì línshí juédìng.
LǏ MÀN: Wǒ tài jīdòng le. Nǐ shénme shíhou lái kàn wǒ?
ALAN: Shénme shíhou dōu xíng. Nǐ juédìng.
LǏ MÀN: Jīntiān wǎnshang xíng ma?

ALAN: Tài bàng le! Nǐ zhù zài shénme dìfang?
LǏ MÀN: Wǒ jiā bù hǎo zhǎo. Wǒ lái jiē nǐ ba.

ALAN: 喂，请找一下李曼。
LI MAN: 我就是。你是谁啊？
ALAN: 我是 Alan. 从英国来的 Alan.
LI MAN: 真的！ 你是什么时候来的？ 我怎么不知道？
ALAN: 上个星期四来的。是临时决定。
LI MAN: 我太激动了。你什么时候来看我？
ALAN: 什么时候都行。你决定。
LI MAN: 今天晚上行吗？
ALAN: 太棒了！ 你住在什么地方？
LI MAN: 我家不好找。我来接你吧。

Vocabulary

wèi	喂	hello [only used on the telephone]
zhǎo	找	to look for
cóng . . . lái	从…来	to come from . . .
línshí	临时	last minute/temporary
juédìng	决定	to decide/decision
jīdòng	激动	to be excited/exciting
shénme shíhou	什么时候	any time/whenever
dōu	都	[emphatic word, see Note 7]
Nǐ juédìng.	你决定	You decide.
Tài bàng le!	太棒了！	Superb!
shénme dìfang	什么地方	whereabouts [*lit.* 'what place']
jiā	家	home/family
bù hǎo zhǎo	不好找	not easy to find
jiē	接	to collect/to meet [somebody]

Notes to Dialogue 1

1 Use of Wèi

This word is only used to open a telephone conversation. It is basically a way of catching the attention of the person on the other end of the phone. For example:

***Wèi*, nǐ shì Běijīng Fàndiàn ma?** *Hello*. Is that the Beijing Hotel?
***Wèi*, Xiǎo Liú zài ma?** *Hello*. Is Xiao Liu there?

2 Some telephone expressions

If you want to speak to someone, you can say one of the following:

Qǐng zhǎo yīxià Lǐ Màn?
Lit. Please look for Li Man?
Could you get Li Man please?

Note that the expression **yīxià** has the same effect, i.e. mitigating the abruptness, as it had in Lesson 3.

Qǐng wèn, Lǐ Màn zài ma? Is Li Man around please?

If you happen to be the one who answers the telephone and speak first, you can say one of the following:

Qǐng wèn, nǐ zhǎo shéi?
Lit. Please ask, you look for who?
Whom do you want to speak to, please?

Wéi, nǐ shì nǎli?
Lit. Hello, you are whereabout?
Hello, who is calling?

3 Use of . . . cóng . . . lái . . .

In English, prepositional phrases such as *from England* come after the verb. In Chinese, they occur before the verb. For example:

Wáng xiǎojie *cóng* Xiāng Gǎng *lái*.
Lit. Wang Miss from Hong Kong come.
Miss Wang *comes from* Hong Kong.

Suppose you do not know where Miss Wang comes from. The unknown information is 'Hong Kong'. Thus, the question should be:

Wáng xiǎojie cóng *nǎr* lái?
Lit. Wang Miss from where come?
Where does Miss Wang come from?

4 More on the link word de

In the dialogue, Alan explains who he is by saying **Cóng Yīngguó lái *de* Alan** (The Alan from Britain). The word **de** links the verbal phrase with the noun (see Note 4 in Lesson 11). The complete sentence should be:

Wǒ shì cóng Yīngguó lái *de* Alan.
I am the Alan from Britain.

Now you can see that the above sentence can be taken apart into two simple sentences:

(a) **Wǒ shì Alan.**
(b) **Wǒ cóng Yīngguó lái.**

5 *Construction* shì . . . de

This construction has many usages. Let us look at two of them here. First, it is used in interrogative sentences which ask about the time, the place or manner of an action that happened in the past. The word **shì** is placed before the phrase that is being emphasized and **de** comes either at the end of the sentence or after the verb. For example:

Nǐ *shì* shénme shíhou lái Běijīng *de*?
Nǐ *shì* shénme shíhou lái *de* Běijīng?
} When did you arrive in Beijing?

Nǐ *shì* zěnme lái *de*? How did you get here?

Without **shì . . . de**, the above first two sentences become:

Nǐ shénme shíhou lái Běijīng?
When are you coming to Beijing?

And the last sentence becomes **Nǐ zěnme lái?**, which means 'How do you get here?' or 'How are you going to get here?'

Second, the construction is used in positive sentences that emphasize the time or manner of a past action. For example:

Wǒ *shì* bābā nián kāishǐ xué Zhōngwén *de*.
I started to learn Chinese in eighty-eight.

Wǒ *shì* qí zìxíngchē lái *de*.
I came by bike.

Note that **shì** is often omitted in the above two cases. Thus we have:

Tā jǐ diǎn xià bān *de*?
What time did he leave work?

Wǒ zuò gōnggòng qìchē lái *de*.
I came by bus.

Let us compare the use of **le** and **shì . . . de** in describing a past action:

Tā zuótiān lái *le*.	She turned up yesterday.
Tā *shì* zuótiān lái *de*.	She arrived yesterday.

Tā zuótiān lái le is merely a statement about a past event (i.e. to confirm that something happened yesterday), whilst **Tā shì zuótiān lái de** emphasizes the time 'yesterday' as opposed to any other time.

6 Use of shì *at the beginning of sentences*

You may have noticed that the pronoun 'it' is seldom used in Chinese. Thus, the structure 'It is/was . . .' is sometimes replaced by **Zhè shì** . . . (This is/was . . .). For example:

***Zhè shì* línshí juédìng ma?** *Was it* a last-minute decision?

The pronoun **zhè** is often omitted. So **shì** occurs at the beginning of a sentence:

***Shì* línshí juédìng.**	*It was* a last-minute decision.
***Shì* Wáng Fāng ma?**	*Is that* Wang Fang?

7 More on question words used in statements

Certain question words, when used in statements, especially in conjunction with the emphatic word **dōu**, function as indefinite pronouns. Note how the meaning changes accordingly:

Word item	*In questions*	*In statements*
shénme shíhou	when	whenever / at any time
nǎr	where	wherever
zěnme	how	by whatever means

For the moment, let us concentrate on how to use **shénme shíhou** in conjunction with **dōu**, which can be placed after **shénme shíhòu**. For example:

***Shénme shíhou dōu* xíng.**
Lit. Whenever be fine.
Whenever you like.

Dōu can also be placed after the verb, that is, if a verb is used. For example:

Zánmen shénme ***shíhou*** **yóuyǒng** ***dōu*** **xíng.**
(verb: yóuyǒng)
Lit. We whenever swim be fine.
It's fine with me *whenever* we go swimming.

You can also use **shénme shíhou** in the first part of a sentence, and **dōu** in the second part. For example:

Nǐ ***shénme shíhou*** **lái,** **wǒ** ***dōu*** **zài.**
Lit. You whenever come, I be in.
Whenever you come, I'll be in.

If you want to negate the sentences with **shénme shíhou** and **dōu**, put the negation word after **dōu**. For example:

Xiǎo Lǐ shénme shíhou dōu ***méi yǒu*** **kòng.**
Lit. Xiao Li whenever not have time.
Xiao Li *never has* time.

8 *Question word* shénme dìfang

Literally, **shénme dìfang** means 'what place'. In addition to 'what place', it also means 'whereabouts' or 'where exactly'. For example:

Nǐ zhù zài Běijīng ***shénme dìfang*****?**
Where exactly in Beijing do you live?

Nǐ qù le Měiguó ***shénme dìfang*****?**
What places in America did you go to?

9 *Use of* jiā

Depending on the context, **jiā** can mean either 'home' or 'family'. For example:

Nǐ fùmǔ de ***jiā*** **zài shénme dìfang?**
Whereabouts is your parents' *home*?

Wǒ ***jiā*** **yǒu hěnduō rén. Wǒ yǒu yī ge dà** ***jiā*****.**
There are many people in my family. I have a big *family*.

10 Use of bù hǎo *+ verb*

As you know, **bù hǎo** means 'not good'. However, when you have the pattern 'something + **bù hǎo** + verb', it means 'It is not easy to do something'. For example:

Huǒchē zhàn ***bù hǎo zhǎo.***
verb

Lit. Railway station not easy find.
It's not easy to find the railway station.

Zhōngwén ***bù hǎo xué.***
verb

Lit. Chinese not easy learn.
It's not easy to learn Chinese.

11 Use of jiē

Jiē means 'to collect' or 'to meet', usually, somebody. For example:

Jīntiān wǎnshang bā diǎn bàn, wǒ yào qù huǒchē zhàn ***jiē*** **wǒ māma.**
I'm going to go to the station *to meet* my mother at half past eight tonight.

Nǐ xūyào wǒ qù ***jiē*** **nǐ ma?**
Do you need me to go and *collect* you?

Exercises

Exercise 1

Complete the following telephone dialogues in as many ways as you can think of:

(a) A: ____________ ?
B: Wǒ jiù shì Lǐ Màn.
(b) A: Nǐ shì Běijīng Dàxué Zhōngwén Xì ma?
B: ____________ ?
A: Qǐng zhǎo yīxià Hú Xīnháng.
(c) A: ____________ ?
B: Duìbùqǐ. Jane bù zài.
(d) A: ____________ ?
B: Wǒ shì cóng Yīngguó lái de Alan.

Exercise 2

Combine the two sentences in each group to make them into one sentence by using **de**:

Example: Wǒ shì Alan. Wǒ cóng Yīngguó lái.
→ Wǒ shì cóng Yīngguó lái *de* Alan.

(a) Sīfāng shì Zhōngguórén. Sīfāng cóng Xīnjiāpō lái.
(b) Linda shì dà xuésheng. Linda xué Zhōngwén.
(c) Wǒde Zhōngwén lǎoshī shì Zhōngguórén.
Tā cóng Zhōngguó dàlù lái. (**dàlù** means 'mainland China')

Exercise 3

Translate the following sentences into Chinese:

(a) When did David leave?
(b) I came to work by bike this morning.
(c) Whenever you like. You decide.
(d) He does not like to take a bus, no matter when.
(e) Could you come to collect me?
(f) What time and where exactly shall we meet?

Exercise 4

How do you ask Xiao Li the following in Chinese:

(a) What time did you leave work yesterday?
(b) How did you get to work yesterday?
(c) Was it last night that your younger sister arrived?
(d) When did your younger sister start learning English?

Exercise 5

Make up as many sentences as you can using **bù hǎo** to mean 'It is not easy to . . .' and write the English translation after each sentence.

Dialogue 2
Diànhuà hàomǎ 电话号码 Telephone numbers

Jane works in the Hong Kong office of a Canadian telecommunications company. Most of the local employees in the office can speak Mandarin Chinese. It is a busy day today and all the phones are engaged

JANE: Yǒngměi, nǐ yòng wán diànhuà le ma?
YǑNGMĚI: Yòng wán le.
JANE: Wǒ gěi zánmen lǎobǎn dǎ ge diànhuà.
YǑNGMĚI: Tā jīntiān bù zài bàngōngshì.
JANE: Shì ma? Nǐ yǒu tā jiā de diànhuà hàomǎ ma?
YǑNGMĚI: Méi yǒu. Nǐ kěyi dǎ diànhuà wèn tāde mìshū.
JANE: Hǎo zhǔi.
SECRETARY: Èr-liù-bā fēnjī. Qǐng wèn, nǎ yī wèi?
JANE: Wǒ shì Jane. Wǒ yǒu yī jiàn jí shì tóng Fāng jīnglǐ shāngliang. Tīngshuō tā jīntiān bù zài bàngōngshì. Nǐ kěyǐ gàosu wǒ tā jiā de diànhuà hàomǎ ma?
SECRETARY: Kěyǐ. Qǐng děng yīxià. Tīng hǎo. Hàomǎ shì sì-liù-èr-yāo-bā-sān.
JANE: Sì-liù-èr-yāo-bā-sān.
SECRETARY: Duì.

JANE: 你用完电话了吗？
YONGMEI: 用完了。
JANE: 我给咱们老板打个电话。
YONGMEI: 他今天不在办公室。
JANE: 是吗？你有他家的电话号码吗？
YONGMEI: 没有。你可以打电话问他的秘书。
JANE: 好主意。
SECRETARY: 二六八分机。请问，哪一位？
JANE: 我是 Jane。我有一件事同方经理商量。听说他今天不在办公室。你可以告诉我他家的电话号码吗？
SECRETARY: 可以。请等一下。听好。号码是四六二幺八三。
JANE: 四六二幺八三。
SECRETARY: 对。

Vocabulary

yòng	用	to use
wán	完	[see Note 12]
lǎobǎn	老板	boss
dǎ diànhuà	打电话	to make telephone calls/to telephone
bàngōngshì	办公室	office
hàomǎ	号码	number
mìshū	秘书	secretary
fēnjī	分机	extension
Nǎ yī wèi?	哪一位?	Who is calling?
jí shì	急事	urgent matter
tóng	同	with/and
shāngliang	商量	to discuss/to consult
tīng hǎo	听好	to listen carefully [*lit.* 'listen well']
yāo	幺	one

Notes to Dialogue 2

12 Use of wán *after the verb*

When you put **wán** after a verb, it indicates that the action is completed. It is similar to the English phrase *to have finished with/doing something*. Whenever **wán** is used after a verb, **le** must be placed after whatever has been finished. For example:

Nǐ chī *wán* wǎnfàn *le* ma?
Lit. You eat finish supper [question word]?
Have you *finished* having your supper?

Wǒ yòng *wán* wèishēng jiān *le*. Nǐ qù yòng ba.
Lit. I use finish bathroom. You go use please.
I've *finished* with the bathroom. Do go and use it.

13 More on the preposition gěi

A phrase beginning with **gěi** . . . is always placed before the verbal phrase (see Lessons 5 and 8). Thus, if you want to say 'to telephone somebody' or 'to make a phone call to somebody', you say **gěi** + somebody + **dǎ diànhuà**. For example:

Bié wàng le *gěi nǐ māma* dǎ diànhuà.
Don't forget to phone your mum.

Míngtiān wǒ yīdìng *gěi nǐ* dǎ diànhuà.
I'll definitely give you a call tomorrow.

If you want to mention the number of phone calls made or to be made, put the numerals together with the measure word **gè** before **diànhuà**. For example:

Zuótiān wǒ gěi zánmen láobǎn dǎ le *liǎng ge* diànhuà.
Yesterday, I made two phone calls to our boss.

14 More on the omission of de

The word **de**, which indicates the ownership relationship, is usually omitted before **jiā** (home/family). For example:

***Nǐ jiā* bù hǎo zhǎo.**
It's not easy to find *your home*.

***Wǒ fùmǔ jiā* zài Xiāng Gǎng.**
My parents' home is in Hong Kong.

However, it is not wrong to use **de**. For example, it is perfectly right to say **Nǐde jiā bù hǎo zhǎo**. But, **de** must be kept before **diànhuà hàomǎ** (telephone number). The reason is that the concept of **jiā** is associated with people whilst **diànhuà hàomǎ** is just an object (see Note 3 in Lesson 5). For example:

***Wǒde* diànhuà huài le.**
My telephone has been out of order.

***Nǐ jiā de* diànhuà hàomǎ shì shénme?**
What is *your home* telephone number?

15 More on the measure word wèi

We learnt this measure word in Lesson 9. The question **Nǎ yī wèi?** (*lit.* 'Which one?') is actually a polite way of asking 'Who is it?' on the telephone. For example:

Wéi, *nǎ yī wèi*? Hello. *Who is it, please*?

It is also appropriate to ask **Nǐ shì nǎ yī wèi?** (*lit.* 'You are which one?').

16 *Preposition* tóng

You may have noticed by now that prepositional phrases (e.g. Note 13 above) appear before verbal phrases. **Tóng**, meaning 'with' or 'and', is a preposition. Thus **tóng** + somebody is a prepositional phrase. This phrase must be placed before the verbal phrase. For example:

Wǒ xiǎng *tóng nǐde mèimei* shāngliang yī jiàn shì.
Lit. I want with your younger sister discuss one matter.
I'd like to discuss something *with your younger sister.*

Nǐ xiǎng *tóng wǒ* qù yóuyǒng ma?
Lit. You want with me go swim [question word]?
Would you like to go swimming *with me*?

Note that **tóng** and **hé** (and/with) are interchangeable.

17 Qǐng tīng hǎo

Literally, this phrase means 'Please listen well'. It is like a sort of warning before you pass on a piece of important information on the telephone. It is similar in meaning to the English phrase 'Here it is' or 'Ready?' For example:

A: **Qǐng gàosu wǒ Xiǎo Lǐ de diànhuà hàomǎ?**
Please tell me Xiao Li's telephone number?
B: ***Qǐng tīng hǎo.* Bā-sì-líng-wǔ-liù-yāo.**
Here it is: eight-four-zero-five-six-one.

18 *Use of the number* yāo

Yāo is a substitute for **yī** (one). **Yāo** is used when the number 'one' occurs in telephone numbers, room numbers, bus and train numbers, etc. The reason is that the pronunciation of **yī** is likely to be mixed up with **qī** (seven) when a series of numbers is uttered. For example, **yāo** is used in the following:

***yāo*-líng-qī fángjiān**
room *1*07

***yāo-yāo*-sān lù diànchē**
tram no. *11*3

Wǒ jiā de diànhuà hàomǎ shì qī-qī-líng-wǔ-bà-*yāo*.
My home telephone number is 77058*1*.

Exercises

Exercise 6

Decide which **de** (if any) can be omitted in the following sentences. Rewrite the sentence if a **de** can be omitted:

(a) Wǒde jiějie shì dǎoyóu.
(b) Wǒménde jīnglǐ de bàngōngshì zài èr céng.
(c) Wǒde diànhuà huài le.
(d) Tāde fùmǔde jiā hěn piàoliang.
(e) Wáng Píng shì cóng Běijīng lái de lǎoshī.

Exercise 7

Fill in the blanks using the prepositions **tóng** or **gěi**:

(a) Tā méi _____ tāde nǚ péngyou mái lǐwù.
(b) Qǐng ______ wǒ jièshào yīxià nǐde tàitai.
(c) Wǒ méi yǒu kòng _____ nǐ qù yóuyǒng.
(d) Qǐng yīdìng _____ wǒ dǎ diànhuà.
(e) Xiǎo Lǐ xiǎng ____ Lǐ jīnglǐ shāngliang yī jiàn shì.

Exercise 8

Rewrite the following sentences using **wán**. Then translate the rewritten sentences into English:

(a) Nǐ chī wǎnfàn le ma?
(b) Tā yòng diànhuà le.
(c) Tā diǎn cài le.
(d) Xiǎo Lǐ xiū diàndēng le.

Exercise 9

Translate the following sentences into Chinese:

(a) It is very expensive to make phone calls in England.
(b) What is your telephone number?
(c) Your father telephoned you last night.
(d) Is there a telephone at your home?

Exercise 10

Re-arrange the words in each group below so that they make meaningful sentences and then translate them into English:

(a) gěi lǎobǎn, wàng le, David, dǎ diànhuà
(b) diànhuà, kěyi, wǒ, hàomǎ, nǐde, nǐ, gàosu, ma [question word]
(c) tā, bàngōngshì, jīntiān, zài, bù

Characters

Exercise 11

Fill in the blank with the right character, and then translate the sentence into English:

(a) 昨天我去______朋友了。

i) 着 ii) 看 iii) 春

(b) 我______北京住了十年。

i) 在 ii) 左 iii) 存

(c) 我弟弟_______说日文。

i) 舍 ii) 会 iii) 去

Exercise 12

Read the following dialogue in characters and then answer the questions in English:

A: 喂，请问李老师在家吗？我是他的学生张文。
B: 对不起，他不在家。他去银行了。
A: 他什么时候回来？
B: 六点左右。

A: 那，我六点后再打电话。
B: 好的。再见。

Question 1: Who is phoning whom?
Question 2: Where is Mr. (Teacher) Li?
Question 3: What time will he be back?

Reading/listening comprehension

Read the conversation below, and then answer the questions in Chinese. If you have the recording, listen to the conversation first, and then answer the questions in Chinese.

The following telephone conversation is between two Chinese speakers:

A: Qǐng wèn, Wáng Yǔ zài ma?
B: Duìbùqǐ, tā bù zài. Qǐng wèn, nín shì nǎ yī wèi?
A: Wǒ shì Wáng Yǔ de māma.
B: Nín hǎo. Wǒ shì Xiǎo Liú.
A: Nǐ hǎo, Xiǎo Liú. Wáng Yǔ jīntiān shàng bān ma?
B: Shàng bān. Tā qù chī wǔfàn le. Yī diǎn bàn zuǒyòu huílai.
A: Qǐng nǐ gàosu tā, wǒ zuò shíliù cì chē míngtiān wǎnshang liù diǎn shí fēn dào Shànghǎi. Tīng qīng le ma?
B: Tīng qīng le. Nín xūyào tā qù huǒchē zhàn jiē nín ma?
A: Tài xūyào le.
B: Wǒ yīdìng gàosu tā.
A: Duō xiè.

Questions

A Wáng Yǔ zài bàngōngshì ma?
B Shéi gěi Wáng Yǔ dǎ diànhuà le?
C Wáng Yǔ de māma shénme shíhou dào Shànghǎi?
D Wáng Yǔ de māma chéng jǐ cì lièchē dào Shànghǎi?
E Wáng Yǔ de māma xiǎng yào tāde érzi qù jiē tā ma?

14 Shèjiāo 社交

Socializing

By the end of this lesson, you will be able to:

- express the number of times you have done certain things
- describe a past event in a more sophisticated manner
- differentiate between the verbs **lái/qù** and the directional words **lai/qu**
- ask a question requiring a yes or no answer and indicate it is your guess by using **le**
- use **le** to indicate that a new situation has arisen and is still happening
- negate sentences with the adverb **yě**
- recognize some city names and write more characters

Dialogue 1

Xiàyǔ le 下雨了 It's raining

Patrick is American and his wife, Meifang, is Taiwan Chinese. They are currently visiting Meifang's family in Taibei. Today, they have been invited to a barbecue party. At the moment, Patrick is chatting with a Chinese woman called Yulan

YÙLÁN: Zhè shì nǐ dì yī cì lái Táiwān ma?

PATRICK: Bù shì. Wǒ jīhū měi nián dōu lái Táiwān. Qù nián, wǒ lái le liǎng cì.

YÙLÁN: Zhēn de? Wèishénme?

PATRICK: Dì yī cì, wǒmen lái cānjiā wǒ tàitai de mèimei de hūnlǐ. Dì èr cì, lái guò chūnjié.

YÙLÁN:	Zhème shuō, nǐ tàitai shì Táiwānrén le?
PATRICK:	Shì'a.
YÙLÁN:	Nǐmen shì zěnme rènshi de?
PATRICK:	Shuō lái huà cháng. Shí nián qián, tā qù Měiguó shàng dàxué. Wǒmen shì tóngxué. Yǒu yī tiān . . .
YÙLÁN:	Zhēn làngmàn. Āiyō! Xiàyǔ le. Zánmen jìn qu tán ba.

YULAN:	这是你第一次来台湾吗？
PATRICK:	不是。我几乎每年都来台湾。去年，我来了两次。
YULAN:	真的？为什么？
PATRICK:	第一次，我们来参加我太太的妹妹的婚礼。第二次，来过春节。
YULAN:	这么说，你太太是台湾人了？
PATRICK:	是阿。
YULAN:	你们是怎么认识的？
PATRICK:	说来话长。十年前，她去美国上大学。我们是同学。有一天…
YULAN:	真浪漫。哎哟！下雨了。咱们进去谈吧。

Vocabulary

dì yī cì	第一次	the first time/for the first time
jīhū	几乎	almost
měi	每	every
qù nián	去年	last year
cānjiā	参加	to attend/to take part
hūnlǐ	婚礼	wedding
guò	过	to celebrate/to spend
chūnjié	春节	Chinese New Year [*lit.* 'spring festival']
shuō lái huà cháng	说来话长	it's a long story [*lit.* 'speak talk long']
qián	前	ago/before
tóngxué	同学	classmate
yǒu yì tiān . . .	有一天…	one day . . . [*lit.* 'have one day']
làngmàn	浪漫	to be romantic/romantic
āiyō!	哎哟	whoops!
xiàyǔ	下雨	to rain/raining
jìn qu	进去	to go in/to go into
tán	谈	to talk/to chat

Notes to Dialogue 1

1 *Use of* dì . . . cì

Simply add a number between **dì** and **cì** to form expressions such as **dì yī cì** (the first time/for the first time), **dì èr cì** (the second time/for the second time), etc. This phrase is always placed before the verb it modifies or at the beginning of the sentence. For example:

Zhè shì wǒ *dì èr cì* qù Měiguó.
(qù = verb)
Lit. This is I second time go to America.
It will be *the second time* that I go to America.

***Dì yī cì,* wǒ bù zhīdao wǒ yīnggāi gàn shénme.**
Lit. The first time, I not know I should do what.
The first time, I didn't know what I should do.

2 *Use of* cì

If you want to say 'once', 'twice', 'three times', etc., add **cì** to the numeral. Thus we have **yī cì, liǎng cì, sān cì**, etc. These phrases must be placed after the verb. For example:

Měi ge xīngqī, wǒ qí yī cì zìxíngchē.
(qí = verb; zìxíngchē = object)
I ride my bike *once* every week.

If these phrases are used in the past tense, i.e. when **le** or **guo** is used, they can be placed either after **le** or **guo** or at the end of the sentence. For example:

David qù *guo sān cì* Zhōngguó.
David qù *guo* Zhōngguó *sān cì*.
} David has been to China *three times*.

In certain fixed verbal phrases such as **dǎ diànhuà**, you must put **yī cǐ** or **liǎng cǐ** after the verb or the particle **le**. For example:

Zuótiān wǒ gěi wǒ māma dǎ *le liǎng cì* diànhuà.
I phoned my mother *twice* yesterday.

If you want to turn the above sentence into a question, use the question word **jǐ**:

Zuótiān nǐ gěi nǐ māma dǎ le *jǐ* cì diànhuà?
How many times did you phone your mum yesterday?

3 Use of qù *in* qù nián

Literally, **qù nián** means 'gone year'. **Qù nián** is a fixed expression for 'last year'. You can not use **qù** with **yuè** (month) or **xīngqī** (week). When **qù** is used before a noun, it means 'to have gone' or 'to have passed'.

4 More on verbs

As prepositions (e.g. 'at', 'in', 'on') are not extensively used in Chinese, one of the ways to articulate an idea expressed in English with a preposition is by using verbs. For example:

Wǒ xiǎng mǎi yī zhāng *qù* Běijīng de huǒchē piào.
Lit. I want buy one go Beijing train ticket.
I'd like to buy a train ticket *to* Beijing.

Dì èr cì, wǒmen *lài guò* chūnjié.
Lit. The second time, we come spend Spring Festival.
The second time, we came *for* the Spring Festival.

5 le *indicating a guess*

If you want to ask a question requiring a yes or no answer and at the same time indicate that it is your guess, put **le** at the end of a sentence instead of **ma** and use the rising tone. Phrases such as **nàme** (so / in that case), **zhème shuō** (in that case), etc. are often used in this case. For example:

Nàme, nǐ bù xiǎng qù *le*? (↗)
So, you don't wish to go?

Zhème shuō, nǐ jiù shì Wáng jīnglǐ *le*? (↗)
In that case, you must be Mr Wang the manager?

6 Use of měi

When **měi** (every) is used before a noun which requires a measure word, the measure word must be used after **měi** and before the noun. For example:

měi ge (measure word)	rén	*every* person/everyone
měi jiān (measure word)	fángjiān	*every* room
měi ge (measure word)	xīngqī	*every* week

As measure words are not used before **tiān** (day), **nián** (year), **jiā** (family), **fēnzhōng** (minute), etc., you can simply put **měi** before them on its own. For example:

***měi* tiān** *every* day **_měi_ nián** *every* year

If you want to say 'every morning/evening', in Chinese you must say 'every day morning/evening'. For example:

***měi tiān* zǎoshang** *every* morning ***měi tiān* wǎnshang** *every* evening

7 *More on the emphatic word* dōu

In Lesson 7, we learnt the use of **dōu** with **suóyǒude** (all). **Dōu** is also frequently used with **měi** (every). Simply put **dōu** before the verb but after the phrase with **měi**. For example:

Wǒ *měi* ge yuè *dōu* húi jiā kàn wǒ fùmǔ.
Every month, I go home to see my parents.

Tā *měi* fēnzhōng *dōu* zài xiǎng shàng dàxué.
He is thinking about going to university *every* minute.

Note that **zài** in the above sentence indicates the continuous state of the verb **xiǎng** (to think).

8 *More on the verb* lái

You must use **lái** (to come) if you are currently in the place about which you are speaking. For example:

(The speaker is currently at her home:)
Xiǎo Lǐ *lái* guo wǒ jiā sān cì.
Xiao Li *has been* to my home three times.

(The speaker is currently in Taiwan:)
Wǒ *lái* guo liǎng cì Táiwān.
I've been here to Taiwan twice.

If you are in one place and talk about some other place you have been to, use the verb **qù**:

> **Wǒ *qù* guo sān cì Shànghǎi.**
> *I've been* to Shanghai three times.

9 More on the omission of de

The sentence sounds awkward if there are more than two occurrences of **de** – try to omit those which can be omitted. For example, the **de** in **wǒde** can be omitted from **wǒ*de* tàitai *de* mèimei *de* hūnlǐ**. So we have **wǒ tàitai de mèimei de hūnlǐ** (my wife's younger sister's wedding).

10 Use of qián

The word **qián** (ago/before) is always placed after a time expression, a verbal clause or a sentence. For example:

> **Tā shì liǎng nián *qián* lái Yīngguó de.**
> duration of time
> It was two years *ago* that he came to Britain.
>
> **Shàng dàxué *qián*, Liú Xiǎohóng shì dǎoyóu.**
> verbal clause
> *Before* going to university, Liu Xiaohong was a tourist guide.
>
> **Wǒ lái Yīngguó *qián*, méi chī guo xī cān.**
> sentence
> I hadn't had western food *before* I came to Britain.
>
> **Qù Běijīng Dàxué *qián*, xiān chácha dìtú.**
> verbal clause
> Check the map *before* going to Beijing University.

Note that in the third sentence above, since **wǒ**, the subject, appears in the first part of the sentence, it must not be repeated in the second part of the sentence.

11 le *used to indicate a change of state*

When **le** is used in sentences that describe a present event, it indicates that a new situation has appeared. It also implies that something is happening gradually which was not the case previously. It is usually put after a verb–adjective or at the end of a sentence. It can be translated by the 'to be + doing' pattern. For example:

Wŏ lăo ***le.***	I'm getting old.	(i.e. *I was not old before*)
Xiàyŭ ***le.***	It's raining.	(i.e. *previously it was not*)

12 jìn qu ***versus*** jìn lai

Literally, **jìn qu** means 'enter go' and **jìn lai** means 'enter come'. If you are outside a house and wanting to go in, use **jìn qu** (to go in/to go into). If you are inside a house and asking someone else to come in, use **jìn lai** (to come in/to come inside). Here again, **qú** and **lái** are directional words, as we saw in Note 16 of Lesson 7, and they usually become toneless. For example:

Xiàyŭ le. Zánmen ***jìn qu*** **tán, hăo ma?**
It's raining. Shall we *go inside* to talk?
Wàimian hĕn lĕng. Nĭmen wèishénme bù ***jìn lai*****?**
It's cold outside. Why don't you *come in*?

You can negate **jìn qu** or **jìn lai** with **bù**. When **bù** is placed before **jìn qu** or **jìn lai**, it means 'do not go in' or 'do not come in'. When **bù** is placed in between **jìn** and **qù** or **lái**, it means 'cannot go in' or 'cannot come in', in which case **qù** and **lái** keep their tones as **bu** becomes a neutral tone in actual speech. For example:

Xiăo Lĭ jìn ***bu*** **qù tāde bàngōngshì.**
Xiao Li *cannot go into* his office.

Wŏ bù zhīdao tā wèishénme jìn ***bu*** **lái.**
I don't know why she cannot come in.

Exercises

Exercise 1

Insert **le** in each sentence below in an appropriate position. Then translate them into English:

(a) Zuótiān wŏ bàba gĕi wŏ dă diànhuà.
(b) Nĭ kàn. Xiàxuĕ.
(c) Rúguŏ tā míngtiān hái bù dào, wŏ jiù zŏu.
(d) Sān tiān qián, tā chí dào bàn ge xiăoshí.

(e) Wǒ bù xiǎng qù dòngwùyuán. Wǒ lèi.
(f) Zhème shuō, nǐ shì Fēixiá?

Exercise 2

Fill in the blanks below with **dì èr cì** or **liǎng cì**:

(a) Zhè shì Richard ______ dào Táiwān.
(b) Wǒ chī guo ______ Běijīng kǎo yā.
(c) Wǒ ______ wàng le dài yàoshi.
(d) Zhè ge xīngqī, zánmen lǎobǎn de mìshū chí dào le ______.
(e) Dì yī cì, shì lái Běijīng lǚyóu, ______, shì lái gōngzuò.

Exercise 3

Fill in the blanks with **lái** or **qù** either as the verb or the directional word:

(a) Míngtiān, wǒ dài nǐ ______ guàng shāngdiàn.
(b) Zhèr hěn lěng. Zánmen jìn ______ tán, hǎo ma?
(c) (*On the phone*) Nǐ kěyi ràng Xiǎo Lǐ dài nǐ ______ wǒ jiā.
(d) Zāogāo, wǒ méi dài yàoshi. Jìn bù ______ wǒde bàngōngshì.
(e) (*Feixia knocks at Lao Wang's door. Lao Wang opens the door:*)

Fēixiá: Wǒ yǒu yī jiàn shì xiǎng tóng nǐ tántan. Nǐ yǒu kòng ma?
Lǎo Wáng: Yǒu kòng. Qǐng jìn ______ tán.

Exercise 4

Translate the following into Chinese:

(a) I go to work at eight o'clock every morning.
(b) Everybody likes him.
(c) I got to know her two years ago.
(d) She went to Hong Kong twice last year.
(e) I telephone my parents every two weeks.
(f) She is going to her parents' for the Chinese New Year.

Dialogue 2
Nǐ zuì xǐhuan nǎ ge dìfang?
你最喜欢哪个地方? Which place do you like most?

Graham has just come back from a tour in China. He is in Boston today to meet his Chinese friend Chen Ailin. At the moment, he is knocking at Ailin's door

AìLÍN: Nǐ hǎo, Graham. Zhēn gāoxìng jiàndào nǐ. Kuài jìn lai. Zuò, zuò.
GRAHAM: Hǎo de. Nǐ hǎo ma, Aìlín?
AìLÍN: Bù cuò. Xièxie. Nǐ xiǎng hē diǎnr shénme?
GRAHAM: Zhōngguó chá, xièxie.
AìLÍN: (*whilst making the tea*) Shuōqǐ Zhōngguó, nǐde Zhōngguó zhī xíng zěnme yàng?
GRAHAM: Hěn chénggōng.
AìLÍN: Nǐ qù le nǎ jǐ ge chéngshì?
GRAHAM: Běijīng, Shànghǎi, Xī'ān, Guìlín hé Guǎngzhōu.
AìLÍN: Nǐ zuì xǐhuan nǎ ge dìfang?
GRAHAM: Zhè ge wèntí hěn nán huídá. Wǒ hěn xǐhuān Guìlín. Nàlǐ fēngjǐng hěn měi. Dāngdì rén yě hěn yǒuhǎo. Tóng tāmen tánhuà hěn yǒu yìsi.
AìLÍN: Wǒ méi qù guo Guìlín. Xià cì yīdìng qù. Nǐ juéde Guǎngzhōu zěnme yàng?
GRAHAM: Wǒ bù tài xǐhuan Guǎngzhōu. Rén tài duō, yě tài rè.
AìLÍN: Wǒ yě bù xǐhuan Guǎngzhōu. Tīngshuō Chángchéng hěn xióngwěi. Shì ma?
GRAHAM: Shì de. Shífēn zhuàngguān. Wǒ pāi le xǔduō zhàopiān . . .

AILIN: 你好, Graham 。真高兴见到你。快进来。坐,坐。
GRAHAM: 好的。你好吗,爱琳?
AILIN: 不错。谢谢。你想喝点儿什么?
GRAHAM: 中国茶(...) 谢谢。
AILIN: (...)说起中国,你的中国之行怎么样?
GRAHAM: 很成功。
AILIN: 你去了哪几个城市?
GRAHAM: 北京,上海,西安,桂林和广州。
AILIN: 你最喜欢哪个地方?
GRAHAM: 这个问题很难回答。我很喜欢桂林。那里风景很美。当地人也很友好。同他们谈话很有意思。
AILIN: 我没去过桂林。下次一定去。你觉得广州怎么样?

GRAHAM:	我不太喜欢广州。人太多，也太热。
AILIN:	我也不喜欢广州。听说长城很雄伟。是吗？
GRAHAM:	是的。十分壮观。我拍了许多照片…

Vocabulary

diǎnr	点儿	a little/some
chá	茶	tea
shuōqǐ	说起	talking about/to talk about
zhī xíng	之行	the trip to . . . [*lit.* 'of trip']
chénggōng	成功	to be successful/success
chéngshì	城市	city
huídá	回答	to answer
fēngjǐng	风景	scenery
měi	美	to be beautiful/beautiful
dāngdì	当地	local
tánhuà	谈话	to talk
yǒuhǎo	友好	to be friendly/friendly ['**yǒu**', third tone in isolation]
xià cì	下次	next time
Chángchéng	长城	the Great Wall [*lit.* 'long city wall']
xióngwěi	雄伟	to be grandiose
shífēn	十分	extremely
zhuàngguān	壮观	to be magnificent
pāi	拍	to take/to shoot
zhàopiān	照片	photograph

Notes to Dialogue 2

13 Lack of qǐng *in many expressions*

In Chinese, the word **qǐng** (please), as has been mentioned before, is seldom used among friends and on informal occasions. The omission of **qǐng** does not suggest any lack of politeness or warmth in expressions such as **Kuài jìn lai**, **Zuò**, etc. These expressions are often repeated to make the guest feel that he/she is very welcome. For example:

(At the dinner table, the hostess says:)
***Chī, chī.* Bié kèqi.**
Lit. Eat, eat. Don't be polite.
Help yourself. Don't be polite.

(Inviting your guest to come in:)
Jìn lai, jìn lai.
Lit. Come in, come in.
Come in, please.

(Inviting your guest to some tea:)
Hē chá, hē chá.
Lit. Drink tea, drink tea.
Do have some tea.

14 Use of zuò

In English, phrases such as *to call in*, *to come around*, *to go to see*, etc. are used to talk about informal visits. In Chinese, the literal translation of similar expressions is 'to go someone's home sit sit' or 'sit for a while'. For example:

Wǒ kěyǐ dào nǐ jiā *zuòzuo* ma?
Could I *come around* to see you?

Zuówǎn, Guāngmèn lái *zuò* le yīhuìr.
Guangmen *called in* for a while last night.

15 Use of retroflex ending r

The sound **r**, pronounced with the tongue rolled backward a bit, is often added to phrases such as **yīdiǎn**, **yǒu yīdiǎn**, **yīhuì** (a while), etc. In such cases, **yī** is usually omitted. For example:

Nǐ xiǎng hē diǎn*r* shénme?	What would you like to drink?
Wǒ yǒu diǎn*r* è.	I'm a bit hungry.
Děng huì*r*.	Wait for a second.

Note that when ***r*** is added to **diǎn**, the nasal **n** sound gets dropped off.

16 Use of . . . zhī xíng

Although this is very much a written expression, it is often used in colloquial speech to refer to a particular trip. Simply put the place name before **zhī xíng**. For example:

Tīngshuō nǐde Zhōngguó *zhī xíng* hěn chénggōng.
I've heard that your *trip to* China was very successful.

17 Use of nǎ jǐ . . .

Literally, **nǎ jǐ** + a measure word means 'which several'. It can be used to ask about either places or people when the questioner assumes that only a few places or people will be named in the reply. For example:

Nǐ qù guo Yīngguó *nǎ jǐ ge* chéngshì?
Which cities in Britain have you been to?

Nǐ zài *nǎ jǐ jiā* gōngsī gōngzuò guo?
For which companies have you worked?

18 More on the 'topic structure'

The topic or theme of a sentence always occurs at the beginning of that sentence. In English, for example, you can say *It is difficult to answer this question*; but in Chinese, you must say 'This question is difficult to answer' or 'Answering this question is difficult'. For example:

	Tāde Yīngwén	**hěn**	**nán**	**dǒng.**
	Topic			
Lit.	His English	very	be difficult	understand.

It's very difficult to understand *his English*.

	Zài Zhōngguó,	***mǎi huǒchē piào***	**hěn**	**nán.**
		Topic		
Lit.	In China,	buy train tickets	very	be difficult.

Getting train tickets in China is very difficult.

19 Nǐ juéde . . . zěnme yàng?

This question can be translated as 'What do you think of . . .?'. For example:

***Nǐ juéde* Zhāng Hóng *zěnme yàng*?**
What do you think of Zhang Hong?

***Nǐ juéde* Měiguó *zěnme yàng*?**
What do you think of America?

20 rén tài duō

The complete sentence should be ***Guǎngzhōu de* rén tài duō** (*lit.* 'Guangzhou's people too many'). The reason that **Guǎngzhōu de** is omitted is that it can be elicited from the context. Whenever you wish to say 'There are too many . . . in . . .', use the pattern something + **tài duō**. For example:

Běijīng de zìxíngchē *tài duō*.
There are too many bikes *in* Beijing.

A: **Táiwān zěnme yàng?**
How is/was Taiwan?

B: **Hěn yǒu yìsi. Dànshì, rén *tài duō*.**
Very interesting. But *too many* people.

21 Negative sentences with yě

In English, 'also' is used in positive sentences whilst *either* or *neither* are used in negative sentences; in Chinese, the adverb **yě** (also) is used in both sentence types. When the sentence with **yě** is negated, the negation word **bù**, **méi yǒu** or **méi** is placed after **yě**. Let us compare **yě** used in both positive and negative sentences:

Wǒmen *yě* xiǎng qù cānjiā Xīn Hǎi de hūnlǐ.
We would like to attend Xin Hai's wedding *too*.

Tā *yě bù* xǐhuan Zhōngguó fàn.
She doesn't like Chinese food *either*.

Lǎo Lǐ zuótiān méi lái. Xiǎo Wáng *yě méi* lái.
Lao Li didn't come yesterday and Xiao Wang didn't come *either*.

Exercises

Exercise 5

What do you say on the following occasions:

(a) A friend of yours knocks at your door and you invite him in.
(b) Your neighbour comes around for a chat, and you invite her to sit down.

(c) Your friends have come to see you. You ask them what they would like to drink.
(d) You tell your mother that you are going round to Lao Li's.
(e) You are hosting a dinner party, and you ask your guests to help themselves.

Exercise 6

You ask your Chinese friend what she thinks of:

(a) America
(b) summer in Hong Kong
(c) the Beijing Hotel
(d) the locals
(e) David's Chinese

Exercise 7

Negate the following sentences with **bù** or **méi yǒu**:

(a) Wǒ yě xǐhuan Zhōngguó fàn.
(b) Tā māma yě qù cānjiā Àilīn de hūnlǐ le.
(c) Tā yě zhīdao yóuyǒng chí jǐ diǎn kāimén.
(d) Xiǎo Zhāng yě chí dào le.

Exercise 8

Translate the following into Chinese:

(a) It is very interesting to talk to the locals.
(b) Which cities did you go to?
(c) How was your trip to Taiwan?
(d) There are too many people in Guangzhou. It's very noisy and very hot in the summer.

Characters

1 Learning to write hěnduō and dǒng

The adjective **hěnduō** (many/much)

The left part of **hěn** 彳 is called the 'double person radical'. This is the same **hěn** as in **hěn hǎo** (very good/well) and in **hěn xǐhuan** (to like . . . very much).

The verb **dǒng** (to understand)

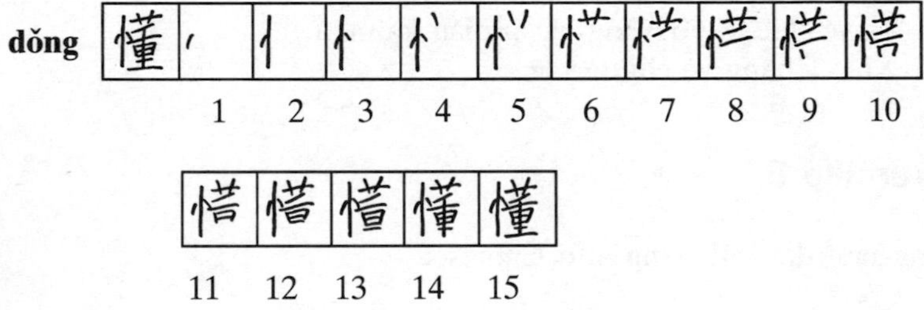

The left part of **dǒng** 忄 is called the 'vertical heart radical' which often occurs in characters that have to do with thoughts and emotions. The right part 董, which can be used as a surname, is also pronounced **dǒng** when used in isolation. Quite a number of characters have this feature, namely, the left part gives some indication of the meaning and the right part gives some indication of the pronunciation.

2 Recognizing the following city/place names

Reading/listening comprehension

1 Read the following passage (if you have the recording, listen first) and then answer the following questions in Chinese:

Shufang tells her friend about her wedding

Wǒ hé Dàyǒng shì dàxué tóngxué. Wǒmen shì qù nián jiéhūn de. Dàyǒng de fùmǔ zhù zài Táiwān. Tāmen cóng Táiwān lái cānjiā le wǒmen de hūnlǐ. Nà shì wǒ fùmǔ hé Dàyǒng de fùmǔ dì yī cì jiànmiàn. Tāmen xiāngchǔ de hěn hǎo. Wǒmen hái qǐng le hěnduō péngyou cānjiā wǒménde hūnlǐ. Hūnlǐ hòu, wǒ hé Dàyǒng qù Guìlín dù le liǎng ge xīngqī mìyuè.

Vocabulary

xiāngchǔ	to get along
dù	to spend
mìyuè	honeymoon [*lit.* 'honey month']

Questions

A Dàyǒng de fùmǔ zhù zài shénme dìfang?
B Dàyǒng de fùmǔ cānjiā Shūfāng hé Dàyǒng de hūnlǐ le ma?
C Shūfāng de fùmǔ hé Dàyǒng de fùmǔ shì dì èr cì jiànmiàn ma?
D Shūfāng hé Dàyǒng qù shénme dìfang dù mìyuè le? Qù le duō jiǔ?

2 Read the following phrases aloud and add the correct tone marks:

(a) **womende hunli**	our wedding
(b) **gaosu wo nide Zhongguo zhi xing**	to tell me about your China trip
(c) **qing le xuduo pengyou**	to have invited many friends

15 Hǎiwài láixìn
海外来信
Letter from abroad

By the end of this lesson, you will be able to:

- write a simple letter
- use the correct format to write names and addresses on an envelope
- express a continuous action in the past
- express more sophisticated sentences such as 'When I was in China, I . . .'
- recognize some place/country names and write a post-card in characters

Text
Wǒ bǎozhèng 我保证 I promise

Elena and Liu Xiaomei are very close friends. They met when Elena was studying Chinese at a university in Beijing. Although Elena is back in Italy, they write to each other very often. Below is a letter from Elena to Xiaomei.

TO: People's Republic of China

Yóubiān: 100081
Zhōngguó Běijīng Dōng Zhí Mén Wài Dàjiē 22 Hào 16 Dòng 1 Hào

Liú Xiǎoméi Shōu

Crosa Maccarina, Milan, Italy

TO: People's Republic of China
邮编：100081
中国北京东直门外大街22号16栋1号
刘晓梅 收

Qīn'àide Xiǎoméi:

Nǐ hǎo!

Nǐde láixìn shōu dào le. Wǒ zhēn gāoxìng nǐ xǐhuan nǐde xīn gōngzuò.

Wǒ yīqiè hái hǎo, jiù shì gōngzuò tài máng. Shàng ge xīngqī, wǒ yīzhí zài Lúndūn kāi huì. Huílai hòu, máng zhe xiě yī fèn bàogào. Měi tiān zǎoshàng liù diǎn bàn qǐchuáng, wǎnshang shí'èr diǎn cái shuìjiào. Wǒ bìxū zài xīngqīwǔ zhī qián xiě wán zhè fèn bàogào. Wǒ zhīdao wǒ hǎo jiǔ méi gěi nǐ xiě xìn le, qǐng bié shēngqì. Děng zhè ge zhōumò wǒ xiūxi de shíhou, yīdìng gěi nǐ xiě yī fēng cháng xìn. Wǒ bǎozhèng.

Hǎo yǒu,

Àilìnà

94. 1. 26

亲爱的晓梅:

你好!

你的来信收到了。我真高兴你喜欢你的新工作。

我一切还好，就是工作太忙。上个星期，我一直在伦敦开会。回来后，忙着写一份报告。每天早上六点半起床，晚上十二点才睡觉。我必须在星期五之前写完这份报告。我知道我好久没给你写信了，请别生气。等这个周末我休息的时候，一定给你写封长信。我保证。

好友，
爱丽娜

94, 1, 26

Vocabulary

qīn'àide	亲爱的	dear [*lit.* 'close loved one']
xìn	信	letter
láixìn	来信	letter [*lit.* 'come letter', see Note 3]
shōu dào	收到	to receive
xīn	新	new/to be new
yīqiè	一切	everything
jiù shì	就是	the only thing is . . ./but/except for
shàng ge	上个	last
yīzhí	一直	all the time
Lúndūn	伦敦	London
kāi huì	开会	to attend a meeting/ to attend a conference
hòu	后	after/in/. . . later
zhe	着	[grammar word, see Note 9]
xiě	写	to write
fèn	份	[measure word for documents]
bàogào	报告	report
qǐchuáng	起床	to get up
cái	才	[emphatic word, see Note 10]

shuìjiào	睡觉	to sleep/sleep
bìxū	必须	must
zài . . . zhī qián	在...之前	before . . ./by . . .
shēngqì	生气	to be angry/to be cross
. . . de shíhou	...的时候	when/while
zhōumò	周末	weekend
zhè ge zhōumò	这个周末	this weekend
xiūxi	休息	to rest/to take time off work
fēng	封	[measure word for letters]
cháng	长	long/to be long
bǎozhèng	保证	to promise
hǎo yǒu	好友	good friend [same **yǒu** as in **péngyou**]
yóubiān	邮编	postcode
Dōng Zhí Mén Wài	东直门外	[street name]
dàjiē	大街	avenue
dòng	栋	block
hào	号	number
shōu	收	to be received by . . ./to receive

Notes to text

1 Writing a letter

When writing a letter or postcard to a Chinese person, there is usually no need to write 'Dear' (**qīn'àide**) in front of the person's name. You simply use the form of address that is usually used (e.g. **Xiǎo Liú**, **Liú Xiǎoméi**, or **Xiǎoméi**.). The term **qīn'àide** (dear), you may be surprised to learn, is only reserved for close family and friends. A colon (:), instead of a comma, is used after the person's name. The greeting expression **Nǐ hǎo** is usually used to open a letter and appears in the second line. You can start the main part of the letter either on the same line after **Nǐ hǎo** if the space is a problem, or on the next line. The closing phrase usually takes up a separate line. The commonly used closing phrases are **Duō bǎozhòng** (Take care), **Zhù hǎo** (Best wishes), **Zhù shēntǐ jiànkāng** (Wishing you good health), **Hǎo yǒu** (Good friend), etc. After the closing phrase, you sign your name and then date the letter underneath your signature. Note that you do not need to put your address in a personal letter (as opposed to a business letter).

2 Writing an envelope

When writing a name and address on an envelope in Chinese, you first write the recipient's address in one line at the top of the envelope (use a second line if it is a long address); then write the recipient's name in the centre of the envelope and finally put the sender's address, which is put at the bottom of the envelope towards the right-hand corner. The word **shōu** is usually put after the recipient's name and it means 'to be received by . . .'. For example:

Recipient's address: XXXXXXXXXXXXXXXXXXXXXXX
XXXXXXX

Recipient's name: XXX Shōu

Sender's address:XXXXXXXXXXXX

In writing the address, the largest unit comes first. So you put the country first (if you write from abroad) followed by the city, then the street name (or name of an organization), and finally the flat number. Note that the recipient's postcode is placed before the address but the sender's postcode goes after the address. For example, if you write to Mr Wang Lisheng whose address is 26 Dongdan Ave., Beijing, postcode 816001 and your address is Flat 6, Block 10, Xi'an Foreign Languages College, postcode 716001, the envelope should look like this:

Yóubiān: 816001 Běijīng Dōngdān Dàjiē 26 Hào

Wáng Lìshēng Shōu

Xī'ān Wàiguóyǔ Xuéyuàn 10 Dòng 6 Hào
Yóubiān:716001

If you send a letter from abroad, all you need to do is to put 'To: People's Republic of China' in English or in the language that is spoken wherever you are at the top of the envelope (see the envelope in the Text).

3 *Difference between* xīn, láixìn *and* qùxīn

The word **xìn** means 'letter'. Literally, **láixìn** means 'come letter' and **qùxìn** means 'go letter'. **Láixìn** refers to the letter you have received; and **qùxìn** refers to the letter you have written to someone. The measure word for letters is **fēng**. For example:

Zhèr yǒu nǐde yī fēng *xìn*.
Lit. Here have your one letter.
Here is a *letter* for you.

Xièxie nǐde *láixìn*.
Thank you for your *letter*.

Wǒde *qùxīn* nǐ shōu dào le ma?
or **Nǐ shōu dào wǒde *qùxìn* le ma?**
Have you received my *letter*?

Whilst **láixìn** and **qùxìn** are very different, **xìn** can always replace **láixìn** or **qùxìn**.

4 Wǒ yíqiè hái hǎo

This is a very common expression used in writing personal letters to mean 'Everything is all right with me'. You can also turn it into a question. For example:

Nǐ yīqiè hái hǎo ma?
Is everything all right with you?

5 *Use of* jiù shì

When a general positive statement is followed by another sentence beginning with **jiù shì**, a mild criticism is expected because **jiù shì** in this context means 'the only thing is . . .', 'but' or 'except for/except that . . .'. For example:

Xiāng Gǎng hěn yǒu yìsi, *jiù shì* xiàtiān tài rè.
Hong Kong is very interesting. *The only thing is* that it's too hot in the summer.

Nà ge yóuyǒng chí hěn hǎo, ***jiù shì*** **yǒu diǎnr yuǎn.**
That swimming pool is very good *except that* it's a bit far away.

6 Different terms for 'last', 'next' and 'this'

You can use **shàng ge** (last), **xià ge** (next) and **zhè ge** (this) together with **xīngqī** (week) and **yuè** (month), but not with **tiān** (day) and **nián** (year). Below is a chart illustrating the differences:

Chinese	*English*	*Chinese*	*English*
zuó**tiān**	yesterday	***shàng ge*** **yuè**	last month
jīn**tiān**	today	***zhè ge*** **yuè**	this month
míng**tiān**	tomorrow	***xià ge*** **yuè**	next month
shàng ge **xīngqi**	last week	***qù*** **nián**	last year
zhè ge **xīngqī**	this week	***jīn*** **nián**	this year
xià ge **xīngqī**	next week	***míng*** **nián**	next year

7 Use of yīzhí

When you want to emphasize the continuation of an event, use **yīzhí** in front of **zài** to mean 'all the time'. For example:

Zuótiān wǎnshàng, wǒ ***yīzhí zài*** **xiě xìn.**
I was writing letters all night last night.

However, if you want to say 'He was attending a conference in Taiwan last month', you must say **Tā shàng ge yuè** ***yīzhí zài*** **Táiwān kāi huì**. Since **zài** is used in **zài Táiwān** to mean 'in Taiwan', the continuous indicator **zài** must not be used. Thus you cannot say **Tā shàng ge yuè yīzhí** ***zài*** **Táiwān** ***zài*** **kāi huì**.

8 Use of hòu

In English, *after* or *in* is placed before a phrase or a sentence (e.g. ***In*** *three days' time* . . ., ***After*** *he came back* . . .) and *later* is placed after a phrase or a sentence (e.g. *A week* ***later*** . . .). But in Chinese, **hòu** (after/in/. . . later) always occurs at the end of a phrase or a sentence. For example:

Cóng Bālí huílai ***hòu*****, wǒ shēntǐ bù tài hǎo.**
I haven't been very well *since* I came back from Paris.

Sān tiān *hòu*, wǒ gěi nǐ dǎ diànhuà.
I'll telephone you *in* three days' *time*.

Yī ge xīngqī *hòu*, Xiǎo Fāng jiàndào le tāde mèimei.
Xiao Fang met her younger sister a week *later*.

9 *Grammar word* zhe

Zhe is placed between the verb–adjective **máng** (to be busy) and a verb to mean 'to be busy doing something'. For example:

Wǒ máng *zhe* zhǎo gōngzuò. I'm busy looking for a job.
Tā máng *zhe* xué Zhōngwén. She is busy learning Chinese.

10 *Emphatic word* cái

Cái is an adverb used to indicate that something happens too late (e.g. 'start, end, etc. too late'). Sometimes, it can be broadly translated as 'only' or 'just', but other times, it can be translated as '. . . until . . .' For example:

Nǐ zěnme *cái* qǐchúang?
How come you *just* got up?
Wǒ māma měi tiān wǎnshang shí'èr diǎn *cái* shuìjiào.
Every night, my mother doesn't go to bed *until* 12 o'clock.
David zuótiān cái zǒu.
David *only* left yesterday.

The sentence **David zuótiān cái zǒu** implies that he planned to leave earlier. Another thing to notice is that the past particle **le** cannot be used with **cái** if the event described happened in the definite past.

11 *Use of* zài . . . zhī qián

The phrase **zài . . . zhī qián** means 'before . . .' or 'by . . .', which emphasizes that something must be done by a certain date/day. That certain date/day is always placed between **zài** and **zhī qián**. For example:

***Zài* nǐ qù Zhōngguó *zhī qián*, kěyi gěi wó dǎ ge diànhuà ma?**
Could you give me a ring *before* you go to China?

Tā bìxū *zài* xīngqīwǔ *zhī qián* xiě wán zhè běn shū.
She must finish writing this book *by* Friday.

12 Use of . . . de shíhou

The expression **. . . de shíhou** (when/while) is placed at the end of the first half of a phrase or sentence. It can be used to describe present, past or future events. For example:

> **Shàng dàxúe** ***de shíhou,*** **wǒ hěn xǐhuan yóuyǒng.**
> I liked swimming very much *when* I was at university.

> **Bù gāoxìng** ***de shíhou,*** **yǒuxiē rén xǐhuan guàng shāngdiàn.**
> Some people like to go shopping *when* they are unhappy.

When **. . . de shíhou** is used to describe a future event, the verb **děng** (to wait) is usually put at the very beginning of a phrase or sentence. For example:

> ***Děng*** **zhè ge zhōumò wǒ yǒu kòng** ***de shíhou,*** **yīdìng gěi nǐ xiě fēng cháng xìn.**
> I'll definitely write you a long letter *when* I have time this weekend.

Exercises

Exercise 1

Write a short letter to your family or friend.

Exercise 2

Write the following information on an envelope:

Recipient's name: Huang Weilei; recipient's address: Apt. 3, Block 46, 6 Chang An Avenue, Xi'an, postcode 710061, P.R. China. You are the sender and are currently in another country (make up your own address).

Exercise 3

Fill in the blanks with **xìn**, **láixìn** or **qùxìn**:

(a) (*Telling someone*) Zuótiān, wǒ shōu dào le sān fēng __________.
(b) (*Writing to someone*) Wǒ zhēn gāoxìng shōu dào le nǐde __________.

(c) (*Telling someone*) Wǒde nán péngyou bù xǐhuan xiě __________.

(d) (*Writing to someone*) Wǒde __________ nǐ shōu dào le ma?

Exercise 4

Match the words in the left column with those in the right column (there are several possible combinations):

(a) qù	1 tiān (*day*)
(b) shàng ge	2 nián (*year*)
(c) míng	3 xīngqī (*week*)
(d) xià ge	4 yuè (*month*)
(e) zuó	

Exercise 5

Translate the following sentences into Chinese:

(a) Your home is beautiful but it is not easy to find.
(b) I was at home writing letters all night last night.
(c) I like writing letters to good friends.
(d) Don't be cross.
(e) I went to the market after work.
(f) Our boss is busy making phone calls.
(g) I only received my parents' letter yesterday.
(h) I often cycled when I was in China.
(i) He will definitely return you that book by next Monday.

Characters

1 Learning to write yóubiān (postcode), jiē (avenue) and shōu (to be received by . . .)

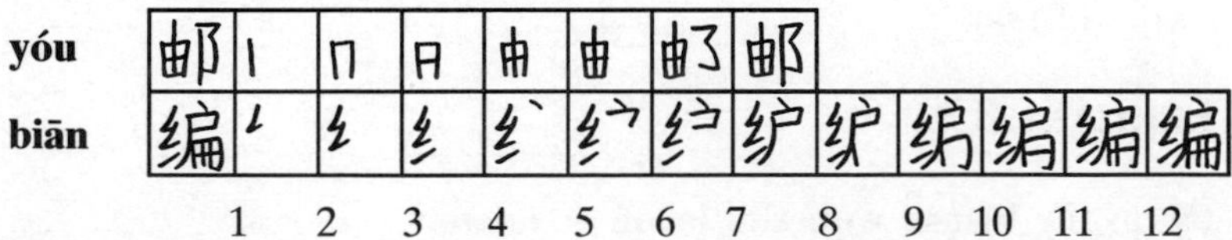

The character **yóu** has 阝, informally known as the 'ear radical' (possibly because it looks a bit like an ear). Note that the radical is on the right side. The left part of **yóu** 由 gives a clue to the pronunciation because it is pronounced **yóu** in isolation. The 'ear radical' sometimes appears on the left side. For example, the family name **Chen**, 陈 has the 'ear radical' on the left. The character **biān** has the 'silk radical' 纟 on the left and the right part 扁 is pronounced **biǎn** on its own.

jiē 街

1 2 3 4 5 6 7 8 9 10 11 12

This character consists of three parts and each part takes up approximately the same amount of space.

shōu

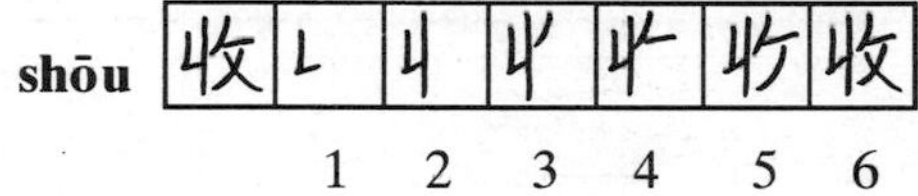

1 2 3 4 5 6

2 Recognizing some place/country names

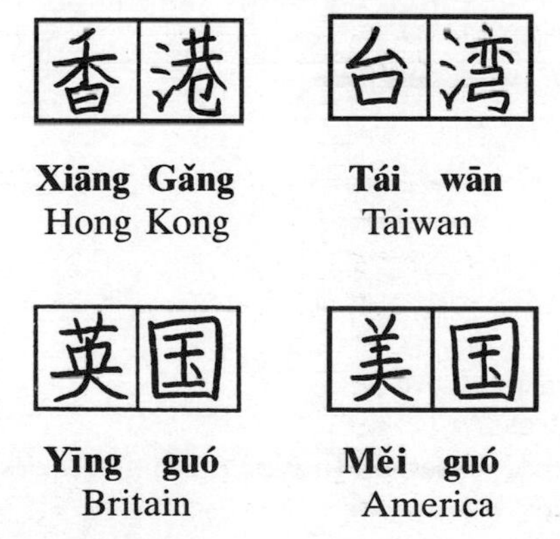

Xiāng Gǎng
Hong Kong

Tái wān
Taiwan

Yīng guó
Britain

Měi guó
America

Exercise 6

Write a postcard or short letter in characters. Ask your tutor or a Chinese friend to check it.

Reading comprehension

Read this postcard and then answer the questions in English:

Bóbīn:

Nǐ hǎo! Hǎo jiǔ méi yǒu shōu dào nǐde xìn le. Nǐ yīqiè hái hǎo ma? Wǒ xià ge yuè bā hào zuǒyòu yào qù Guǎngzhōu kāi huì. Rúguó nǐ dào shíhou yǒu kòng dehuà, wǒ hěn xiǎng jiànjian nǐ. Qǐng huí xìn gàosu wó nǐde diànhuà hàomǎ.

Zhù hǎo

Zhāng Xīn

94. 6. 18

Yóubiān: 510450
Guǎngzhōu Zhōngshān Dàxué
Yīngwén Xì 10 Hào Xìnxiāng

Lín Bóbīn

Běijīng Qián Mén 1 Hào
Yóubiān:100081

Vocabulary

dào shíhou	then/around that time
jiànjian	to meet
huí xìn	to reply [*lit.* 'return letter']
zhù hǎo	best wishes [*lit.* 'wish well']
xì	department
xìnxiāng	post box

Questions

A Who is the recipient of this postcard?
B What is the recipient's address?
C Where does the recipient work (based on the recipient's address)?
D Where does Zhang Xin live?
E Why is Zhang Xin going to Guangzhou?
F When is Zhang Xin going to Guangzhou?
G Does Zhang Xin know Bobin's telephone number?

Grammar summary

This is not an exhaustive summary of Chinese grammar. It is just a summary of the main grammatical concepts which have been introduced in this book.

The *pinyin* alphabet

Letter	*Example*	*Letter*	*Example*
a	bā	**n**	nǎ
b	bǐ	**o**	wǒ
c	cāi	**p**	píng
d	dì	**q**	qī
e	tè	**r**	rì
f	fā	**s**	sān
g	gē	**t**	tán
h	hē	**u**	tú
i	tī/sì/zhī	**ü**	lǜ
j	jǐ	**x**	xià
k	kè	**y**	yǒu
l	lèi	**z**	zǒu
m	mā		

Word order

It is easier to talk about the word order with the help of some grammatical terms. Let us first define the following terms:

Subject – the topic of a sentence. Nouns, noun phrases, verbal phrases can all function as the subject in Chinese.
Verb – a doing word.
Object – a noun or its equivalent acted upon by (a) a verb whose meaning is incomplete unless followed by something (e.g. in

'I play table-tennis', 'table-tennis' is the object of the verb 'play'); or (b) a preposition (e.g. in 'I'm not against him', 'him' is the object of the preposition 'against').
Prepositional phrase – a preposition followed by a noun or equivalent such as place names, etc. (e.g. 'in London').

Word order in Chinese is quite fixed. The common patterns are:

subject + verb + object

Wǒ mǎi dōngxi.	I buy things.

subject + time + verb + object

Wǒ *liù diǎn* qù mǎi dōngxi.	I'm going shopping *at six o'clock*.
Tā *qù nián* lái de Yīngguó.	She came to Britain *last year*.

subject + prepositional phrase + verb + object

Wǒ *zài Běijīng* jiàndào le tā.	I saw him *in Beijing*.

object + subject + verb (to emphasize the object)

***Xìn* wǒ xiě le.**	I did write *the letter*.

Topic structure

In English, the topic or theme of a sentence can be put at the end of the sentence by using the *It is . . . to . . .* pattern (e.g. in *It is very interesting to talk to him*, *to talk to him* is the topic.) In Chinese, since the 'It is . . . to . . .' pattern is not used, the topic always occurs at the beginning of a sentence:

***Nǐ jiā* hěn nán zhǎo.**	It is difficult to find your house.
***Qí zìxíngchē* hěn yǒu yìsi.**	It is very interesting to cycle.

Nouns

Nouns are the same regardless of number:

Wǒ yǒu yī ge *mèimei*.	I have one younger *sister*.
Wǒ yóu liǎng ge *mèimei*.	I have two younger *sisters*.

Articles

Articles such as *the*, *a* or *an* in English do not exist in Chinese. Whether something is specfic or general can be inferred from the context:

Tā hái méi huán gěi wǒ *shū*.	She still hasn't returned me *the book*.
Wǒ qù shūdiàn mǎi *yī běn shū*.	I'm going to the bookshop to buy *one book*.
Wǒ qù mǎi *shū*.	I'm going to buy *some books*.

Adjectives

Adjectives are always placed before nouns. **De** is usually inserted between the adjective and the noun (a) if the adjective is modified by an adverb; and (b) if a two-syllable adjective is used to modify a noun:

***hǎo* zhǔyi**	good idea
***hěn* hǎo *de* zhǔyi**	very good idea
xióngwěi *de* guǎngchǎng	the magnificent square

Verb–adjectives

In English, adjectives can be preceded by the verb *to be*; in Chinese, some adjectives can incorporate the verb 'to be' and they become verb–adjectives. For example, the word **lǎo** is an adjective when it means 'old', but it is a verb–adjective when it means 'to be old'. Thus, the verb **shì** (to be) is not used in this case. When these verb–adjectives are used, they are usually modified by adverbs such as **hěn** (very), **tǐng** (rather), etc. in front of them:

Wǒ hěn *máng*.	I *am* very *busy*.
Dāngdì rén hén *yǒuhǎo*.	The locals *are* very *friendly*.

Measure words

Measure words are a distinctive feature of the Chinese language. A measure word is usually used between (a) a numeral and a noun; and (b) a demonstrative pronoun (i.e. **zhè** (this) or **nà** (that)) and a noun. The most common measure word is **gè**:

Wǒ yǒu sān *ge* dìdi.	I have three younger brothers.
Zhè *ge* rén hěn qíguài.	This person is very strange.

Different measure words are used with different nouns. Below are some commonly used measure words:

Pinyin	*Character*	*Category*	*Nouns (e.g.)*
bǎ	把	objects with a handle	toothbrush, knife, umbrella, chair
bāo	包	parcel, packet	cigarettes, noodles
bēi	杯	cup, glass	tea, orange juice
běn	本	volume	book, dictionary
bù	部		film, encyclopedia
fèn	份		newspaper, report
fēng	封		letter
gè	个	people, things which do not fall into other categories; substitute measure word.	girl, man
jiā	家	organization	company, factory
jiān	间	space	room
jiàn	件	piece	jumper, luggage
jù	句	phrase	remarks, comments
kē	棵	plants, trees	tree, spring onion
kuài	块	square piece	soap, field
liàng	辆	things with wheels	bike, bus
píng	瓶	bottles, jars	beer, jam
qún	群	crowd	people, cattle
tái	台	machines	television, washing-machine
tào	套	set	flat, furniture
tiáo	条	long and winding	fish, river
tóu	头	big animals	pig, elephant
wèi	位	people (polite)	teacher, leader
zhāng	张	flat	paper, map, ticket, blanket
zhāng	章		chapter
zhī	只	small animals	chicken, cat
zuò	座	solid things, architecture	mountain, bridge

Currency words, unit words and nouns such as **tiān** (day), **nián** (year), etc. do not require measure words:

bā *yuán*	eight *yuan*	**sì *jīn***	two *kilos*
liǎng *tiān*	two *days*	**wǔ *nián***	five *years*

Pronouns

1 Personal pronouns

wǒ	I, me
nǐ	you (singular)
nín	you (polite form)
tā	he/she/, him/her
wǒ*men*	we, us
nǐ*men*	you (plural)
tā*men*	they, them

These personal pronouns can be used in both subject and object positions:

***Wǒ* xiǎng wǒde māma.**	*I* miss my mother.
Wǒde māma xiǎng *wǒ*.	My mother misses *me*.

Ta is seldom used to mean 'it' as a subject. It occasionally occurs in the object position:

Mōmo *tā*.	Touch *it*.

Most of the time, any reference to 'it' can be inferred from the context:

Wǒ xǐhuan Zhōngguó fàn. *Hěn hǎochī.*	I like Chinese food. *It's very tasty.*

Similarly, **tāmen** is rarely used to refer to things.

2 Possessive adjectives and possessive pronouns

Possessive adjective and possessive pronoun	*Possessive adjective (in front of nouns)*	*Possessive pronoun (at the end of the sentence)*
wǒ*de*	my	mine
nǐ*de*	your	yours
tā*de*	his/her	his/hers

wǒmén*de*	our	ours
nǐmén*de*	your	yours
tāmén*de*	their	theirs

To form possessive adjectives and possessive pronouns, simply add **de** to personal pronouns **wǒ**, **nǐ**, **tā**, **wǒmen**, **nǐmen**, **tāmen**:

***Wǒde* shū diū le.**	*My* book is missing.
Zhè běn shū shì *wǒde*.	This book is *mine*.

3 Demonstrative pronouns

zhè	this
nà	that
zhèxiē	these
nàxiē	those

Zhè or **nà** never occurs in object positions. **Zhè** is used in many cases where 'it' is used in English:

***Zhè* hěn yǒu yìsi.**	*It* is very interesting.

When the measure word **ge** is added to **zhè** and **nà**, we have **zhè ge** and **nà ge**. These then are demonstrative adjectives:

***Nà ge* rén hěn gāo.**	*That person* is very tall.
***Zhè liàng* zìxíngchē huài le.**	*This bike* is broken.

Numbers

1 Cardinal numbers

0–99:

0–9		*10–19*		*20–29*	
líng	zero	**shí**	ten	**èrshí**	twenty
yī	one	**shíyī**	eleven	**èrshíyī**	twenty-one
èr (liǎng)	two	**shí'èr**	twelve	**èrshí'èr**	twenty-two
sān	three	**shísān**	thirteen	**èrshísān**	twenty-three
sì	four	**shísì**	fourteen	**èrshísì**	twenty-four
wǔ	five	**shíwǔ**	fifteen	**èrshíwǔ**	twenty-five
liù	six	**shíliù**	sixteen	**èrshíliù**	twenty-six
qī	seven	**shíqī**	seventeen	**èrshíqī**	twenty-seven
bā	eight	**shíbā**	eighteen	**èrshíbā**	twenty-eight
jiǔ	nine	**shíjiǔ**	nineteen	**èrshíjiǔ**	twenty-nine

The numbers 30, 40, etc. up to 90 are formed by adding **shí** (ten) to **sān** (three), **sì** (four), etc. Thus we have **sānshí** (thirty), **sìshí** (forty), etc. to **jiǔshí** (ninety). The numbers 31–9, 41–9, etc., use the same principle as 21–9 above. An apostrophe (') is used to mark the break between two syllables whenever there is ambiguity in pronunciation. Thus we have ***shí'èr*** (twelve) instead of ***shíèr***.

100–10,000
The same pattern continues with **bǎi** (hundred), **qiān** (thousand) and **wàn** (ten thousand):

yībǎi èrshí	one hundred and twenty
wǔqiān líng liùshí	five thousand and sixty

2 Ordinal numbers

Simply add **dì** to cardinal numbers:

dì **yī**	first
dì **shíyī**	eleventh
dì **èrshí'èr**	twenty-second

Verbs

Chinese verbs remain the same regardless of first-, second-, or third-person pronouns, singular or plural:

wǒ ***shì***	I *am*
tā ***shì***	he/she *is*
tāmen ***shì***	they *are*

Verbs do not indicate tenses. Let us take the verb **qù** (to go) for example:

Wǒ míngtiān ***qù*** **Zhōngguó.**	I *am going* to China tomorrow.
Zuótiān, wǒ méi ***qù*** **kàn péngyou.**	Yesterday, I *didn't go* to see my friends.
Tā ***qù*** **túshūguǎn le.**	He *has gone* to the library./ He *went* to the library.

The future and the past are indicated by the time phrases such as **míngtiān** (tomorrow), and **zuótiān** (yesterday) and some grammar words such as **le** (see Grammar Words below).

Grammar words (particles)

1 **le** indicates that:

(a) an action happened in the past:

Wǒ zuótiān mǎi *le* yī liàng zìxíngchē. I bought a bike yesterday.

(b) an action has happened and may still be happening:

Tā qù túshūguǎn *le*. He has gone to the library. (He has not come back yet.)

(c) there is a change of state (when used at the end of a sentence):

Xiàyǔ *le*. It's raining. (It wasn't raining before.)
Wǒ lèi *le*. I'm getting tired. (I wasn't tired before.)

2 **guo**, although also indicating a past event, puts emphasis on the aspect that something has been experienced:

Wǒ chī *guo* Zhōngguó fàn. I have had Chinese food.
Tā qù *guo* Měiguó liǎng cì. He has been to America twice.

3 **zài** indicates the continuous state of a verb. It is placed before the verb:

Wǒ *zài* chī wǎnfàn. I am having supper.

Negation words

1 **bù** is used with most verbs and verb–adjectives:

Wǒ *bù* xǐhuan zhè ge chéngshì. I *don't* like this city.
Tā *bù* máng. He is *not* busy.

2 **méi** is used to negate the verb **yǒu** (to have):

Wǒ méi yǒu gēge. I *do not* have brothers.

3 **méi yǒu** or **méi** is used to indicate that:

(a) something has not happened:

Wǒ *méi yǒu* (or *méi*) chī guo Zhōngguó fàn.
I haven't had Chinese food.

(b) something did not happen:

Tā zuótiān *méi yǒu* (or *méi*) lái shàng bān.
She did not come to work yesterday.

Questions

To form questions that require a 'yes' or 'no' answer, simply add the particle **ma** to the end of a sentence:

Nǐ shì Yīngguó rén.	→	**Nǐ shì Yīngguó rén *ma*?**
You are British.		Are you British?

Another way of forming a yes/no question is to repeat the verb with the negation word **bù** or **méi** as appropriate inserted in between:

Nǐ *chī bù chī* dàsuàn?	Do you eat garlic?
Nǐ *yǒu méi yǒu* jiějie?	Do you have elder sisters?

When question words such as **shénme** (what), **shénme shíhou** (when), **nǎr** (where), etc. are used to ask questions, the sentence order is not changed. The question word occupies the position in the sentence where the information required should appear in the reply:

A: **Nǐ jiào *shénme*?**
What are you called?

B: **Wǒ jiào *Lǐ Xīng*.**
I am called *Li Xing*.

A: **Nǐ *shénme shíhou* qù Zhōngguó.**
When are you going to China?

B: **Wǒ *míngtiān* qù Zhōngguó.**
I'm going to China *tomorrow*.

Directional words

In English, words such as *in* and *out* are used to indicate the direction of a verb, for example, *Please come **in*** and *I'd like to go **out***. In Chinese, directional words such as **lái** (*lit.* 'come'), **qù** (*lit.* 'go'), etc. are used after a verb in these cases:

Qǐng jìn *lai*.
Please *come in*.

Wǒ xiǎng chū *qu* yīhuìr.
I'd like to *go out* for a while.

Adverbs

1 When adverbs describe adjectives, they are placed before adjectives:

Tā ***fēicháng*** **piàoliang.** She is extremely good-looking.

2 When adverbs describe the manner of an action:

(a) they are placed before the verb in an imperative sentence (i.e. order, suggestion):

Kuài **zǒu. Wǒmen yào chí dào le.**
Lit. Quickly walk. We will late arrive.
Hurry up. We'll be late.

(b) they are placed after the verb and the linking word **de** if the degree or result of an action is indicated:

Wǒ zuótiān wǎnshang shuì de ***hǎo.*** I slept well last night.

Many adverbs usually have the same form as adjectives.

Prepositions

Prepositions are not used as often as in English. The preposition **zài** (at/in) can also be used in the object position, in which case it means 'to be at/in':

Wǒ ***zài*** **Běijīng dāi le sì tiān.** I stayed in Beijing for four days.
(*zài*: preposition)

Tā zuówǎn bù ***zài.*** He wasn't in last night.
(*zài*: preposition)

Key to the exercises and reading/listening comprehension questions

Lesson 1

Exercise 1

(a) (i) Zhāng jīnglǐ/Zhāng xiānsheng/Zhāng Gōngmín; (ii) Lín xiǎojie/Lín Fāng/Xiǎo Lín; (iii) Xiǎo Gǒng/Qíbīn. (b) Nǐ hǎo, Wáng Lín. (c) Hěn gāoxìng jiàndào nǐ.

Exercise 2

(a) shì; (b) tā; (c) Shì de.

Exercise 3

(a) Nǐ shì Wáng xiānsheng ma? (b) Tā hěn gāoxìng jiàndào nǐ ma? (c) Tāmen lái Zhōngguó ma?

Exercise 4

(a) Wǒ yě hěn gāoxìng jiàndào nǐ. (b) Qǐng jiào wǒ David. (c) Huānyíng nǐ lái Zhōngguó.

Exercise 5

(a) Nǐ lèi ma? (Lèi *or* Bù lèi). (b) Nǐ gāoxìng ma? (Gāoxìng *or* Bù gāoxìng.) (c) Nǐ xiǎng hē kāfēi ma? (Xiǎng *or* Bù xiǎng.)

Exercise 6

(a) B: Nǐ hǎo. (b) B: Bù kèqi. (c) B: Shì de . . . (d) B: Bù shì . . . (e) B: Xiǎng, xièxie.

Exercise 7

(a) Lǎo Wáng bù xiǎng hē kāfēi. (b) David *bù* hěn gāoxìng. (c) David hěn *bù* gāoxìng. (d) Wǒde yīlù *bù* hěn shùnlì. (e) Wǒde yīlù hěn *bú* shùnlì. (f) Tā *bù* shì Jones xiānsheng.

Exercise 8

(a) Hěn lèi. (b) Yǒu yīdiǎn lèi. (e) Bù tài lèi.

Exercise 9

(a) wǒde, tāde; (b) Tāde; (c) wǒde, Andrew de.

Reading/listening comprehension questions

A John. B No, he had a very rough trip. C He asks John if he would like a coffee. D He says that he would very much like a coffee.

Lesson 2

Exercise 1

1(c) Germany; 2(h) Italy; 3(b) France; 4(a) Japan; 5(e) Hong Kong; 6(d) Australia; 7(f) New Zealand; 8(g) Singapore.

Exercise 2

(a)Yīngguórén; (b) Měiguórén; (c) Zhōngguórén; (d) Yìdàlìrén; (e) Táiwānrén; (f) Xiānggǎngrén; (g) Aǒdàlìyàrén; (h) Rìběnrén.

Exercise 3

(a) Yīngwén; (b) Yīngwén; (c) Zhōngwén; (d) Yìdàlìwén; (e) Zhōngwén; (f) Fǎwén; (g) Zhōngwén/Yīngwén/Guǎngdōnghuà (Cantonese); (h) Rìwén.

Exercise 4

(a) Nǐ jiào shénme? (b) Nǐ shì nǎli rén? (c) Nǐ huì shuō Yīngwén ma?

Exercise 5

(a) yīdiǎn; (b) yǒu yīdiǎn; (c) yǒu yīdiǎn; (d) yīdiǎn.

Exercise 6

(a) A: Nǐ shì nǎ guó rén? (b) A: Tā shì nǎli rén? (c) B: Nǎli, nǎli. (d) B: Bù huì.

Exercise 7

(a) Nǐ zhīdao Amy shì nǎ guó rén ma? (b) Wǒ bù huì shuō Yīngwén. (c) Tā bù shì Rìběnrén. (d) Wǒ bù zhīdao tā jiào shénme.

Exercise 8

For your reference only:
Amy shì Měiguórén. Tā jīn nián èrshíyī suì le. Tā huì shuō yīdiǎn Zhōngwén. Tā hěn gāoxìng rènshi Fāng Chūn. Fāng Chūn shì Zhōngguó Běijīngrén. Tā sānshí'èr suì. Tā kànshangqu hěn niánqīng. Tā yě hěn gāoxìng rènshi Amy.

Exercise 9

(a) B: Nǎli, nǎli/Guòjiang. (b) B: Sānshí suì zuǒyòu. (c) B: Bù duì.

Exercise 10

(a) zhīdao; (b) rènshi/zhīdao; (c) zhīdao; (d) rènshi.

Exercise 11

(a) Tā jiào shénme? (b) Xiǎo Fāng shì nǎli rén? (c) Amy jīnnián duō dà le?

Exercise 12

(a) Tā kànshangqu bù hěn gāoxìng. (b) Simon kànshangqu hěn niánqīng. (c) Nǐ kànshangqu yǒu yīdiǎn lèi.

Reading/listening comprehension questions

1 A Yes, she does. B Britain. C Yes, a little. D No, she does not. E Yes, she very much likes to.

2 *Tones* (a) xièxie (fourth, neutral); (b) bù zhīdao (fourth, first, neutral); (c) bú duì (second, fourth); (d) Yīngguórén (first, second, second); (e) shuō Zhōngwén (first, first, second); (f) tài hǎo le (fourth, third, neutral); (g) zàijiàn (fourth, fourth); (h) wó yě shì (second, third, fourth).

Lesson 3

Exercise 1

For your reference only:
(a) Hǎo jiǔ bù jiàn. Nǐ zěnme yàng? / Nǐ hǎo ma? Zhēn gāoxìng jiàndào nǐ. (b) Ràng wǒ jièshào yīxià. Xiǎo Lín, zhè shì wǒde hǎo péngyou, Amy. Amy, zhè shì wǒde Zhōngguó péngyou, Xiǎo Lín.

Exercise 2

(a) John SHÌ bù tài máng. (John is *not* very busy.) (b) Shūlán de gōngzuò SHÌ hěn máng. (Shulan *is* very busy with her work.) (c) Wáng Lín kànshangqu SHÌ tǐng lǎo. (Wang Lin *does* look rather old.)

Exercise 3

(a) A: Nǐ zuótiān qù nǎr le? / Zuótiān nǐ qù le nǎr?
B: Qù Lúndūn le. / Qù le Lúndūn.
(b) A: Nǐ xià ge xīngqī qù nǎr? / Xià ge xīngqī nǐ qù nǎr?
B: Zhōngguó. / Qù Zhōngguó.
(c) A: Yánzhōng qù nǎr le?
B: Tā qù Měiguó le.

Exercise 4

(a) Andrew qù le Měiguó. / Andrew qù Měiguó le. (Andrew went to America. / Andrew has gone to America.) (b) Elena hē le kāfēi. / Elena hē kāfēi le. (Elena had her coffee. / Elena has had her coffee.) (c) Zuótiān Xīnháng shuōqi le Tiānyī. (Xinhang mentioned Tianyi yesterday.)

Exercise 5

(a) jiàndào; (b) jiànmiàn; (c) jiànmiàn; (d) jiàndào.

Exercise 6

(a) Rènshi. Tāmen shì hǎo péngyou. (b) Bù rènshi. (c) Méi jiéhūn. (d) Tā shì WP gōngsī de fù jīnglǐ, yě shì Rachel de nán péngyou.

Exercise 7

(a) shíwǔ ge Měiguórén; (b) liǎng ge Zhōngguórén; (c) sān ge nán de; (d) bā bēi kāfēi; (e) sì ge hǎo péngyou.

Exercise 8

(a) Yǒu. (b) Méi yǒu. (c) Zhēn kěxī!

Exercise 9

(a) Yánzhōng qù nǎr le? (b) Shèi shì WP gōngsī de fù jīnglǐ? (c) Shūlān shì nǎ guó rén? (d) Nǐ xià ge xīngqī qù nǎr?

Exercise 10

(a) Wǒ xià ge xīngqī *bú* qù Zhōngguó. (I'm not going to China next week.) (b) Jane *méi yǒu* jiéhūn. (Jane hasn't got married.) (c) Xiǎo Fāng *méi* yǒu Yìdàlì kāfēi. (Xiao Fang hasn't got Italian coffee.) (d) Wáng Pín *bú* rènshi Měixīn. (Wang Pin does not know Meixin.) (e) Zuótiān wǒmen *méi* qù Lúndūn. (We didn't go to London yesterday.) (f) Wǒ *bù* xiǎng hē kāfēi. (I don't want to have coffee.)

Exercise 11

(a) jiù; (b) SHÌ; (c) SHÌ; (d) jiù.

Exercise 12

(a) 女人

(b) 中国人

(c) 你好

(d) 我说中文

Reading/listening comprehension questions

A true; B false; C false; D true; E false; F true; G false.

Lesson 4

Exercise 1

(a) shí diǎn èrshíwǔ (fēn); (b) liǎng diǎn bàn / liǎng diǎn sānshí (fēn); (c) shí'èr diǎn sān kè / shí'èr diǎn sìshíwǔ / shí'èr diǎn chà shíwǔ / shí'èr diǎn chà yī kè; (d) liù diǎn shí fēn; (e) sì diǎn yī kè / sì diǎn shíwǔ (fēn); (f) jiǔ diǎn wǔ fēn / jiǔ diǎn líng wǔ (fēn).

Exercise 2

(a) 4 jiǔ diǎn yī kè; (b) 6 sì diǎn chà wǔ fēn; (c) 5 liǎng diǎn sìshíwǔ; (d) 2 shíyī diǎn èrshí fēn; (e) 1 bā diǎn líng wǔ; (f) 3 shí'èr diǎn bàn.

Exercise 3

(a) Zǎoshang hǎo. (b) Xiànzài jǐ diǎn le? (c) Qǐng wèn, nǐ jiào shénme? (d) Bù kèqi / Bù xiè.

Exercise 4

(a) cóng . . . dào . . . (The breakfast is from seven to eight thirty.) (b) fēnzhōng (We have five minutes for coffee.) (c) Xiànzài . . . (It's half past six now.) (d) yǐjing (She is already married.)

Exercise 5

(a) Cāntīng jǐ diǎn kāimén? (b) Nǐ zhīdao cāntīng jǐ diǎn kāimén ma? (c) Alan yǐjing sānshí suì le. (d) Qǐng kuài lái Yīngguó.

Exercise 6

(a) Dùibùqǐ. (b) Qǐng wèn, yóuyǒng chí jǐ diǎn kāimén? (c) Dùibùqǐ.

Exercise 7

For your reference only:
(a) Wǒ qī diǎn èrshí chī zǎofàn. (b) Wǒ shí'èr diǎn bàn zuǒyòu chī wǔfàn. (c) Wǒ bā diǎn chī wǎnfàn. (d) Wǒ sān diǎn zuǒyòu yóuyǒng.

Exercise 8

(a) Běijīng yǒu èrshí ge dà fàndiàn. (b) Wǒmén(de) fàndiàn yǒu liǎng ge cāntīng. (c) Zhè ge gōngsī yǒu Zhōngguórén ma? (d) Běijīng Fàndiàn méi yǒu yóuyǒng chí.

Exercise 9

(a) Tā shì bù shì Yīngguórén? (Is he/she British?) (b) Nǐ zuìjìn máng bù máng? (Have you been busy recently?) (c) Zhāng Bīn yǒu méi yǒu nǔ péngyou? (Does Zhang Bin have a girl-friend?) (d) Nǐ xiǎng bù xiǎng qù Zhōngguó? (Do you want to go to China?)

Exercise 10

(a) Duìbùqǐ. (b) Xiànzài jǐ diǎn le? (c) Cāntīng jǐ diǎn kāimén? (d) Huíjiàn.

Exercise 11

(a) Shí'èr diǎn bàn chī wǔfàn, xíng bù xíng? / xíng ma? / hǎo ma? / hǎo bù hǎo? / zěnme yàng? (b) Xiàwǔ sì diǎn qù yóuyǒng, hǎo ma? / hǎo bù hǎo? / xíng bù xíng? / xíng ma? / zěnme yàng? (c) Jiào nǐ 'Xiǎo Lǐ', xíng ma? / xíng bù xíng?

Exercise 12

你想说中文吗？

Reading/listening comprehension questions

I A (b) bù hěn máng; B (a) yóuyǒng; C (c) chī wǔfàn; D (b) shí'èr diǎn sānshí; E (a) shí'èr diǎn yī kè; F (b) sān diǎn.

2 *Tones* (a) huíjiàn (second, fourth); (b) cāntīng (first, first); (c) duìbùqǐ (fourth, fourth, third); (d) dà de (fourth, neutral).

Lesson 5

Exercise 1

1 jiějie = (b) elder sister; 2 dìdi = (d) younger brother; 3 gēge = (a) elder brother; 4 yéye = (e) grandfather; 5 mèimei = (c) younger sister; 6 ā'yí = (h) aunt; 7 nǎinai = (f) grandmother; 8 shūshu = (g) uncle.

Exercise 2

(a) Wǒ māma zài hē kāfēi. (My mum is having coffee.) (b) Yīngméi zài chī zǎofàn ma? (Is Yingmei having her breakfast?) (c) Tā bú zài yóuyǒng. (He/she isn't swimming.) (d) Nǐ bàba zài gōngzuò ma? (Is your father working?)

Exercise 3

(a) shàng / qù; (b) shàng; (c) qù / shàng; (d) shàng.

Exercise 4

(a) Jié(hūn) le. (b) Yīlìshābái / Elizabeth. (c) Měiguórén. (d) Yǒu. (e) Nǚ'ér jiào Měilíng. Érzi jiào Zhìgāng. (f) Bù shì. Tā shì dà xuésheng. (g) Yīngméi shì Shàotáng de mèimei.

Exercise 5

(a) Lǎo Zhāng dāng le Běijīng Fàndiàn de jīnglǐ. (b) Tāmen yóu liǎng ge háizi. Liǎng ge háizi dōu yǒu Zhōngwén míngzi. (c) Wǒmen dōu tuìxiū le. (d) Tāmen bù gōngzuò le. (e) Wǒ dìdi hái méi shàng xiǎoxué. (f) Shàngxué hěn yǒu yìsi. (g) Nǐ xué shénme zhuānyè? (h) Qǐng gěi wǒ jiǎngjiang nǐde zhàngfu. (i) Lúndào wǒ shuō Zhōngwén le.

Exercise 6

(a) He/she does not live in Beijing. (b) Are your parents still working? (c) Ma Lan is having her breakfast. (d) Wang Lin works at the Beijing Hotel.

Exercise 7

(a) Lǎo Wáng yóu jǐ ge háizi? (b) Nǐ zài Běijīng Fàndiàn zhù le jǐ tiān? (c) Tā hē le jǐ bēi kāfēi? (d) Lǐ Píng yǒu jǐ ge gēge?

Exercise 8

(a) Nǐ yǒu shíjiān qù yóuyǒng ma? (b) Duìbùqǐ, wǒ méi yǒu shíjiān. (c) Nǐ gàn shénme gōngzuò? (d) Qǐng wèn nǐ fùmú hǎo.

Exercise 9

(a) [no measure word needed]; (b) ge; (c) jiā / ge; (d) ge; (e) bēi.

Exercise 10

(a) Wǒ hěn xǐhuan wǒde gōngzuò. (b) Wǒ xiǎng qù kàn wǒ fùmǔ. (c) Tā huì lái kàn wǒ ma? (d) Fāng Shū zài Běijīng Lǚyóu Jú gōngzuò. (e) Nǐ zhù zài nǎr?

Exercise 11

(a) 我想去中国.

(b) 她想去哪儿？

Reading/listening comprehension questions

A Gu Liang is a translator/interpreter. B Gu Liang is working for Beijing Silk Trading Company. C Yang Ning has got married. D Yang Ning's wife is a primary-school teacher. E Gu Liang is going to meet Yang Ning's wife tomorrow night at Yang Ning's home.

Lesson 6

Exercise 1

(a) Jīntiān shì xīngqītiān. / Jīntiān shì xīngqīrì. (b) Jīntiān shì liùyuè jiǔ hào. (c) Wǒ qī hào qù Zhōngguó. (d) Wǒ māma xīngqīyī lái Táiwān.

Exercise 2

(a) sān tiān [no measure word] (Xiao Fang stayed in Shenzhen for three days.) (b) sān ge yuè (I've got three months.) (c) liǎng ge xīngqī / liǎng xīngqī (My husband wants to travel in China for two weeks.) (d) sì nián [no measure word] (My younger brother worked in Xi'an for four years.) (e) wǔ ge gēge (Wang Dongping has five elder brothers.) (f) bāyuè [no measure word] (Paul wants to go to Taiwan in August.)

Exercise 3

(a) Fēixiá zài Guǎngzhōu zhù le jǐ nián? (b) Míngtiān shì xīngqīsì. (c) Andrew xué le jǐ ge yuè Zhōngwén? (d) Wǒ xiǎng jīnnián sān yuè qù Zhōngguó. (e) Xià ge xīngqīwǔ shì jǐ hào? (f) Wǒ zhàngfu (*or* àiren) yǒu liǎng ge dìdi hē yī ge jiějie.

Exercise 4

(a) wǒ zuì hǎo de péngyou; (b) tèbié da de yóuyǒng chí / fēicháng dà de yóuyǒng chí; (c) xiǎo cāntīng / xiǎo fàndiàn; (d) nà ge niánqīng hē piàoliang de dà xuésheng; (e) zuì lǎo de nán rén.

Exercise 5

(a) Mick dǎsuàn *shénme shíhou* qù Zhōngguó? (When is Mick going to China?) (b) Zhāng Jūn zài Táiwān gōngzuò le *duō jiǔ*? (For how long did Zhang Jun work in Taiwan?) (c) Lǎo Lǐ de nǚ'ér *shénme shíhou* shàngxué? (When is Lao Li's daughter starting school?) (d) Nǐ xiǎng zài Shànghǎi dāi *duō jiǔ*? (For how long do you want to stay in Shanghai?)

Exercise 6

(a) zuǒyòu; (b) dàyuē; (c) zuǒyòu; (d) dàyuē.

Exercise 7

(a) Nǐ xiǎng shí'èr diǎn háishi yī diǎn chī wǔfàn? (b) Nǐ cháng yóuyǒng ma? / Nǐ chángchang yóuyǒng ma? (c) Nǐ zěnme bù gāoxìng? / Nǐ wèishénme bù gāoxìng? (d) Jìrán nǐ bù è, wǒ jiù xiān chī.

Exercise 8

For your reference only:

好 妈 她 吗

Reading/listening comprehension questions

1 A Xià ge xīngqīsan. B Bù shì. C Bù shì. Tā qù gōngzuò jiā kàn péngyou. D Liǎng ge xīngqī zuǒyòu. E Hěn rè. Bùguò, hěn yǒu yìsi. F Bù zài Měiguó.

2 *Tones* (a) yīyuè (first, fourth); (b) sān ge yuè (first, neutral, fourth); (c) tèbié dà de fàndiàn (fourth, second, fourth, neutral, fourth, fourth); (d) xīngqī'èr (first, first, fourth).

Lesson 7

Exercise 1

(a) Píngguǒ liǎng kuài qī máo wǔ yī jīn. (b) Bōluó liù kuài yī jīn. (c) Xiāngjiāo sì kuài liù máo wǔ yī jīn. (d) Cǎoméi sān kuài yī máo yī jīn. (e) Lízi liǎng kuài líng wǔ yī jīn. (f) Wǔ kuài yī máo jiǔ yī jīn.

Exercise 2

(a) yào; (b) xiǎng / yào; (c) yào; (d) xiǎng / yào.

Exercise 3

(a) Wǒ xiǎng mǎi yīxiē Hǎinán Dǎo xiāngjiāo. (b) Tā bù yào cǎoméi. (c) Wǒ mǎi le liǎng jīn píngguǒ. (d) Nǐ hái yào biéde ma? (e) Wǒ bù zhīdao zhè ge duō shǎo qián. (f) A: Gěi nǐ wǔ kuài. B: Zhǎo nǐ liǎng máo wǔ.

Exercise 4

(a) Wǒ xiǎng mǎi yī tiáo zhēn sī lǐngdài. / Wǒ yào . . . (b) Wǒ xiǎng mǎi liǎng jīn xiāngjiāo. / Wǒ yào . . . (c) Wǒ xiǎng mǎi liǎng tiáo wéijīn. / Wǒ yào . . .

Exercise 5

(a) Nǐ kěyi dài wǒ qù bǎihuò shāngdiàn ma? (b) Nǐ kěyi dài wǒ qù yínháng ma? (c) Nǐ kěyi dài wǒ qù yóujú ma?

Exercise 6

(a) Tài guì le. Wǒ bù yào. (b) Wǒ yào le. (c) Xiǎojie, yǒu lìzhī ma? (d) Nǐ tài hǎo le. Duō xiè.

Exercise 7

(a) gěi tāde nǚ péngyou (He bought a pure silk scarf for his girl-friend.) (b) mǎi yīxiē dōngxi (I should go to the department-store and do some shopping.) (c) suǒyǒude, dōu (All the banks are open on Sundays.) (d) jǐ bēi (Xiao Wang has had several cups of coffee.) (e) dài wǒ māma lái (My elder brother will bring my mother over to see us.)

Reading/listening comprehension questions

A a night gown; B a hundred and eighty-five yuan; C very nice and not expensive; D several table-cloths.

Lesson 8

Exercise 1

(a) Zhōngguó bǐ Měiguó dà. / Měiguó bǐ Zhōngguó xiǎo. (b) Bōluó bǐ píngguǒ guì. (c) John bǐ Wáng Lín gāo. (d) Zhè ge yóuyǒng chí bǐ nà ge yóuyǒng chí dà. (e) Rachel bǐ Línlin dà. / Línlin bǐ Rachel niánqīng. / Línlin bǐ Rachel xiǎo.

Exercise 2

For your reference only:
(a) Wǒ zuì xǐhuan lán yánsè. (I like the blue colour most.) (b) Wǒ bǐjiào xǐhuan Zhōngguó fàn. (I quite like Chinese food.) (c) Zhōngwén bǐ Fǎwén nán. (Chinese is more difficult than French.) (d) Shì de. (Yes, it is.)

Exercise 3

(a) with 4 lán tiān (blue sky); (b) with 1 or 3 lǜ píngguǒ; lǜ chá; (c) with 2 huáng xiāngjiāo; (d) with 1 or 3 hóng píngguǒ; hóng chá (black tea).

Exercise 4

(a) Nǐ kěyi jiè gěi wǒ liǎng ge píngguǒ ma? (b) Tā bù xǐhuan jiè gěi péngyou qián. (c) Tā shénme shíhou huán gěi wǒ qián? / Tā shénme shíhou huán wǒ qián? (d) Wǒ wàng le dài qiánbāo. (e) Xièxie nǐ dài lái yīxiē Zhōngguó chá. (f) Tā dài máoyī le ma? (g) Liú Hóng kànshangqu bǐ Paul niánqīng. / Liú Hóng bǐ Paul kànshangqu niánqing.

Exercise 5

(a) shàng; (b) guàng; (c) qù; (d) shàng.

Exercise 6

(a) Duìbùqǐ. Wǒ chí dào le. (b) Méi wèntí. (c) Zhōngwén zěnme shuō 'good bargain'? (d) Wǒ míngtiān yīdìng huán gěi nǐ qián.

Exercise 7

(a) Zhè tiáo lǐngdài hán bǎifēnzhī wǔshí de sī. (This tie contains 50 per cent silk.) (b) Wǒ guàng le guàng shāngdiàn. (I had a look around in the shops.) (c) Táng Bǐn jié gěi le wǒ èrshí kuài qián. (Tang Bin lent me twenty yuan.) (d) Tā jīntiān zǎoshang chí dào le èrshí fēnzhōng. (She was twenty minutes late this morning.)

Exercise 8

(a) gòu; (b) zúgòu de; (c) A: gòu; B: gòu; (d) zúgòu de.

Exercise 9

1 Tā méi yǒu shénme hǎo péngyou. 2 Míngtiān wǒ bù shàng bān. Wǒ kěyi chōu kòng qù yóuyǒng. 3 Wǒ cāi tā wǔshí duō suì. 4 Duìbùqǐ. Shēng lán sè de máoyī mài guāng le. Hēi sè xíng ma? 5 Zhēn hésuàn. Hái yǒu ma?

Exercise 10

(a) iii) 天 ; My mother will come to see me tomorrow.

(b) ii) 去 ; He doesn't want to go shopping.

Exercise 11

我喜欢学中文.

Reading/listening comprehension questions

A (b); B (c); C (a); D (b); E (c); F (b); G (a).

Lesson 9

Exercise 1

(a) Wǒ yào yī bēi chénzi zhī. (b) Wǒ yào yī píng píjiǔ. (c) Wǒ yào liǎng bēi bái pútao jiǔ. (d) Wǒ yào yīxiē Zhōngguó chá.

Exercise 2

For your reference only:
Wǒ yào yī ge húntún tāng, yī ge yǔ tóu shāo dòufu hé yī ge jīdān chǎo fàn.

Exercise 3

(a) Qǐng zuò. (b) Wǒ xiǎng kànkan càidān. / Wǒ xiǎng kàn yīxià càidān. / Wǒ kěyi kàn yīxià càidān ma? (c) Qǐng gēng wǒ lái. (d) Wǒ è sǐ le. (e) Qǐng shāo děng. / Děng yīxià. / Děngdeng.

Exercise 4

(a) Alan qù guo Zhōngguó ma? (b) Linda zuō tiān qù Lúndūn le. (c) Tā méi yǒu chī guo Zhōngguó fàn. (d) A: Nǐ chī zǎofàn le ma? B: Hái méi chī.

Exercise 5

(a) Wǒ chī bǎo le. / Wǒ bǎo le. (b) Wǒ zài yào yīxiē bǐng. / Wǒ hái xiǎng yào yīxiē bǐng. (c) Qǐng dì géi wǒ jiàng. (d) Duìbùqǐ, wǒ zài yào yī píng píjiǔ. (e) Duō chī yīxiē.

Exercise 6

(a) Rúguǒ nǐ yǒu shíjiān dehuà, zánmen qù chī kǎo yā, hǎo ma? (b) Nǐ děi lái kàn wǒmen. (c) Jīntiān zǎoshang wǒ shàng bān chí dào le èrshí fēnzhōng. (d) Rúguó nǐ è dehuà, zánmen xiān chī wǔfàn, hǎo bù hǎo? (e) Xiǎo Zhāng bù xiǎng qǐng Lǎo Wáng.

Exercise 7

(a) Yóuyǒng chí jīntiān zǎoshang kāi de hěn zǎo. (b) Qǐng zǎo lái. / Qǐng zǎo yīxiē lái. (c) Jīntiān zǎoshang wǒ lái de hěn chí. (d) John shuō de hěn kuài.

Exercise 8

(a) Nǐ shuō de bù duì. (b) Wǒ mèimei lái de bù hěn zǎo. (c) Yīngguó de xiàtiān bù hěn rè. (d) Tāde fùmǔ tuìxiū de bù hěn zǎo. (e) Xiǎohuá bù gāoxìng.

Exercise 9

(a) 我妈妈是中国人.

(b) 她没有空.

(c) A: 你去买东西吗?
B: 是的.

Reading/listening comprehension questions

A Niúnǎi. B Méi chī guo. C kāfēi. D Xiánròu, jiān jīdàn hé yīdiǎn mógu.

Lesson 10

Exercise 1

(a) Qǐng wèn, cèsuǒ zài nǎr? (b) Qǐng wèn, fùjìn yǒu gōngyòng diànhuà ma? (c) Qǐng wèn, shí lù chē zài nǎr? (d) Qǐng wèn, qù huǒchē zhàn zěnme zǒu? (e) Qǐng wèn, qù Běijīng Fàndiàn zuò jǐ lù chē?

Exercise 2

(a) Lǎo Zhāng zài Maria de zuǒ biān. (b) Maria zài Lǎo Zhāng de yòu biān. (c) Linda zài Xiǎo Fāng de zuǒ biān.

Exercise 3

I (a) Cèsuǒ zài gōngyòng diànhuà de zuǒ biān. (b) Gōngyòng diànhuà zài cèsuǒ de yòu biān. / Gōngyòng diànhuà zài cāntīng de zuǒ biān. (c) Cāntīng zài gōngyòng diànhuà de yòu biān.

II (a) Dì èr ge hónglǜdēng wǎng zuó guǎi, zài wǎng yòu guǎi. (b) Dì èr ge hónglǜdēng wǎng yòu guǎi.

Exercise 4

(a) Tā bù jìde wǒde míngzi. (He doesn't remember my name.) (b) Nǐ bù yòng gěi wǒ mǎi lǐwù. (You don't need to buy me any presents.) (c) Fùjìn méi yǒu bǎihuò shāngdiàn. (There's no department store near by.) (d) Wǒ méi kàn jiàn huǒchē zhàn. (I didn't see the railway station.) (e) Wǒ kàn bù jiàn hónglǜ dēng. (I can't see the traffic lights.)

Exercise 5

1 Nàr yǒu yī ge yóujú. 2 Tā huì shuō Zhōngwén. 3 Wǒ bù néng gàosu nǐ tāde qíngkuàng. 4 Dì yī ge lùkǒu wǎng yòu guǎi. Shíwǔ fēnzhōng jiù dào le.

Exercise 6

(a) Qǐng wèn, qí zìxíngchē qù Zhōngshān Dàxué xūyào duō jiǔ? (b) Qǐng wèn, zǒulù qù huǒchē zhàn xūyào duō jiǔ? (c) Qǐng wèn, zuò chē qù Tiān'ānmén xūyào duō jiǔ?

Exercise 7

(a) borrow; (b) lend; (c) borrow; (d) lend.

Exercise 8

(a) Wǒ bù xìn (or bù xiāngxìn) nǐ méi yǒu zìxíngchē. (b) Xià ge xīngqīliù wǒ yào qù Shànghǎi. (c) Frank méi zhǎo dào Zhōngshān Dàxué. (d) Nǐ zuìhǎo chá yīxià dìtú. (e) Qí zìxíngchē dào wǒde dàxué yào yī ge duō xiǎoshí. (f) Zhè shì yī ge hǎo zhǔyi.

Exercise 9

1 (f); 2 (b); 3 (d); 4 (c); 5 (a); 6 (e).

Reading/listening comprehension questions

1 A (c); B (b); C (a); D (b); E (c).

2 *Tones* (a) Qǐng zuò. (third, fourth); (b) È sǐ le. (fourth, third, neutral); (c) yǒu kòng (third, fourth); (d) chī de kuài (first, neutral, fourth); (e) nàr (fourth, neutral); (f) Wǒ bú xìn. (third, second, fourth).

Lesson 11

Exercise 1

(a) Wǒ mǎi sān zhāng qù dòngwùyuán de piào. (I'll buy three tickets for the zoo.) (b) Nà ge gāng dào de nánhái shì Lǎo Liú de érzi. (The boy who has just arrived is Lao Liù's son.) (c) Wáng jīnglǐ bù xǐhuan nàxiē chángchang chí dào de rén. (Manager Wang doesn't like those who are always late.)

Exercise 2

(a) tiáo; (b) zhāng; (c) liàng; (d) píng.

Exercise 3

(a) Zāogāo! Wǒ zuò cuò chē le. (b) Zāogāo! Wǒ diǎn cuò cài le. (c) Zāogāo! Wǒ jiào cuò tāde míngzi le. (d) Zāogāo! Wǒ mǎi cuò kāfēi le.

Exercise 4

(a) Bié jí. (b) Bié zuò gōnggòng qìchē. (c) Bié gàosu Lǎo Wáng wǒ duō dà le. (d) Bié shuō Yīngwén. (e) Bié jiè gěi Liú Hóng nǐde zìxíngchē.

Exercise 5

(a) Xià yī zhàn shì dòngwùyuán. (b) Wǒ bù zhīdao nǐ xià liǎng ge xīngqī yào chūmén. (c) Nǐ xūyào xià yī zhàn xià chē. Huàn shí'èr lù gōnggòng qìchē. (d) Zhè ge fàndiàn yǒu rén jiào Kàn Jiā ma? (e) Duìbùqǐ, wǒ méi tīng qīng. (f) Qǐng màn yīdiǎn shuō.

Exercise 6

(a) Wǒ xiǎng mǎi liǎng zhāng qù Běijīng de piào. (b) Wǒ xiǎng mǎi yī zhāng sānyuè bā hào qù Shànghǎi de piào. (c) Wǒ xiǎng mǎi sān zhāng qù Guìlín de yìngwò. (d) Wǒ xiǎng mǎi liǎng zhāng èrshíliù cì lièchē de piào.

Exercise 7

(a) Qīngdǎo píjiǔ bǐ Běijīng píjiǔ guì liù máo.
Běijīng píjiǔ bǐ Qīngdǎo píjiǔ piányi liù máo.
Běijīng píjiǔ méiyǒu Qīngdǎo píjiǔ guì.

(b) Xiǎoméi bǐ Andrew dà yī suì.
Andrew bǐ Xiǎoméi xiǎo yī suì.
Andrew méi Xiǎoméi dà.

(c) Lǎo Wáng juéde Zhōngguó fàn bǐ xīcān hǎochī.
Lǎo Wáng juéde xīcān méi Zhōngguó fàn hǎochī.

(d) Běijīng de xiàtiān bǐ Lúndūn de xiàtiān rè.
Lúndūn de xiàtiān méi Běijīng de xiàtiān rè.

Exercise 8

(a) Huǒchē dì èr tiān shísān diǎn líng wǔ fēn dào Guìlín. (b) Wǒ xīngqīwǔ zǒu, jiù shì sānyuè èrshíwǔ hào. (c) Wǒde fùmǔ shēntǐ bù cuò. (d) Liùshíqī cì chē jǐ diǎn fāchē?

Exercise 9

For your reference only:

好看; 好吃; 好人; 买票

Reading/listening comprehension questions

1 A Shí cì lièchē. B Shíqī diǎn líng wǔ fēn fāchē. C Èrshí diǎn shí fēn fāchē? D Bù shì. Qī diǎn sìshí wǔ fēn fāchē. E Qù Wūlǔ mùqí?

2 (a) true; (b) false; (c) false; (d) true.

Lesson 12

Exercise 1

(a) Dān jiān dài wèishēng jiān bāshíwǔ yuán yī tiān. (b) Shuāng jiān dài wèishēng jiān yī bǎi bāshíwǔ yuán yī tiān. (c) Dān jiān bú dài wèishēng jiān wǔshíwǔ yuán yī tiān.

Exercise 2

(a) Wǒ yào yī jiān dān jiān dài wèishēng jiān. (b) Wǒ yào yī jiān shuāng jiān dài wèishēng jiān. (c) Wǒ yào yī jiān dān jiān, zhù sān tiān.

Exercise 3

(a) Nǐmen yǒu kòng fángjiān ma? (b) Wǒde fángjiān bú dài diànhuà. / Wǒde fángjiān méi yǒu diànhuà. (c) Nǐde fángjiān zài sì céng. (d) Zuǒ biān dì sān liàng zìxíngchē shì wǒde.

Exercise 4

(a) diàndēng; (b) chúlǐ; (c) fàndiàn; (d) Shénme shíhou?

Exercise 5

(a) 3 xiū diàndēng; (b) 1 chúlǐ zhè jiàn shì; (c) 5 yǒu kòng fángjiān; (d) 2 mái lǐwù; (e) 6 kàn péngyou; (f) 4 děng gōnggòng qìchē.

Exercise 6

(a) Wǒde fángjiān li yǒu ge diàndēng huài le. / Wǒde fángjiān li de diàndēng huài le. (b) Gébì fángjiān hěn chǎo. / Gébì de rén hěn chǎo. (c) Wǒde fángjiān hěn lěng.

Exercise 7

(a) Zhēn bàoqiàn. (b) Lǎoshí shuō . . . (c) Nǐ shuì de hǎo ma? (d) Kàn qíngkuàng. (e) Sīfāng ràng wǒ gàosu nǐ tā xià ge xīngqīsì zǒu. (f) Wǒde qiánbāo li méi yǒu qián. (g) A: Hái yǒu biéde wèntí ma? B: Zànshí méi yǒu.

Exercise 8

For your reference only:
(a) Zuótiān wǒde fángjiān hěn lěng. (b) Zuówǎn, wǒ bù xiǎng chūmén. (c) Zuówǎn, gébì hěn chǎo. (d) Wǒde fángjiān méi yǒu wèishēng jiān.

Reading comprehension questions

The odd words or phrases are in italics and the words or phrases that replace them are in the parentheses. If a word/phrase needs crossing out, it is indicated in the parentheses.

RECEPTIONIST:	Nǐ hǎo.
EMILY:	*Xièxie* (Ní hǎo). Nǐmen yǒu kòng fángjiān ma?
RECEPTIONIST:	Yào kàn qíngkuàng. Nǐ yào *wèishēng jiān* (dān jiān) háishi shuāng jiān?
EMILY:	Yào dān jiān. Dān jiān dài *yóuyǒng chí* (wèishēng jiān) ma?
RECEPTIONIST:	Dāngrán dài. Nǐ dǎsuàn zhù jǐ tiān?
EMILY:	Liǎng *ge* tiān. (cross out 'ge')

RECEPTIONIST: Ràng *nǐ* (wǒ) chácha. Yǒu kòng fángjiān.
EMILY: Duō shǎo qián yī tiān?
RECEPTIONIST: Yī bǎi bāshí Kuài. Xíng ma?
EMILY: Xíng. Wǒ yào le.

Lesson 13

Exercise 1

(a) A: Qíng zhǎo yīxià Lǐ Màn? / Qǐng wèn, Lǐ Màn zài ma? (b) B: Shì de. Nǐ zhǎo shéi? (c) A: Qǐng wèn, Jane zài ma? / Qǐng zhǎo yīxià Jane? (d) A: Qǐng wèn, nǐ shì shéi? / Qǐng wèn, nǐ shì náli?

Exercise 2

(a) Sīfāng shì cóng Xīnjiāpō lái *de* Zhōngguórén. (b) Linda shì xué Zhōngwén *de* dà xuésheng. (c) Wǒde Zhōngwén lǎoshí shì cóng Zhōngguó dàlù lái *de* Zhōngguórén.

Exercise 3

(a) David shì shénme shíhou zǒu de? (b) Jīntiān zǎoshang, wǒ shì qí zìxíngchē lái shàng bān de. (c) Shénme shíhou dōu xíng. Nǐ juédìng. (d) Tā shénme shíhou dōu bù xǐhuan zuò gōnggòng qìchē. (e) Nǐ kěyi lái jiē wǒ ma? (f) Wǒmen jǐ diǎn zài shénme dìfang jiànmiàn?

Exercise 4

(a) Nǐ zuótiān jǐ diǎn xià bān de? / Nǐ zuótiān shì jǐ diǎn xià bān de? (b) Nǐ zuótiān shì zěnme qù shàng bàn de? / Nǐ zuótiān zěnme qù shàng bān de? (c) Nǐ mèimei shì zuótiān wǎngshang lái de ma? (d) Nǐ mèimei shì shénme shíhou kāishǐ xué Yīngwén de?

Exercise 5

For your reference only:
(a) Zhōngwén bù hǎo xué. (It's not easy to learn Chinese.) (b) Shànghǎi huǒchē zhàn bù hǎo zhǎo. (It's not easy to find Shanghai railway station.) (c) Guǎngdōnghuà bù hǎo dǒng. (It's not easy to understand Canton dialect.)

Exercise 6

(a) Wǒ jiějie shì dǎoyóu. (b) Wǒmen jīnglǐ de bàngōngshì zài èr céng. (c) [cannot omit]; (d) Tā fùmǔde jiā hěn piàoliang. (e) [cannot omit].

Exercise 7

(a) gěi; (b) gěi; (c) tóng; (d) gěi; (e) tóng.

Exercise 8

(a) Nǐ chí wán wǎnfàn le ma? (Have you finished with your supper?) (b) Tā yòng wán diànhuà le. (She has finished with the phone.) (c) Tā diǎn wán cài le. (He has finished ordering the dishes.) (d) Xiǎo Lǐ xiū wán diàndēng le. (Xiao Li has finished repairing the light.)

Exercise 9

(a) Zài Yīngguó, dǎ diànhuà hěn guì. (b) Nǐde diànhuà hàomǎ shì shénme? (c) Zuówǎn, nǐ bàba gěi nǐ dǎ diànhuà le. (d) Nǐ jiā yǒu diànhuà ma?

Exercise 10

(a) David wàng le gěi láobǎn dǎ diànhuà. (David forgot to phone the boss.) (b) Nǐ kěyi gàosu wǒ nǐde diànhuà hàomǎ ma? (Could you tell me your telephone number?) (c) Tā jīntiān bù zài bàngōngshì. (She is not in the office today.)

Exercise 11

(a) ii); I went to visit some friends yesterday.
(b) i); I lived in Beijing for 10 years.
(c) ii); My younger brother can speak Japanese.

Exercise 12

Question 1: Zhangwen is phoning his teacher, Mr. Li.
Question 2: He's gone to the bank.
Question 3: About six o'clock.

Reading/listening comprehension questions

A Bù zài. B Tāde māma. C Míngtiān wǎnshang liù diǎn shí fēn dào Shànghǎi. D Shíliù cì chē. E Xiǎng.

Lesson 14

Exercise 1

(a) Zuótiān wǒ bàba gěi wǒ dǎ diànhuà *le.* (My father phoned me yesterday.) (b) Nǐ kàn. Xiàxuě *le.* (Look, it's snowing.) (c) Rúguǒ tā míngtiān hái bù dào, wǒ jiù zǒu *le.* (If he does not arrive tomorrow, I'm leaving.) (d) Sān tiān qián, tā chí dào *le* bàn ge xiǎoshí. (Three days ago, he was half an hour late.) (e) Wǒ bù xiǎng qù dòngwùyuán. Wǒ lèi *le.* (I don't want to go to the zoo. I'm getting tired.) (f) Zhème shuō, nǐ shì Fēixiá *le*? (In that case, you are Feixia, aren't you?)

Exercise 2

(a) dì èr cì; (b) liǎng cì; (c) liǎng cì; (d) liǎng cì; (e) dì èr cì.

Exercise 3

(a) qù; (b) qu; (c) lái; (d) qù; (e) lai.

Exercise 4

(a) Měitiān zǎoshang, wǒ bā diǎn qù shàng bān. (b) Měi ge rén dōu xǐhuan tā. (c) Liǎng nián qián, wǒ rènshi le tā. (d) Qù nián, tā qù le Xiāng Gǎng liǎng cì. (e) Méi liǎng ge xīngqī, wǒ gěi wǒ fùmǔ dǎ yī cì diànhuà. (f) Tā yào qù tā fùmǔ jiā guò chūnjié.

Exercise 5

(a) Qǐng jìn, qǐng jìn./Kuài jìn lai. (b) Zuò, zuò. (c) Nǐmen xiǎng hē shénme? (d) Wǒ qù Lǎo Lǐ jiā zuòzuo. (e) Chī, chī. Bié kèqi.

Exercise 6

(a) Nǐ juéde Měiguó zěnme yàng? (b) Xiāng Gǎng de xiàtiān zěnme yàng? (c) Běijīng fàndiàn zěnme yàng? (d) Dāngdì rén zěnme yàng? (e) David de Zhōngwén zěnme yàng?

Exercise 7

(a) Wǒ yé bù xǐhuan Zhōngguó fàn. (b) Tā māma yě mèi qù cānjiā Àilín de hūnlǐ. (c) Tā yě bù zhīdao yóuyǒng chí jǐ diǎn kāimén. (d) Xiǎo Zhāng yě méi chí dào.

Exercise 8

(a) Tóng dāngdì rén tánhuà hěn yǒu yìsi. (b) Nǐ qù le ná jǐ ge chéngshì? (c) Nǐde Táiwān zhī xíng zěnme yàng? (d) Guǎngzhōu de rén tài duō. Hěn chǎo, xiàtiān hěn rè.

Reading/listening comprehension questions

1 A Táiwān. B Cānjiā le. C Bù shì, shì dì yī cì. D Guìlín. Tāmen qù le liǎng ge xīngqī.

2 *Tones:* (a) wǒménde hūnlǐ (third, second, neutral, first, third); (b) gàosu wǒ nǐde Zhōngguó zhī xíng (fourth, neutral, third, third, neutral, first, second, first, second); (c) qǐng le xǔduō péngyou (third, neutral, third, first, second, neutral).

Lesson 15

Exercise 1

Check your letter with a Chinese speaker if you can find one. Otherwise, go back to the book and check the letter yourself by going through the vocabulary and the language points.

Exercise 2

TO: People's Republic of China

Yóubiān: 710061
Xī'ān Cháng Ān Jiē 6 Hào 46 Dòng 3 Hào

Huáng Wěiléi Shōu

126 SE, 42 Place, Bellevue, WA 98006, USA

Exercise 3

(a) xìn/láixìn; (b) láixìn/xìn; (c) xìn; (d) qùxìn/xìn.

Exercise 4

(a) *with* 2 qù nián; (b) *with* 3 or 4 shàng ge xīngqī / shàng ge yuè; (c) *with* 1 or 2 míngtiān / míng nián; (d) *with* 3 or 4 xià ge xīngqī / xià ge yuè; (e) with 1 zuótiān.

Exercise 5

(a) Nǐde jiā hěn piàoliang, jiù shì bù hǎo zhǎo. (b) Zuówǎn wǒ yīzhí zài jiā xiě xìn. (c) Wǒ xǐhuan gěi hǎo péngyou xiě xìn. (d) Bié shēngqì. (e) Xià bān hòu, wǒ qù le zìyóu shìchǎng. (f) Wǒménde láobǎn máng zhe dǎ diànhuà. (g) Wǒ zuótiān cái shōu dào wǒ fùmǔ de xìn. (h) Zài Zhōngguó de shíhou, wǒ chángchang qí zìxíngchē. (i) Tā yīdìng huì zài xià ge xīngqīyī zhī qián huán gěi nǐ nà běn shū de.

Reading/listening comprehension questions

A Lin Bobin. B Post Box 10, English Department, Zhongshan University, Guangzhou, Postcode: 510450. C English Department of Zhongshan University in Guangzhou. D Beijing. E To attend a conference. F Around 8 July. G No, he does not.

Chinese–English glossary

-a	啊	[auxiliary word]
ai	唉	[exclamation word]
āiyō!	唉 哟	whoops!
ba	吧	[auxiliary word]
bā	八	eight
bàba	爸 爸	father/dad
bǎi	百	hundred
bái mǐ fàn	白 米 饭	boiled rice
bǎifēnzhī	百 分 之	per cent
bǎihuo shāngdiàn	百 货 商 店	department store
bàn	半	half
bàn jīn	半 斤	a quarter of a kilo
bàngōngshì	办 公 室	office
bànyè	半 夜	midnight
bǎo	饱	to be full
bàogào	报 告	report
bǎozhèng	保 证	to promise
bāozi	包 子	steamed bread with fillings
bāyuè	八 月	August
Běijīngrén	北 京 人	Beijing person/people
běn	本	[measure word for books]
bǐ	比	to be compared with
biān	边	side
bié	别	do not
biéde	别 的	anything else/other
bǐjiào	比 较	quite/rather/relatively
bǐng	饼	pancake
bìxū	必 须	must
bù	不	no/not
bù cuò	不 错	quite good/quite well
bù duì	不	no/incorrect

bù háo zhǎo	不好找	not easy to find
bù jiàn	不见	no see
bù kèqi	不客气	you are welcome
bù yòng	不用	no need/do not need
bùguò	不过	however/but
cāi	猜	to guess
cái	才	[emphatic word]
càidān	菜单	menu
cānguǎn	餐馆	restaurant
cānjiā	参加	to attend/to take part
cāntīng	餐厅	restaurant/dining-room
cǎoméi	草莓	strawberry
céng	层	floor/layer
cèsuǒ	厕所	toilet
chá	茶	tea
chá	查	to check
cháng	常	often/always/frequently
cháng	尝	to taste
cháng	长	long/to be long
Chángchéng	长城	the Great Wall
chǎo	吵	to be noisy
chǎo	炒	to stir-fry
chē	车	car/bus
chéng	乘	to take/to catch
chénggōng	成功	to be successful/success
chéngshì	城市	city
chéngzi zhī	橙子汁	orange juice
chī	吃	to eat
chí	迟	late/to be late
chōu kòng	抽空	to make time
chuān	穿	to wear
chǔlǐ	处理	to see to/to handle
chūmén	出门	to be away/to go away
chún máo	纯毛	pure wool
chūnjié	春节	Chinese New Year [*lit.* 'spring festival']
chūntiān	春天	spring
cì	次	number
cóng . . . dào . . .	从 ...到 ...	from . . . to . . .
cóng . . . lái	从 ...来 ...	to come from . . .
cuò	错	wrongly/to be wrong
dà	大	big/large/old
dà	大	to be big/to be large/to be old

dà de	大 的	the large one/the big one
dǎ diànhuà	打 电 话	to make telephone calls/to telephone
dà xuésheng	大 学 生	university student
dāi	待 /呆	to stay
dài	带	to include/to have
dài (qu)	带 (去)	to take
dài (lai)	带 (来)	to bring
dàjiē	大 街	avenue
dāng	当	to become
dāngdì	当 地	local
dāngrán	当 然	of course
dānrén	单 人	single
dànshì	但 是	but
dào	到	to arrive/to get there
dào	到	until/up to
dǎoyóu	导 游	tourist guide
dǎsuàn	打 算	to plan
dàxiā	大 虾	king prawn
dàxué	大 学	university
dàyuē	大 约	approximately/about/around
de	的	[grammar word]
de shíhou	的时候	when/while
děi	得	to have got to/must
dì	递	to pass
dì èr tiān	第 二天	the following day
dì yī	第 一	first
dì yī cì	第 一 次	the first time/for the first time
diǎn	点	o'clock
diàn	店	restaurant/snack-bar/shop
diǎn cài	点 菜	to order[food]
diànchē	电 车	tram/streetcar
diàndēng	电 灯	light bulb
diànhuà	电 话	telephone
dian(r)	点 儿	a little/some
dìtú	地 图	map
dǒng	懂	to understand
dòng	栋	block
dōng	东	east
Dōng Zhí Mén Wài	东 直 门 外	[street name]
dōngtiān	冬 天	winter
dòngwùyuán	动 物 园	the zoo
dōngxi	东 西	things

dōu	都	all
dōu	都	[emphatic word]
dòufu	豆腐	tofu
duì	对	be correct
duì le	对了	right/by the way
duìbùqǐ	对不起	I'm sorry/Excuse me
duō	多	how
duō	多	more
duō	多	more than/over
duō jiǔ	多久	how long?
duō shǎo	多少	how much?/how many?
Duō shǎo qián?	多少钱	How much is it?
duō xiè	多谢	many thanks
è	饿	to be hungry/hungry
è sǐ le	饿死了	starving
èrshíyī	二十一	twenty-one
èrshí	二十	twenty
érzi	儿子	son
fāchē	发车	to depart/departure
fàndiàn	饭店	hotel
fángjiān	房间	room
fēicháng/tèbié	非常/特别	extremely/very
fēn	分	minute
fēn	分	[currency word]
fèn	份	[measure word for documents]
fēng	封	[measure word for letters]
fēngjǐng	风景	scenery
fēnjī	分机	extension
fēnzhōng	分钟	minute
fù	副	deputy/vice
fùjìn	附近	near by/close by
fùmǔ	父母	parents
gàn	干	to do
gāng	刚	just
gānghǎo	刚好	to happen to/by chance/just as well
gàosu	告诉	to tell
gāoxìng	高兴	to be pleased/glad/happy
ge	个	[measure word]
gè zhǒng	各种	various kinds
gébì	隔壁	next door
gēge	哥哥	elder brother
gěi	给	for/to/to be for/to be to

gěi nǐ	给你	here you are
gēn	跟	to follow
gōngsī	公司	company
gōngyòng	公用	public
gōngzuò	工作	work/to work
gòu	够	to be enough
guàng	逛	to look around
guǎnlǐ	管理	management/to manage
guānmén	关门	to be closed/to close
guì	贵	to be expensive
guò	过	to celebrate/to spend
guó	国	country
guo	过	[grammar word]
guòjiǎng	过奖	I'm flattered
hái	还	still/also
hái hǎo	还好	to be all right
Hǎinán Dǎo	海南岛	Hainan Island
háishi	还是	or [question word]
hǎixiān	海鲜	seafood
háizi	孩子	children
hán	含	to contain
hǎo	好	good/fine/well
hǎo	好	to be good/to be well/to be fine
hǎo	好	very
hào	号	date
hào	号	number
hǎo ba	好吧	alright/fine
hǎo bù hǎo?	好不好	Is it alright/fine?
hǎo yǒu	好友	good friend
hǎo zhǔyi	好主意	good idea
hǎochī	好吃	tasty
hǎokàn	好看	to be nice/to be good-looking
hàomǎ	号码	number
hé	和	and
hē	喝	to drink
hěn	很	very
hěn	很	very much
hěnduō	很多	many/much/a lot
hésuàn	合算	good bargain
hónglǜ dēng	红绿灯	traffic light
hòu	后	after/in/ . . .later
huài le	坏了	to have broken/does not work

huàn	还	to change
huán	还	to return
huáng	黄	yellow
huānyíng	欢迎	to welcome
huì	会	can/to be able to
huì	会 ...的	will
huídá	回 答	to answer
huíjiàn	回 见	see you later
huílai	回 来	to return
hūnlǐ	婚 礼	wedding
huǒchē piào	火 车 票	train ticket
huǒchē zhàn	火 车 站	railway station
jǐ	几	how many?
jí	急	hurry/to be urgent/urgent
jī	鸡	chicken
jǐ	几	several
jī dīng	鸡 丁	diced chicken
jí shì	急 事	urgent matter
jiā	家	[measure word]
jiā	家	home/family
jiā	加	plus
jiàn	件	[measure word for clothes]
jiān	间	[measure word for rooms]
jiàn	件	[measure word for matters]
jiàndào	见 到	to meet
jiàng	酱	sauce
jiǎngjiang	讲 讲	to tell
jiànmiàn	见 面	to meet
jiào	叫	to call/to be called
jìde	记 得	to remember
jīdòng	激 动	to be excited/exciting
jiē	接	to collect/to meet [somebody]
jiè	借	to lend
jiè	借	to borrow
jiéhūn	结 婚	to be married
jièshào	介 绍	to introduce
jīhū	几 乎	almost
jìjié	季 节	season
jīn	斤	half a kilo
jīn nián	今 年	this year
jin qu	进 去	to go in/to go into
jīnglǐ	经 理	manager

jīntiān	今天	today
jīntiān wǎnshàng	今天晚上	this evening/tonight
jìrán . . . jiù . . .	既然 ...就 ...	as . . .then
jiǔ	久	long
jiù	就	[emphatic word]
jiù . . . le	就 ...了	[emphatic structure]
jiù shì	就是	the only thing is . . .
jiù shì	就是	that is
jú	局	bureau/office
juéde	觉得	to think/to feel
juédìng	决定	to decide/decision
kāfēi	咖啡	coffee
kāi	开	to be open/to open
kāi huì	开会	to attend a meeting/to attend conference
kāimén	开门	to be open/to open
kàn	看	to see/to visit/to watch/to read
kàn de jiàn	看得见	to be able to see
kànshangqu	看上去	to look/to seem
kǎo	烤	to roast
kè	刻	quarter
kěxī	可惜	pity that . . .
kěyi	可以	could/can/may
kòng	空	vacant/free
kǒngpà	恐怕	I'm afraid . . .
kuài	快	soon/quickly/to be fast/to be quick
kuài	快	nearly
kuài	块	[currency word]
lái	来	to come/to come to
lái	来	to arrive
láixìn	来信	letter
làngmàn	浪漫	to be romantic/romantic
lǎo	老	to be old/old
lǎobǎn	老板	boss
lǎoshí shuō	老实说	frankly speaking/to be honest
le	了	[grammar word]
lèi	累	to be tired
lěng	冷	to be cold/cold
lǐ	里	inside
liǎng	两	two
liàng	辆	[measure word for vehicle]
liǎng	两	[unit of weight]

lièchē	列车	train
lǐngdài	领带	tie
línshí	临时	last minute/temporary
lǐwù	礼物	presents/gifts
lìzhī	荔枝	lychee
lù	路	route/road
lǜ	绿	green
lùkǒu	路口	crossroads
lúndào . . .	轮到	it is [somebody's] turn to . . .
Lúndūn	伦敦	London
lǚyóu	旅游	tourism/to travel
ma	吗	[question word]
mǎi	买	to buy
mài	卖	to sell
mǎi dōngxi	买东西	go shopping/do shopping
mài guāng le	卖光了	to be sold out
māma	妈妈	mother/mum
màn	慢	slowly/slow/to be slow
máng	忙	to be busy/busy
máo	毛	[currency word]
màoyi	贸易	trading/trade
máoyī	毛衣	sweater/jumper
měi	美	to be beautiful/beautiful
měi	每	every
méi guānxi	没关系	It doesn't matter./It's all right./It's OK.
méi shénme	没什么	nothing
méi tīng qīng	没听清	did not hear clearly
mél wèntí	没问题	no problem
méi yǒu	没有	not
Měiguórén	美国人	American people
miàntiáo	面条	noodles
míng nián	明年	next year
míngtiān	明天	tomorrow
míngzi	名子	name
mìshū	秘书	secretary
mòshangqu	摸上去	it feels . . .
nà	那	in that case
nà	那	that
nǎ (něi)	哪	which
nà ge nǚ de	那个女的	that woman
Nǎ yī wèi?	哪一位	Who is it speaking?
náli	哪里	where/whereabouts

náli	哪里	not really/not at all
nàme	那么	in that case
nán	男	male
nán	难	to be difficult/difficult
nán de	男的	the man
nǎr	哪儿	where
néng	能	can/could
nǐ	你	you
nǐ hǎo	你好	How do you do?/Hello
Nǐ juédìng.	你决定	You decide.
nǐ kàn	你看	have a look
Nǐ tài duì le.	你太对了	You are so right.
nǐ zuìhǎo	你最好	you'd better
nián	年	year
niánqīng	年轻	to be young/young
nǐde	你的	your/yours
nǐménde	你们的	your/yours [plural]
nín	您	you [polite form]
Nín ne?	您呢	What about you?/And you?
niúròu	牛肉	beef
nǚ	女	female
nǚ'ér	女儿	daughter
pāi	拍	to take/to shoot
péngyou	朋友	friend
piānyi	便宜	to be cheap/cheap
piào	票	ticket
piàoliang	漂亮	to be beautiful/beautiful
píjiǔ	啤酒	beer
píng	瓶	[measure word]
píngguǒ	苹果	apple
qī	七	seven
qí	骑	to ride
qián	前	ago/before
qián	钱	money
qiánbāo	钱包	wallet/purse
qiánmian	前面	ahead
qǐchuáng	起床	to get up
qīn'àide	亲爱的	dear
qǐng	请	to invite
qǐng	请	please
qīngchǔ	清楚	to be clear/clearly
qíngkuàng	情况	situation/present condition

qíshí	其实	in fact
qítā	其它	other
qiūtiān	秋天	autumn
qīyuè	七月	July
qù	去	to go/to go to
qù nián	去年	last year
ràng	让	to let/to allow
ràng rén	让人	to send for someone
rè	热	to be hot/hot
rén	人	person/people
rènshi	认识	to know [somebody]
ruǎnwò	软卧	soft-sleeper
rúguǒ	如果	if
sānshí'èr	三十二	thirty-two
shàng	上	to go to/to attend
shàng bān	上班	go to work/be at work
shàng ge	上个	last
shāngdiàn	商店	shop
shāngliang	商量	to discuss/to consult
shāo děng	稍等	just a second
shéi/shuí	谁	who
shēng	深	dark/deep/to be dark/to be deep
shēngqì	生气	to be angry/to be cross
shénme	什么	what
shénme	什么	any/anything
shénme dìfang	什么地方	whereabout/what place
shénme shíhou	什么时候	when
shénme shíhou	什么时候	any time/whenever
shēntǐ	身体	health
shì	是	be (am, is, are)
shí	十	ten
shì	事	thing/matter
shì de	是的	yes
Shì ma?	是吗	Is that so?
shì'a	是啊	yes
shícài	什菜	seasonal vegetables
shìchǎng	市场	market
shífēn	十分	extremely
shíjiān	时间	time
shíyuè	十月	October
shōu	收	to be received by . . ./to receive
shōu dào	收到	to receive

shòupiào chù	售 票 处	ticket office
shū	书	book
shuài	帅	to be smart/smart
shuāngrén	双 人	double
shūdiàn	书 店	bookshop
shūfu	舒 服	comfortable/to be comfortable
shuíguǒ	水 果	fruit
shuìjiào	睡 觉	to sleep/sleep
shùnlì	顺 利	to be smooth
shuō	说	to speak/to say
shuō lái huà cháng	说 来 话 长	it's a long story
shuōqǐ	说 起	to mention/to talk
shuōqǐ	说 起	talking about/to talk about
sīchóu	丝 绸	silk
suānlà	酸 辣	hot and sour
suì	岁	years old
suóyǒude	所 有 的	all
tā	他	he/she/it
tài . . . le	太 ... 了	extremely/very much/too
Tài bàng le!	太 棒 了	Superb!
tài hǎo le	太 好 了	wonderful
tàitai	太 太	wife/Mrs
támen	他 们	they/them
tāmen	它们	they (inanimate objects)
tán	谈	to talk/to chat
tāng	汤	soup
tángcù	糖 醋	sweet and sour
tánhuà	谈 话	to talk
tāozi	桃子	peach
tèbié	特别	extremely
tiān	天	very
tiáo	条	[measure word]
tīng	听	to listen to
tīng hǎo	听 好	to listen carefully
tīngshuō	听 说	to have heard
tóng	同	with/and
tóngxué	同 学	classmate
tuìxiū	退 休	to be retired/retired
wán	完	[the completion of an action]
wàng	忘	to forget
wǎng . . . guǎi	往 ...拐	to turn
wǎnshang	晚 上	evening

wèi 位 [measure word]
wèi 喂 hello [only used on the telephone]
wéijīn 围巾 scarf
wèishēng jiān 卫生间 bathroom
wèishénme 为什么 why
wèn 问 to ask
wèntí 问题 problem
wǒ 我 I/me
wǒ xiǎng 我想 I think . . .
wǒmen 我们 we
wǒménde 我们的 our/ours
wǔfàn 午饭 lunch
xià bān 下班 to finish work
xià chē 下车 to get off
xià cì 下次 next time
xià ge 下个 next
xià yī zhàn 下一站 next stop
xiān 先 first of all
xiǎng 想 to think
xiǎng (+ verb) 想 would like/to want
xiāngjiāo 香蕉 banana
xiāngxìn 相信 to believe
xiānsheng 先生 Mr/husband
xiànzài 现在 now
xiǎo 小 little/small/young
xiǎo 小 to be little/to be small/to be young
xiǎo lóng 小笼 small steam-container
xiǎohái 小孩 small children
xiǎojie 小姐 Miss
xiǎoshí 小时 hour
xiàtiān 夏天 summer
xiàwǔ 下午 afternoon
xiàxuě 下雪 to snow
xiàyǔ 下雨 to rain/raining
xiě 写 to write
xièxie 谢谢 thank you
xǐhuan 喜欢 to like
xìn 信 letter
xīn 新 new/to be new
xíng 行 to be OK/can do/will do
xíng ma? 行吗？ Is it OK?
xīngqī 星期 week

xīngqī'èr	星期二	Tuesday
xīngqītiān	星期天	Sunday
xīnxiān	新鲜	fresh
xiū	修	to repair
xiūxi	休息	to rest/to take time off work
xué	学	to learn/to study
xūyào	需要	to require/to need
yā	鸭	duck
yánsè	颜色	colour
yāo	幺	one
yào	要	to want
yào	要	to be going to
Yào kàn qíngkuàng.	要看情况。	It depends.
yàoshi	钥匙	key
yě	也	also/too
yěxǔ	也许	perhaps
yī bēi	一杯	one cup/one glass
yī xiǎo pán	一小盘	a small plate
yīdiǎn	一点	a little bit
yīdìng	一定	definitely/must
yīgòng	一共	altogether
yǐjing	已经	already
yījiǔjiǔsì nián	一九九四年	nineteen ninety-four
Yīlìshābái	伊丽莎白	Elizabeth
yīlù	一路	journey/trip
yīnggāi	应该	should/ought
Yīngguó	英国	Britain
Yīngguórén	英国人	British people
yìngwò	硬卧	hard-sleeper
yínháng	银行	bank
yīqiè	一切	everything
yīxià	一下	one second
yīxiē	一些	some
yīyàng	一样	to be the same/same
yīyuè	一月	January
yīzhí	一直	all the time
yòng	用	to use
yǒu	有	to have
yǒu kòng	有空	to have time/to be free
yǒu rén	有人	anybody/somebody
yǒu yī tiān . . .	有一天	one day . . .
yǒu yīdiǎn	有一点	a little bit

yǒu yìsi	有意思	to be interesting
yóubiān	邮编	postcode
yǒuhǎo	友好	to be friendly/friendly
yóujú	邮局	post-office
yóuyǒng	游泳	to swim
yóuyǒng chí	游泳池	swimming pool
yú	鱼	fish
yuè	月	month
zài	在	[continuous particle]
zài	在	to be at/to be in/at/in
zài	再	once again
zài . . . zhī qián	在...之前	before . . ./by . . .
zàijiàn	再见	goodbye
zánmen	咱们	we [colloquial term]
zànshí	暂时	at the moment/temporarily
zǎo	早	early
zǎofàn	早饭	breakfast
zāogāo	糟糕	Damn it!
zǎoshang	早上	morning
zěnme	怎么	how
zěnme	怎么	why
Zěnme huí shì?	怎么回事？	What's the matter?
Zěnme yàng?	怎么样？	How are you?/How are things?
Zěnme zǒu?	怎么走？	How do I get there?/How do I get to . . .?
zhá	炸	to deep fry
zhāng	张	[measure word]
zhàngfu	丈夫	husband
zhǎo	找	to look for
zhǎo	找	to return [the change]
zhǎo dào	找到	to succeed in finding something
zhàopiān	照片	photograph
zhè	这	this
zhe	着	[grammar word]
zhè cì	这次	this time
zhè ge zhōumò	这个周末	this weekend
zhè jiàn shì	这件事	this matter
zhème	这么	so
zhème shuō	这么说	in that case
zhēn	真	really
zhēn bàoqiàn	真抱歉	many apologies
zhēn de?	真的？	really?

Zhēn kěxī!	真可惜!	What a shame!
zhēn qiǎo	真巧	What a coincidence!/coincidentally
zhēn sī	真丝	pure silk
zhèxiē	这些	these
zhī xíng	之行	the trip to
zhīdao	知道	to know/to be aware of
zhǐyǒu	只有	only
zhǒng	种	kind
Zhōngguó	中国	China
Zhōngwén	中文	Chinese [as a language]
zhōngxué	中学	secondary/middle school
zhōngyú	终于	at last/finally
zhōumò	周末	weekend
zhù	住	to live
zhuàngguān	壮观	to be magnificent
zhuānyè	专业	subject/major
zìxíngchē	自行车	bicycle
zìyóu	自由	free/freedom/to be free
zǒu	走	to leave
zǒu	走	to walk
zúgòu de	足够的	enough
zuì	最	most
zuì hǎo	最好	best
zuìhǎo	最好	ideally
zuìhòu	最后	the last
zuìjìn	最近	recently
zuò	坐	to sit/to sit down
zuò	坐	to take (e.g. bus)
zuǒ	左	left
zuótiān	昨天	yesterday
zuǒyòu	左右	about/approximate

English–Chinese glossary

a little/some	**diǎnr**
a little bit	**yīdiǎn/yǒu (yī)diǎn**
a quarter of a kilo	**bàn jīn**
a small plate	**yī xiǎo pán**
about, approximate	**zuǒ yòu**
after/in/. . . later	**hòu**
afternoon	**xiàwǔ**
ago/before	**qián**
ahead	**qiánmian**
all	**dōu**
all	**suǒyǒude**
all right	**hái hǎo**
all right/fine	**hǎo ba**
all the time	**yīzhí**
almost	**jīhū**
already	**yǐjing**
also, too	**yě**
altogether	**yīgòng**
American	**Měiguórén**
and	**hé**
answer	**huídá**
any/anything	**shénme**
anybody/somebody	**yǒu rén**
anything else	**biéde**
any time/whenever	**shénme shíhou**
apple	**píngguǒ**
approximately/ about/around	**dàyuē**
arrive	**dào/lái**
as . . . then	**jìrán . . . jiù . . .**
ask	**wèn**
ask	**ràng**
at/in	**zài**
at last/finally	**zhōngyú**
at the moment/ temporarily	**zànshí**
attend/to take part	**cānjiā**
attend a meeting/ to attend a conference	**kāi huì**
August	**bāyuè**
autumn	**qiūtiān**
avenue	**dàjiē**
banana	**xiāngjiāo**
bank	**yínháng**
bathroom	**wèishēng jiān**
be (am, is, are)	**shì**
beautiful/to be beautiful	**piàoliang**
become	**dāng**
beef	**niúròu**
beer	**píjiǔ**
before . . ./by . . .	**zài . . . zhī qián**
Beijing person/ people	**Běijīngrén**
bicycle	**zìxíngchē**
big/large	**dà**
block	**dòng**
boiled rice	**bái mǐ fàn**
book	**shū**
bookshop	**shūdiàn**

boss **lǎobǎn**
breakfast **zǎofàn**
bring/take **dài**
Britain **Yīngguó**
British **Yīngguórén**
bureau/office **jú**
busy/to be busy **máng**
but **dànshì**
buy **mǎi**
call/to be called **jiào**
can/could **néng**
can/to be able to **huì**
car/bus **chē**
celebrate/to spend **guò**
change **huàn**
cheap/to be cheap **piányi**
check **chá**
chicken **jī**
children **háizi**
China **Zhōngguó**
Chinese (as a language) **Zhōngwén**
Chinese New Year **chūnjié**
city **chéngshì**
classmate **tóngxué**
coffee **kāfēi**
collect/to meet (somebody) **jiē**
colour **yánsè**
come/to come to **lái**
come from . . . **cóng . . . lái**
comfortable/to be comfortable **shūfu**
company **gōngsī**
contain **hán**
could/can/may **kěyi**
country **guó**
crossroads **lùkǒu**
Damn it! **zāogāo**
dark/to be dark **shēng**
date **hào**
daughter **nǚ'ér**
day **tiān**
dear **qīn'àide**
decide/decision **juédìng**
deep fry **zhá**
deep/to be deep **shēng**
definitely/must **yīdìng**
depart/departure **fāchē**
department store **bǎihuò shāngdiàn**
deputy/vice **fù**
diced chicken **jī dīng**
did not hear clearly **méi tīng qīng**
difficult/to be difficult **nán**
discuss/to consult **shāngliang**
do **gàn**
do not **bié**
Do/Does/Are/Is . . .or . . .? **háishi**
double room **shuāngrén fángjiān**
drink **hē**
duck **yā**
early/to be early **zǎo**
east **dōng**
eat **chī**
eight **bā**
elder brother **gēge**
Elizabeth **Yīlìshābái**
enough **zúgòu de**
evening **wǎnshàng**
every **měi**
everything **yīqiè**
expensive/to be expensive **guì**
extension **fēnjī**
extremely **shífēn**
extremely/very **fēicháng/tèbié**
extremely/very much/too **tài . . . le**
father/dad **bàba**
female **nǚ**

finish work	**xià bān**	have broken/does not work	**huài le**
first	**dì yī**	have heard	**tīngshuō**
first of all	**xiān**	have time/to be free	**yǒu kòng**
fish	**yú**	have/has	**yǒu**
floor/layer	**céng**	he/him	**tā**
follow	**gēn**	health	**shēntǐ**
forget	**wàng**	hello (only used on the telephone)	**wéi**
frankly speaking/ to be honest	**lǎoshí shuō**	here you are	**géi nǐ**
free/freedom/ to be free	**zìyóu**	home/family	**jiā**
fresh	**xīnxiān**	hot and sour	**suānlà**
friend	**péngyou**	hotel	**fàndiàn**
from . . . to	**cóng . . . dào . . .**	hour	**xiǎoshí**
fruit	**shuíguǒ**	how	**zěnme**
get off	**xià chē**	how are you?/ how are things?	**zěnme yàng?**
get up	**qǐchuáng**	How do I get there?/How do I get to . . .?	**Zěnme zǒu?**
glad/to be glad	**gāoxìng**	How do you do?/ hello	**ní hǎo**
go/to go to	**qù**	how long	**duōjiǔ**
go in/to go into	**jìn qu**	how many?	**jǐ**
go shopping/do shopping	**mǎi dōngxi**	how much?/how many?	**duōshǎo**
go to/to attend	**shàng**	How much is it?	**Duōshǎo qián?**
go to work	**shàng bān**	however/but	**búguò**
good/fine	**hǎo**	hundred	**bǎi**
good bargain	**hésuàn**	hungry/to be hungry	**è**
good friend	**hǎo yǒu**	hurry/urgent	**jí**
good idea	**hǎo zhǔyi**	husband	**zhàngfu/ xiānsheng/ àiren**
good-looking/to be good-looking	**hǎokàn**	I/me	**wǒ**
goodbye	**zàijiàn**	I think . . .	**wó xiǎng**
green	**lǜ**	I'm afraid . . .	**kǒngpà**
guess	**cāi**	I'm flattered	**guò jiǎng**
Hainan Island	**Hǎinán Dǎo**		
half	**bàn**		
half a kilo	**yī jīn**		
happen to/by chance/just as well	**gānghǎo**		
happy/to be happy	**gāoxìng**		
hard-sleeper	**yìngwò**		
have to/must	**děi**		
have a look	**nǐ kàn**		

I'm sorry/ Excuse me	**duìbùqǐ**	lend	**jiè**
		let/to allow	**ràng**
ideally	**zuìhǎo**	letter	**xìn**
if	**rúguǒ**	letter	**láixìn**
in fact	**qíshí**	light bulb	**diàndēng**
in that case	**nà/zhème shuō/nàme**	like	**xǐhuān**
		listen carefully	**tīng hǎo**
include/to have	**dài**	listen to	**tīng**
inside	**lǐ**	little/small/young	**xiǎo**
introduce	**jièshào**	live	**zhù**
Is it all right?/OK?	**hǎo bù hǎo?**	local	**dāngdì**
Is it OK?	**xíng ma?**	London	**Lúndūn**
Is that so?	**Shì ma?**	long	**jiǔ**
It depends	**Yào kàn qíngkuàng**	long/to be long	**cháng**
		look around	**guàng**
It doesn't matter/ It's all right/ It's OK	**méi guānxi**	look for	**zhǎo**
		look/to seem	**kànshangqu**
		lunch	**wǔfàn**
it feels . . .	**mōshangqu**	lychee	**lìzhī**
it is (somebody's) turn to . . .	**lúndào . . .**	make telephone calls/to telephone	**dǎ diànhuà**
it's a long story	**shuō lái huà cháng**	make time	**chōu kòng**
		male	**nán**
January	**yīyuè**	man	**nán de**
journey/trip	**yīlù**	management	**guǎnlǐ**
July	**qīyuè**	manager	**jīnglǐ**
just	**gāng**	many apologies	**zhēn bàoqiàn**
just a second	**shāo děng**	many thanks	**duō xiè**
key	**yàoshi**	many/much	**hěnduō**
kind	**zhǒng**	map	**dìtú**
king prawn	**dàxiā**	market	**shìchǎng**
know (somebody)	**rènshi**	meet	**jiànmiàn**
know/to be aware of	**zhīdao**	meet(somebody)	**jiàndào**
		mention/to talk	**shuōqǐ**
last	**shàng ge**	menu	**càidān**
last minute/ temporary	**línshí**	minute	**fēn**
		minute	**fēnzhōng**
last year	**qù nián**	Miss	**xiǎojie**
late	**chí**	money	**qián**
learn/to study	**xué**	month	**yuè**
leave	**zǒu**	more	**duō**
left	**zuǒ**	more than/over	**duō**

morning	**zǎoshàng**	one cup	**yī bēi**
most	**zuì**	one day . . .	**yǒu yī tiān . . .**
mother/mum	**māma**	only	**zhǐyǒu**
Mr	**xiānsheng**	open/to be open	**kāi**
Mrs	**tàitai**	orange juice	**chéngzi zhī**
must	**bìxū**	order (food)	**diǎn cài**
name	**míngzi**	other	**qítā/biéde**
near by/close by	**fùjìn**	our/ours	**wǒménde**
nearly	**kuài**	pancake	**bǐng**
new/to be new	**xīn**	parents	**fúmǔ**
next	**xià ge**	pass	**dì**
next door	**gébì**	peach	**táozi**
next stop	**xià yī zhàn**	per cent	**bǎifēnzhī**
next time	**xià cì**	perhaps	**yěxǔ**
next year	**míng nián**	person/people	**rén**
nice/to be nice	**hǎo/hǎokàn**	photograph	**zhàopiān**
nineteen ninety-four	**yījiǔjiǔsì nián**	pity that . . .	**kěxī**
		plan	**dǎsuàn**
no	**bù shì**	please	**qǐng**
no/incorrect	**bù duì**	pleased/to be pleased	**gāoxìng**
no need/do not need	**bù yòng**	plus	**jiā**
no problem	**méi wèntí**	post-office	**yóujú**
noodles	**miàntiáo**	postcode	**yóubiān**
not	**bù**	presents	**lǐwù**
not	**méi/méi yǒu**	problem	**wèntí**
not bad	**bù cuò**	promise	**bǎozhèng**
not easy to find	**bù háo zhǎo**	public	**gōngyòng**
not really/not at all	**nálǐ**	pure silk	**zhēn sī**
nothing	**méi shénme**	pure wool	**chún máo**
now	**xiànzài**	quarter	**kè**
number	**hàomǎ/cì/hào**	quite/rather/relatively	**bǐjiào**
o'clock	**diǎn**		
October	**shíyuè**	quite good/quite well	**bù cuò**
of course	**dāngrán**		
office	**bàngōngshì**	railway station	**huǒchē zhàn**
often/always/frequently	**cháng**	rain/raining	**xiàyǔ**
		really	**zhēn**
OK	**hǎo de**	really?	**zhēn de?**
old/to be old	**lǎo/dà**	receive	**shōu dào**
once again	**zài**	recently	**zuìjìn**
one	**yāo**	remember	**jìde**

repair	**xiū**	single	**dān**
report	**bàogào**	sit/to sit down	**zuò**
require/need	**xūyào**	situation/present condition	**qíngkuàng**
rest/to take time off work	**xiūxi**	sleep/to sleep	**shuìjiào**
restaurant	**cānguǎn**	slowly/slow/ to be slow	**màn**
restaurant/ dining-room	**cāntīng**	small children	**xiǎohái**
retired/be retired	**tuìxiū**	small steam- container	**xiāo lóng**
return	**huílai**	smooth/to be smooth	**shùnlì**
return (the change)	**zhǎo**	snow	**xiàxuě**
return/to give back	**huán**	so	**zhème**
ride	**qí**	soft-sleeper	**ruǎnwò**
right/by the way	**duì le**	some	**yīxiē**
roast	**kǎo**	son	**érzi**
room	**fángjiān**	soon/quickly	**kuài**
route/road	**lù**	soup	**tāng**
same	**yīyàng**	speak/to say	**shuō**
sauce	**jiàng**	spring	**chūntiān**
scarf	**wéijīn**	starving	**è sǐ le**
scenery	**fēngjǐng**	stay	**dāi**
seafood	**hǎixiān**	steamed bread with fillings	**bāozi**
season	**jìjié**	still/also	**hái**
seasonal vegetables	**shícài**	stir-fry	**chǎo**
secondary/middle school	**zhōngxué**	strawberry	**cǎoméi**
secretary	**mìshū**	subject/major	**zhuānyè**
see/to visit/to watch/to read	**kàn**	succeed in finding something	**zhǎo dào**
see to/to handle	**chǔlǐ**	summer	**xiàtiān**
see you again	**huíjiàn**	Sunday	**xīngqītiān**
see you later	**huíjiàn**	Superb!	**Tài bàng le!**
sell	**mài**	sweater/jumper	**máoyī**
send for someone	**ràng rén**	sweet and sour	**tángcù**
seven	**qī**	swim	**yóuyǒng**
several	**jǐ**	swimming pool	**yóuyǒng chí**
she/her	**tā**	take	**dài**
shop	**shāngdiàn**	take/to shoot	**pāi**
should/ought	**yīnggāi**	take/to catch	**zuò/chéng**
side	**biān**	talk/to chat	**tánhuà/tán**
silk	**sīchóu**		

talking about/to talk about **shuōqǐ**
taste **cháng**
tasty **hǎochī**
tea **chá**
telephone **diànhuà**
tell **gàosu**
tell/to narrate **jiǎngjiang**
ten **shí**
thank you **xièxie**
that **nà**
that is **jiù shì**
that woman **nà ge nǚ de**
the first time/ for the first time **dì yī cì**
the following day **dì èr tiān**
the Great Wall **Chángchéng**
the large one/the big one **dà de**
the last **zuìhòu**
the only thing is . . . **jiù shì**
the small one **xiǎo de**
the trip to **zhī xíng**
there **nàr**
these **zhèxiē**
thing/matter **shì**
things **dōngxi**
think/feel **juéde**
thirty-two **sānshí'èr**
this **zhè**
this evening/ tonight **jīntiān wǎnshang**
this matter **zhè jiàn shì**
this time **zhè cì**
this weekend **zhè ge zhōumò**
this year **jīn nián**
ticket **piào**
ticket office **shòupiào chù**
tie **lǐngdài**
time **shíjiān**
to/for **gěi**
to be able to see **kàn de jiàn**
to be angry/ to be cross **shēngqì**
to be at/to be in **zài**
to be away/to go away **chūmén**
to be beautiful/ beautiful **měi**
to be big/to be large **dà**
to be clear/clearly **qīngchǔ**
to be closed/to close **guānmén**
to be cold/cold **lěng**
to be compared with **bǐ**
to be enough **gòu**
to be excited/ exciting **jīdòng**
to be fast **kuài**
to be friendly/ friendly **yǒuhǎo**
to be full **bǎo**
to be going to **yào**
to be good/to be well/to be fine **hǎo**
to be hot/hot **rè**
to be interesting/ interesting **yǒu yìsi**
to be magnificent **zhuàngguān**
to be married **jiēhūn**
to be noisy **chǎo**
to be OK/can do **xíng**
to be open/to open **kāimén**
to be received by . . ./to receive **shōu**
to be romantic/ romantic **làngmàn**
to be smart/smart **shuài**
to be sold out **mài guāng le**
to be successful/ success **chénggōng**
to be the same **yīyàng**

to be tired	**lèi**
to be to/to be for	**gěi**
to be urgent	**jí**
to believe	**xiāngxìn**
to borrow	**jiè**
today	**jīntiān**
tofu	**dòufu**
toilet	**cèsuǒ**
tomorrow	**míngtiān**
tourism/to travel	**lǚyóu**
tourist guide	**dǎoyóu**
trading/trade	**màoyì**
traffic light	**hónglǜ dēng**
train	**lièchē**
train ticket	**huǒchē piào**
tram/streetcar	**diànchē**
Tuesday	**xīngqī’èr**
turn	**wǎng . . . guǎi**
twenty	**èrshí**
twenty-one	**èrshíyī**
two	**liǎng**
understand	**dǒng**
university	**dàxué**
university student	**dà xuésheng**
until/up to	**dào**
urgent matter	**jí shì**
use	**yòng**
vacant	**kòng**
various kinds	**gè zhǒng**
very	**hěn/hǎo**
very much	**hěn**
walk	**zǒu/zǒulù**
wallet/purse	**qiánbāo**
want	**yào**
we/us	**wǒmen**
we (colloquial term)	**zánmen**
wear	**chuān**
wedding	**hūnlǐ**
week	**xīngqī**
weekend	**zhōumò**
welcome	**huānyíng**
well	**hǎo**

what	**shénme**
What a coincidence!/ coincidentally	**zhēn qiǎo**
What a shame!	**Zhēn kěxī!**
What about you?/ And you?	**Nín ne?**
What’s the matter?	**Zěnme huí shì?**
when	**shénme shíhou**
when/while	**. . . de shíhou**
where	**nǎr**
where/whereabouts	**náli**
whereabout/what place	**shénme dìfang**
which	**nǎ/něi**
who	**shéi**
Who is it speaking?	**Nǎ yī wèi?**
whoops!	**āiyō!**
why	**wèishénme**
why	**zěnme**
wife	**tàitai/qīzi/ àiren**
will	**huì**
winter	**dōngtiān**
with/and	**tóng**
wonderful	**tài hǎo le**
work/to work	**gōngzuò**
would like/to want	**xiǎng**
write	**xiě**
wrongly/to be wrong	**cuò**
year	**nián**
years old	**suì**
yellow	**huáng**
yes	**shì de**
yes	**shì’a**
yesterday	**zuótiān**
you	**nǐ**
you [polite form]	**nín**
You are so right.	**Nǐ tài duì le.**

you are welcome	**bù kèqi**	your/yours	**nǐde**
You decide.	**Nǐ juédìng.**	your/yours (plural)	**nǐménde**
you'd better	**nǐ zuìhǎo**		
young/to be young	**niánqīng**	zoo	**dòngwùyuán**

Appendix A Useful signs

The characters introduced in the book are simplified characters. In this appendix, complex characters (traditional form) are placed alongside their simplified versions wherever they differ from their simplified version. This appendix consists of those character signs that are introduced at the end of each lesson in the book and some other useful signs.

Simplified form	*Complex form*	*Pinyin*	*English*	*Lesson*
北京		**Běijīng**	Beijing (Peking)	2
男		**nán**	Men's	3
女		**nǚ**	Ladies'	3
饭店	飯店	**fàndiàn**	hotel	4
餐厅	餐廳	**cāntīng**	dining-room	4
旅游局		**lǚyóu jú**	tourist bureau	5
商店		**shāngdiàn**	shop	7
银行	銀行	**yínháng**	bank	7
邮局	郵局	**yóujú**	post-office	7
菜单	菜單	**càidān**	menu	9
餐馆	餐館	**cānguǎn**	restaurant	9
厕所	厠所	**cèsuǒ**	toilet	10

Simplified form	*Complex form*	*Pinyin*	*English*	*Lesson*
洗手间	洗手間	**xǐshǒu jiān**	toilet	
公用电话	公用電話	**gōngyòng diànhuà**	public telephone	10
火车站	火車站	**huǒchē zhàn**	railway station	10
售票处	售票處	**shòupiào chù**	ticket office	11
公共汽车站	公共汽車站	**gōnggòng qìchē zhàn**	bus station	11
上海		**Shànghǎi**	[place name]	14
西安		**Xī'ān**	[place name]	14
桂林		**Guìlín**	[place name]	14
广州	廣州	**Guǎngzhōu**	[place name]	14
长城	長城	**Chángchéng**	[place name]	14
香港		**Xiāng Gǎng**	[place name]	15
台湾	臺灣	**Táiwān**	[place name]	15
英国	英國	**Yīngguó**	Britain	15
美国	美國	**Měiguó**	America	15
故宫		**Gùgōng**	Forbidden City	
天坛	天壇	**Tiāntán**	Temple of Heaven	
旅行社		**lǚxíng shè**	travel agency	
飞机场	飛機場	**fēijī chǎng**	airport	
进口	進口	**jìnkǒu**	entrance	

Simplified form	*Complex form*	*Pinyin*	*English*	*Lesson*
入口		**rùkǒu**	entrance	
出口		**chūkǒu**	exit	
问询处	問詢處	**wènxún chù**	information/ enquiry	
行李寄存处	行李寄存處	**xínglǐ jìcún chù**	left-luggage	
蔬菜		**shūcài**	vegetable	
肉		**ròu**	meat	
冷饮	冷飲	**lěngyǐn**	cold drinks	
素菜馆	素菜館	**sùcài guǎn**	vegetarian restaurant	
美元		**měi yuán**	US dollars (US$)	
英镑	英鎊	**yīng bàng**	sterling (£)	
医院	醫院	**yīyuàn**	hospital	
警察局		**jǐngchá jú**	police station	
理发店	理髮店	**lǐfà diàn**	barber shop	
发廊	髮廊	**fàláng**	hairdresser	
博物馆	博物馆	**bówùguǎn**	museum	
出租车	出租車	**chūzūchē**	taxi	
书店	書店	**shūdiàn**	bookshop	
图书馆	圖書館	**túshūguǎn**	library	
电影院	電影院	**diànyǐngyuàn**	cinema	
服装店	服裝店	**fúzhuāng diàn**	clothes shop	

Simplified form	*Complex form*	*Pinyin*	*English*	*Lesson*
药店	藥店	**yàodiàn**	chemist	
请勿拍照	請勿拍照	**qǐng wù pāi zhào**	no photographs	
请勿吸烟	請勿吸烟	**qǐng wù xī yān**	no smoking	

Appendix B Additional useful expressions

English	*Chinese* (in pinyin)	*Chinese* (in character)
aeroplane	**fēijī**	飞机
baggage	**xíngli**	行李
boiled water	**kāi shuǐ**	开水
Chinese characters	**hànzì**	汉字
chopsticks	**kuàizi**	筷子
cold water	**liáng shuǐ**	凉水
complex characters	**fántǐ zì**	繁体字
connection	**guānxì**	关系
cough	**késou**	咳嗽
diarrhoea	**lādùzi**	拉肚子
easy	**róngyì**	容易
fever	**fāshāo**	发烧
flu	**gǎnmào**	感冒
foreigner	**wàiguórén**	外国人
headache	**tóuténg**	头疼

English	*Chinese* (in pinyin)	*Chinese* (in character)
I'm ill.	**Wǒ bìng le.**	我 病 了
ice	**bīng**	冰
ice-cream	**bīngjīlíng**	冰激凌
magazine	**zázhì**	杂志
newspaper	**bàozhǐ**	报纸
overseas Chinese	**huáqiáo**	华侨
Peking Opera	**jīng jù**	京剧
post a letter	**jì xìn**	寄信
postcard	**míngxìnpiàn**	明信片
see a doctor	**kàn yīshēng/kàn dàifu**	看医生/看大夫
send a parcel	**jì bāoguǒ**	寄包裹
simplified characters	**jiǎntǐ zì**	简体字
stomach-ache	**dùziténg**	肚子疼
take off	**qǐfēi**	起飞
toothache	**yáténg**	牙疼
tourist guide	**dǎoyóu**	导游
work unit	**dānwèi**	单位

Appendix C

Table of the combinations of the initials and finals in *Putonghua*

F† / I†	*a*	*o*	*e*	*er*	*ai*	*ei*	*ao*	*ou*	*an*	*en*	*ang*	*eng*	*ong*	*i*	*i**	*ia*	*iao*	*ie*	*iu*
	a	o	e	er	ai	ei	ao	ou	an	en	ang	eng		yi		ya	yao	ye	you
b	ba	bo			bai	bei	bao		ban	ben	bang	beng		bi			biao	bie	
p	pa	po			pai	pei	pao	pou	pan	pen	pang	peng		pi			piao	pie	
m	ma	mo	me		mai	mei	mao	mou	man	men	mang	meng		mi			miao	mie	miu
f	fa	fo				fei		fou	fan	fen	fang	feng							
d	da		de		dai	dei	dao	dou	dan	den	dang	deng	dong	di			diao	die	diu
t	ta		te		tai		tao	tou	tan		tang	teng	tong	ti			tiao	tie	
n	na		ne		nai	nei	nao	nou	nan	nen	nang	neng	nong	ni			niao	nie	niu
l	la		le		lai	lei	lao	lou	lan		lang	leng	long	li		lia	liao	lie	liu
z	za		ze		zai	zei	zao	zou	zan	zen	zang	zeng	zong		zi				
c	ca		ce		cai		cao	cou	can	cen	cang	ceng	cong		ci				
s	sa		se		sai		sao	sou	san	sen	sang	seng	song		si				
zh	zha		zhe		zhai	zhei	zhao	zhou	zhan	zhen	zhang	zheng	zhong		zhi				
ch	cha		che		chai		chao	chou	chan	chen	chang	cheng	chong		chi				
sh	sha		she		shai	shei	shao	shou	shan	shen	shang	sheng			shi				
r			re				rao	rou	ran	ren	rang	reng	rong		ri				
j														ji		jia	jiao	jie	jiu
q														qi		qia	qiao	qie	qiu
x														xi		xia	xiao	xie	xiu
g	ga		ge		gai	gei	gao	gou	gan	gen	gang	geng	gong						
k	ka		ke		kai	kei	kao	kou	kan	ken	kang	keng	kong						
h	ha		he		hai	hei	hao	hou	han	hen	hang	heng	hong						

† I stands for 'initial'; F stands for 'final'.

* See p. 4 for pronunciation.

ian	*in*	*iang*	*ing*	*iong*	*u*	*ua*	*uo*	*uai*	*ui*	*uan*	*un*	*uang*	*ueng*	*ü*	*üe*	*üan*	*ün*
yan	yin	yang	ying	yong	wu	wa	wo	wai	wei	wan	wen	wang	weng	yu	yue	yuan	yun
bian	bin		bing		bu												
pian	pin		ping		pu												
mian	min		ming		mu												
					fu												
dian			ding		du		duo		dui	duan	dun						
tian			ting		tu		tuo		tui	tuan	tun						
nian	nin	niang	ning		nu		nuo			nuan				nü	nüe		
lian	lin	liang	ling		lu		luo			luan	lun			lü	lüe		
					zu		zuo		zui	zuan	zun						
					cu		cuo		cui	cuan	cun						
					su		suo		sui	suan	sun						
					zhu	zhua	zhuo	zhuai	zhui	zhuan	zhun	zhuang					
					chu	chua	chuo	chuai	chui	chuan	chun	chuang					
					shu	shua	shuo	shuai	shui	shuan	shun	shuang					
					ru	rua	ruo		rui	ruan	run						
jian	jin	jiang	jing	jiong										ju	jue	juan	jun
qian	qin	qiang	qing	qiong										qu	que	quan	qun
xian	xin	xiang	xing	xiong										xu	xue	xuan	xun
					gu	gua	guo	guai	gui	guan	gun	guang					
					ku	kua	kuo	kuai	kui	kuan	kun	kuang					
					hu	hua	huo	huai	hui	huan	hun	huang					

Appendix D

English translation to dialogues after Lesson 6

Lesson 6

Dialogue 1: What day is it today?

T: What day is it today?
PA: Today is Tuesday.
T: How many days are there in a week?
PB: There are seven days in a week.
T: How many months are there in a year?
PC: There are twelve months in a year.
T: What's tomorrow's date?
PD: Tomorrow is 18th January 1994.
T: How many seasons are there in a year and what are they?
PE: Four seasons, and they are spring, summer, autumn and winter.

Dialogue 2: When . . . ?

M: Is it cold in Beijing in the winter?
L: Extremely cold. It often snows.
M: How about the summer?
L: July and August are very hot.
M: What is the best season?
L: Autumn, around October. Why, are you planning to go to Beijing?
M: Yes
L: When?
M: As you've said that October is best, I'll go in October next year.
L: Are you going there to travel or to work?
M: Travel plus work.
L: How long are you going for?

M: Travelling for two weeks and working for three days. Altogether about three weeks.

Lesson 7

Dialogue 1: How much is it?

S: Hello. What would you like to buy?
A: I'd like to buy some fruit.
S: Have a look. We've got fresh strawberries, Hainan Island bananas and various kinds of apples.
A: What are these?
S: Lychees.
A: How much are they per *jin*?
S: Five *kuai* and eight *mao*.
A: I'll have one *jin* of lychees. How much are strawberries?
S: Three *kuai* and nine *fen* per *jin*.
A: I'll have half a *jin* of strawberries. Do you have peaches?
S: No, sorry. Anything else?
A: No, thank you.
S: Altogether seven *kuai* three *mao* and six *fen*.
A: Here are ten *kuai*.
S: OK. Here is your change – two *kuai* six *mao* and four *fen*.
A: Thanks.

Dialogue 2: It's too expensive

D: Xiao Fan, are shops closed on Sundays?
F: No. All the shops, banks and post-offices are open. Why, do you want to do some shopping?
D: Yes. I'd like to buy several silk scarves for my wife, some presents for the kids and friends.
F: That's not difficult. I can take you to the department store.

D: Miss, how much is this silk tie?
S: Two hundred and fifty *yuan* for one.
D: It's too expensive.
S: Two hundred *yuan*, is that OK?
D: How about three hundred and fifty *yuan* for two?
S: All right, all right.
D: I'll take it.

Lesson 8

Dialogue 1: Which is better?

P: Xiao Liu, these two jumpers, which one do you think is better?
L: I think the green one is better than the yellow one. Green suits you quite well.
P: OK. I'll take your advice.

P: Damn! I forgot to bring my wallet. Xiao Liu, could you lend me some money?
L: No problem. How much do you need?
P: Thirty *yuan*, is that OK?
L: Yes. Is it enough?
P: Yes, it is.
L: Here you are.
P: Thanks a lot. I'll definitely return the money tomorrow.
L: There's no hurry. Shall we go and have a look in the bookshop? I'd like to buy a couple of books.
P: OK.

Dialogue 2: It's a bargain

J: Sorry. I'm late.
Y: That's all right. I've just arrived.
J: I finished work early today and went to have a look-around in the street market.
Y: Is there any good stuff?
J: Yes, a lot. Shame I didn't have enough money with me. I bought er . . . how do you say 'jumper' in Chinese?
Y: *Maoyi.*
J: Right. I bought a jumper.
Y: Let me have a look. (. . . .) Really good. Is it pure wool?
J: No. It contains 80 per cent wool.
Y: It feels very comfortable. How much is it?
J: Over fifty *yuan*.
Y: It's really inexpensive. A real bargain. I like this colour very much. Are there any more of those left?
J: Dark red is sold out. This was the last one. But, there are many other nice colours.
Y: I'm not working tomorrow. I'll find some time to go and have a look.

Lesson 9

Dialogue 1: Ready to order?

W: Good evening! How many of you?
L: Three.
W: Follow me please.

W: Sit down, please. What would you like to drink first?
D: I'd like to have a *Qingdao* beer.
L: Same for me.
W: What would you like to drink, Miss?
J: A glass of orange juice.
W: OK. Please have a look at the menu.

W: Ready to order?
L: Yes. I'll order first. One seafood soup and one beef with fried noodles.

W: What about you, sir?
D: One hot and sour tofu soup, one diced chicken with seasonal vegetables and two *liang* of small steamed bread with fillings. I'm starving.
W: And you, Miss?
J: I'd like to have a small plate of deep-fried king-prawns, one sweet and sour fish and one boiled rice.
W: Alright. Please wait for a while.

Dialogue 2: Have you ever had roast duck?

Q: Have you had Beijing roast duck?
X: No, I haven't
Q: Really. In that case, you've got to give it a taste. Are you free tonight?
X: Yes, I am.
Q: Then, I'm inviting you to have roast duck tonight. How does that sound?
X: Wonderful. Which restaurant are we going to?
Q: How about the Beijing Roast Duck Restaurant?
X: Super!

X: You were so right. It's delicious.
Q: I'm so pleased you like the roast duck. Have some more.
X: OK. Please pass me the sauce.

Q: Are there enough pancakes?
X: Enough for me. I'm nearly full. Ask for some more if you want more pancakes.
Q: In fact I'm already full. I eat faster than you do.

Lesson 10

Dialogue 1: Where's the toilet?

(a) Inside a hotel
YOU: Where is the toilet, please?
CHINESE: On the left of the dining-room.

(b) In the street
YOU: Is there a public telephone nearby?
CHINESE: I'm afraid not. Can you see the traffic light ahead?
YOU: Yes, I can.
CHINESE: When you get to the traffic light, turn right. I remember there is one there.

(c) In the street
YOU: Could you tell me which bus to take to go to the Railway Station?
CHINESE: No need to take the bus. It takes ten minutes to walk there.
YOU: How do I get there?
CHINESE: Turn east at the first traffic light.

Dialogue 2: Borrowing a bike

FRANK: Can I borrow your bike?
FEIXIA: Of course you can. Where are you going?
FRANK: Maybe Zhongshan University on Sunday.
FEIXIA: Do you know how to get there?
FRANK: No. But I think I can find it.
FEIXIA: I don't believe it. You'd better check the map first.
FRANK: Good idea. How long does it take approximately to cycle there?
FEIXIA: About an hour and a half.

Lesson 11

Dialogue 1: Fares, please!

B: Fares, please. Anybody?
A: Yes, I'd like a ticket to the zoo.
B: This bus is not going to the zoo.
A: What? Have I got on the wrong bus?
B: Don't worry. You get off at the next stop and change for Tram No. 18.
A: Sorry, I didn't hear it clearly. Please speak slowly.
B: You get off at the next stop and change for Tram No. 18.
A: Thank you. In that case, one ticket please. How much is it?
B: One *mao*.
P: I happen to change for No. 18. Please come with me.
A: Thank you very much.

Dialogue 2: Buying train tickets

C: Is this the ticket office?
T: Yes, it is.
C: I'd like to get a train ticket to Guilin.
T: When are you leaving?
C: Next Wednesday, that is 4th June.
T: Which number train to you plan to take?
C: I'm not sure. Ideally, round six o'clock in the evening.
T: How about No. 81? It departs at nineteen forty-five.
C: When does it arrive at Guilin?
T: It arrives at sixteen twenty the following day.
C: Good timing. I'll get a ticket for this train.
T: Would you like a hard-sleeper or soft-sleeper?
C: I don't understand.
T: A hard-sleeper is fifty yuan cheaper than a soft-sleeper, but not as comfortable.
C: I'll have one hard-sleeper.

Lesson 12

Dialogue 1: Any vacancies?

J: Do you have any vacancies please?
R: It depends. Do you want a single room or double room?
J: Single room, please.
R: How many days are you staying?
J: Three days.
R: Let me check. ... What good luck! There is one room available.
J: Do single rooms have bathrooms?
R: Yes, they do.
J: How much is it per night?
R: Two hundred and thirty yuan.
J: I'll take it.

R: Here is the key to your room. Your room is on the second floor.

Dialogue 2: The light is not working

D: Good morning. Did you sleep well last night?
J: To be honest. I didn't sleep well.
D: What's the matter?
J: Last night the room next door was very noisy all the time until early this morning.
D: Many apologies. I'll see to this matter.
J: Thanks. Oh, right, a light in my room is not working.
D: Really? I'll definitely send someone to fix it. Any other problems?
J: Not for the moment. See you later.

Lesson 13

Dialogue 1: Hello

A: Hello, could you get Li Man for me please?
L: I AM Li Man. Who is speaking?
A: It's Alan, Alan from Britain.
L: Really? When did you get here? How come I didn't know anything about it?

A: I came last Saturday. It was a last minute decision.
L: I'm so excited. When are you coming to see me?
A: Any time. You decide.
L: How about tonight?
A: Superb! Whereabouts do you live?
L: It's not easy to find my home. I'll come to collect you.

Dialogue 2: Telephone numbers

J: Have you finished with the phone?
Y: Yes, I have.
J: I'll give our boss a call.
Y: He is not in the office today.
J: Is that so? Do you have his home number?
Y: No. You could give his secretary a call and ask her for it.
J: Good idea.
S: Extension 268. Who is speaking please?
J: It's Jane. I've got something to discuss with Manager Zhang. I've heard he is not in the office today. Could you tell me his home number?
S: Yes, I can. Just a second, please. Listen carefully. The number is 462183.
J: 462183.
S: Correct.

Lesson 14

Dialogue 1: It's raining

Y: Is this your first time in Taiwan?
P: No. We come to Taiwan almost every year. Last year, we were here twice.
Y: Really? Why?
P: The first time, we came for my wife's younger sister's wedding. And the second time, it was for the Spring Festival.
Y: In that case, you wife must be Taiwanese, is that so?
P: Yes, she is.
Y: How did you get to know each other?
P: It's a long story. Ten years ago, she went to the States for her university education and we were classmates. One day . . .
Y: Very romantic. Whoops! It's raining. Let's go inside to talk.

Dialogue 2: Which place do you like most?

A: Hi, Graham. So nice to see you. Come on in. Please take a seat.
G: OK. Are you well, Ailin?
A: Quite well, thank you. What would you like to drink?
G: Chinese tea, please.
A: Talking about China, how was your trip to China?
G: Very successful.
A: Which cities did you go to?
G: Beijing, Shanghai, Si'an, Guilin and Guangzhou.
A: Which place did you like most?
G: It's a very difficult question to answer. I liked Guilin very much. The scenery there is beautiful. The locals are very friendly. It's very interesting to talk to them.
A: I haven't been to Guilin yet. I'll definitely go there next time. What do you think of Guangzhou?
G: I don't like Guangzhou that much. Too many people there, and also too hot.
A: I don't like Guangzhou either. I've heard that the Great Wall is very grandiose. Is that right?
G: Yes, it is. It's magnificent. I took a lot of photos . . .

Lesson 15

Text: I promise

Dear Xiaomei:
Hi!
I've received your letter. I'm so please that you like your new job. Everything is fine with me, except that I'm too busy writing a report. Every morning I've been up at six thirty and can't go to bed until twelve at night. I've got to finish this report by Friday. I know I haven't written to you for a long time. Please don't be cross with me. When I have some time off this weekend, I will definitely write you a long letter. I promise.

Good friend,
Elena

26.1.94

Index to grammar and cultural notes

The number in each entry refers to the lesson(s) where that entry occurs